MODEL-DRIVEN ENGINEERING OF INFORMATION SYSTEMS
PRINCIPLES, TECHNIQUES, AND PRACTICE

MODEL-DRIVEN ENGINEERING OF INFORMATION SYSTEMS
PRINCIPLES, TECHNIQUES, AND PRACTICE

Edited by
Liviu Gabriel Cretu, PhD, and Florin Dumitriu, PhD

Apple Academic Press

TORONTO   NEW JERSEY

Apple Academic Press Inc. | Apple Academic Press Inc.
3333 Mistwell Crescent | 9 Spinnaker Way
Oakville, ON L6L 0A2 | Waretown, NJ 08758
Canada | USA

©2015 by Apple Academic Press, Inc.

First issued in paperback 2021

Exclusive worldwide distribution by CRC Press, a member of Taylor & Francis Group
No claim to original U.S. Government works

ISBN 13: 978-1-77463-216-1 (pbk)
ISBN 13: 978-1-77188-083-1 (hbk)

Library of Congress Control Number: 2014946556

Library and Archives Canada Cataloguing in Publication

Model-driven engineering of information systems: principles, techniques, and practice/ edited by Liviu Gabriel Cretu, PhD, and Florin Dumitriu, PhD.

Includes bibliographical references and index.
ISBN 978-1-77188-083-1 (bound)
1. Computer software--Development. 2. Model-integrated computing. 3. Software engineering. I. Cretu, Liviu Gabriel, author, editor II. Dumitriu, Florin, editor

QA76.76.D47M58 2014   005.1   C2014-905297-9

Apple Academic Press also publishes its books in a variety of electronic formats. Some content that appears in print may not be available in electronic format. For information about Apple Academic Press products, visit our website at **www.appleacademicpress.com** and the CRC Press website at **www.crcpress.com**

MODEL-DRIVEN ENGINEERING OF INFORMATION SYSTEMS
PRINCIPLES, TECHNIQUES, AND PRACTICE

Edited by
Liviu Gabriel Cretu, PhD, and Florin Dumitriu, PhD

Apple Academic Press

TORONTO   NEW JERSEY

Apple Academic Press Inc.	Apple Academic Press Inc.
3333 Mistwell Crescent	9 Spinnaker Way
Oakville, ON L6L 0A2	Waretown, NJ 08758
Canada	USA

©2015 by Apple Academic Press, Inc.

First issued in paperback 2021

Exclusive worldwide distribution by CRC Press, a member of Taylor & Francis Group
No claim to original U.S. Government works

ISBN 13: 978-1-77463-216-1 (pbk)
ISBN 13: 978-1-77188-083-1 (hbk)

Library of Congress Control Number: 2014946556

Library and Archives Canada Cataloguing in Publication

Model-driven engineering of information systems: principles, techniques, and practice/ edited by Liviu Gabriel Cretu, PhD, and Florin Dumitriu, PhD.

Includes bibliographical references and index.
ISBN 978-1-77188-083-1 (bound)
1. Computer software--Development. 2. Model-integrated computing. 3. Software engineering. I. Cretu, Liviu Gabriel, author, editor II. Dumitriu, Florin, editor

QA76.76.D47M58 2014   005.1   C2014-905297-9

Apple Academic Press also publishes its books in a variety of electronic formats. Some content that appears in print may not be available in electronic format. For information about Apple Academic Press products, visit our website at **www.appleacademicpress.com** and the CRC Press website at **www.crcpress.com**

ABOUT THE EDITORS

LIVIU GABRIEL CRETU, PhD

Dr. Liviu Gabriel Cretu is currently coordinating the activities of the Software Engineering Lab, Centre for Advanced Information Systems, Financial Reporting and Accounting, Alexandru Ioan Cuza University, Iași, Romania. He lectures on Software Engineering and Information Systems Architecture at the same university, and he is a software architect consultant with a consistent portfolio of clients across Europe. He is a researcher, developer, and author, having published numerous peer-reviewed articles in the fields of enterprise systems, semantic web, enterprise architectures, model-driven engineering, service-oriented architecture, and business process management. He received his PhD in business information systems from the Alexandru Ioan Cuza University, Iași, Romania.

FLORIN DUMITRIU, PhD

Dr. Florin Dumitriu currently leads the Department of Accounting, Business Information Systems and Statistics at Alexandru Ioan Cuza University, Iași, Romania. He lectures on Systems Analysis and Design and Human Resource Management Systems at the same university. He is a researcher, having published numerous peer-reviewed articles in the fields of systems analysis and design, global software development, agile software development, distributed databases, and business process management. He received his PhD in business information systems from the Alexandru Ioan Cuza University, Iași, Romania.

CONTENTS

ACKNOWLEDGMENT AND HOW TO CITE

The editor and publisher thank each of the authors who contributed to this book, whether by granting their permission individually or by releasing their research as open source articles or under a license that permits free use, provided that attribution is made. The chapters in this book were previously published in various places in various formats. To cite the work contained in this book and to view the individual permissions, please refer to the citation at the beginning of each chapter. Each chapter was read individually and carefully selected by the editor; the result is a book that provides a nuanced study of model-driven engineering. The chapters included examine the following topics:

- MDE is usually associated with software product lines where variability and variation points are the main concerns. The proposed E2EDE methodology in Chapter 1 guides the MDE process, explaining how various types of requirements may have a formal representation in the models by means of annotations with metadata. This way, the model will contain enough information for the automation of transformation decisions. The paper includes a case study where QVT is used to implement the mapping rules.
- The authors of Chapter 2 carry out a review of variability modeling methods and related tools, in order to organize the plethora of existing approaches into several classification dimensions, and provide representative examples of Model-Driven Engineering tools and algorithms exploiting them.
- Quality of the input models is as important as the transformation process. Chapter 3 presents a metamodel for quality assessment in MDE automation. This metamodel is developed using Eclipse MOF specification, then a procedure for defect detection is proposed.
- One of the main advantages of MDE is that correctness of complex software may be assessed even before the physical system is actually generated, at the level of abstract models with lower complexity. The authors of Chapter 4 show how formal techniques can be used to establish the correctness of model transformations.
- Chapter 5 applies mathematical theory to MDE where the later is regarded as just another particular instance of the engineering discipline. Two examples are presented, showing categorical arrangement of model management scenarios: model merge and bidirectional update propagation.

- Chapter 6 offers clear guidance for an MDA process implemented with UML and ATL. A metamodel for component-oriented software is discussed and then it is designed in UML using stereotypes and tags. A set of mapping rules is defined and implemented in ATL to transform components (PIM) into CORBA PSM.
- Systematic integration of Model Driven Engineering (MDE) principles within the software development process has proven to be a challenging task. Usually, one of the first questions arising is how to properly organize the MDE process itself. Chapter 7 introduces a pragmatic method to apply MDE using UML, the de-facto standard modeling language in software development. The proposed method is based on the metamodeling approach and uses UML profiles to encapsulate information about typed use cases. A Java example is then provided to validate and illustrate the method
- In Chapter 8 we find an MDD approach aiming to facilitate the reuse of crosscutting AOP frameworks. Two experiments have been conducted to compare the proposed model-based reuse approach with the conventional way of reusing CFs, i.e., manually creating the reusable code. The authors also present productivity gains and reuse of metamodel components from one AOP framework to another.
- In Chapter 9, the authors propose an MDD approach to support automated test generation with domain specific concepts. A framework is provided for building test models using Java language together with a DSM language used to guide test case generation. A MBT tool is used to automatically create a DSM language and to apply the transformation of the test model.
- Chapter 10 presents an approach and a case study for the migration of legacy systems to new technologies. According to the authors, application behavior information can be extracted from any existing system by determining its observable behaviour and stored in the form of requirements-level models conformant to the RSL-AL—an extension of the Requirements Specification Language that serves as an intermediate language between the recovery and migration steps.Specific tools are then used to transform this model back to an application based on the new set of technologies.

LIST OF CONTRIBUTORS

Alain Abran
Department of Software Engineering & Information Technology, École de Technologie Supérieure, Université du Québec, 1100 Notre-Dame Ouest, Montréal QC, Canada H3C 1K3

Adel Alti
Department of Computer Science, Farhat Abbes University of Setif, Algeria

Albert Ambroziewicz
Warsaw University of Technology, Warsaw, Poland

Robert M. Colomb
Faculty of Computer Science and Information Systems, Universiti Technologi Malaysia, Skudai, Malaysia.

Liviu Gabriel Cretu
Business Information Systems Department, Alexandru Ioan Cuza University of Iasi, Bd. Carol I, no 11, Iasi, Romania

Jim Davies
Department of Computer Science, University of Oxford, Oxford, United Kingdom OX1 3QD

Valter Vieira de Camargo
Departmento de Computação, Universidade Federal de São Carlos, Caixa Postal 676, 13.565-905, São Carlos, São Paulo, Brazil

Zinovy Diskin
Network for Engineering of Complex Software-Intensive Systems for Automotive Systems (NEC-SIS), McMaster University, Canada and Generative Software Development Lab, University of Waterloo, Canada

Rafael Serapilha Durelli
Instituto de Ciências Matemáticas e Computação, Universidade de São Paulo, Av. Trabalhador São Carlense, 400, São Carlos, São Paulo, Brazil

Giovanni Giachetti
Centro de Investigación en Métodos de Producción de Software, Universidad Politécnica Valencia, Camino de Vera s/n, 46022 Valencia, Spain

Thiago Gottardi
Departmento de Computação, Universidade Federal de São Carlos, Caixa Postal 676, 13.565-905, São Carlos, São Paulo, Brazil

Abdelgaffar Hamed
College of Computer Science and Information Technology, Sudan University of Science and Technology, Khartoum, Sudan

Norbert Jarzebowski
Warsaw University of Technology, Warsaw, Poland

Jean-Marc Jézéquel
Institut de Recherche en Informatique et Systèmes Aléatoire (IRISA), University of Rennes 1, 35042 Rennes, France

Teemu Kanstrén
VTT, Oulu, Finland

Tahar Khammaci
LINA, Université de Nantes, 2, Rue de la Houssinière, 44322, Nantes, France

Óscar Pastor López
Universidad Politecnica de Valencia, Camino de Vera s/n, Valencia, Spain

Tom Maibaum
Network for Engineering of Complex Software-Intensive Systems for Automotive Systems (NEC-SIS), McMaster University, Canada

Beatriz Marín
Centro de Investigación en Métodos de Producción de Software, Universidad Politécnica Valencia, Camino de Vera s/n, 46022 Valencia, Spain

Wiktor Nowakowski
Warsaw University of Technology, Warsaw, Poland

Oscar Pastor
Centro de Investigación en Métodos de Producción de Software, Universidad Politécnica Valencia, Camino de Vera s/n, 46022 Valencia, Spain

Olli-Pekka Puolitaival
F-Secure, Oulu, Finland

Adel Smeda
LINA, Université de Nantes, 2, Rue de la Houssinière, 44322, Nantes, France

Michał Smiałek
Warsaw University of Technology, Warsaw, Poland

Tomasz Straszak
Warsaw University of Technology, Warsaw, Poland

Chen-Wei Wang
McMaster Centre for Software Certification, McMaster University, Hamilton, Canada L8S 4K1

INTRODUCTION

Model-driven engineering (MDE) is an important research topic in the software engineering field. As an evolutionary step from computer-aided software engineering (CASE) methods, model-driven engineering techniques apply systematic transition from semantically rich but simplified models to other models that include more design and technical details. This approach has been reportedly applied in various fields, from embedded software to denotational semantics definition [1]. In this book we have focused our attention on identifying relevant papers proposing techniques and practical examples that could be useful for the development of information systems, the model-driven way.

Simply said, MDE is the automatic production of software from simplified models of structure and functionality. The key here is "simplified models"—the opposite of the detail-rich UML diagrams needed to execute forward and reverse engineering where the usual software design has to involve enough technical (platform-specific) details for the modeling tool to be able to generate some code. MDE is considered by some authors "the first true generational shift in programming technology since the introduction of compilers" [2], and it can profoundly change the way applications are developed [3]. It mainly involves the automation of the routine and technologically complex programming tasks, thus allowing developers to focus on the true value-adding functionality that the system needs to deliver, instead of continuously debugging various technical details inherent in the use of programming languages or specific technologies.

The core concepts used in MDE are: models and transformations. Bézivin offers a systematic analysis about the transition from "everything is an object" paradigm to "everything is a model" [4]. Just like in the object-oriented world, where an Object is an instance of a Class, in model engineering a Model is an instance of a Metamodel. Metamodels are intended to represent a set of related concepts and each metamodel defines a language for describing a specific domain of interest. If one can specify rules to transform metamodel A into metamodel B, then transformers may be implemented to generate new models in the target-language B from input models written in the source-language A. Similar ideas that MDE is all about models, meta-models and transformation rules may be found in [5] where the author names it the model-driven engineering "megamodel", as well as in popular works such as [6, 7, 8] including the MDA guide [9].

Models are created using domain-specific languages (DSL, sometimes called domain specific modeling languages—DSML—if it is a graphical language). DSLs are tailored to directly represent the concepts of an application domain as modeling primitives. To create a DSL one needs a domain analyst [10] which is a person who examines the needs and requirements of a collection of similar systems. Most DSLs are supported by a DSL compiler, called the application generator [11], that generates applications from DSL programs. Various modeling languages dedicated to MDE have been proposed, such as Alloy [12] and B [13]. While the main advantage of building a compiler or interpreter is that the implementation is completely tailored towards the DSL, an important problem is the cost of building such a compiler or interpreter from scratch, and the lack of re-use from other (DSL) implementations [14]. At the same time, the Unified Modeling Language (UML) remains the widely accepted general-purpose modeling language in the software industry today. The main advantage of UML is that it can be specialized to become a domain-specific language (DSL) using UML profiles. Thus, a standard UML model element may be categorized according to a different metamodel by means of stereotypes and tagged-values. There are many researchers who have identified the natural relationship between UML profiles and the metamodeling phase in MDE [15, 16], while a large number of papers are proposing domain-specific profiles such as for critical infrastructures [17], distributed service models [18], embedded systems [19], web services [20], and semantic web services [21].

Although there are still debates on the terminology, some preferring model-based software development [22], others model-driven development [2, 3, 23] or model-driven engineering [4], it is widely accepted that the Model Driven Architecture (MDA) [24] introduced by Object Management Group, is the reference implementation of MDE. MDA is often described as "the future of software engineering," popular works offering statements such as "MDA is about using modelling languages as programming languages rather than merely as design languages"[25].

The book is organized in two sections. Section one—MDE Principles and Methods—is a collection of papers needed to lay down the theoretical foundation of MDE for researchers and professionals alike. The second part—MDE in Practice—mainly focuses on real-world scenarios where MDE has been applied as well as some lessons learned along the process.

REFERENCES

1. Bisztray, D., Heckel, R., & Ehrig, H. (2009). Compositionality of model transformations. Electronic Notes in Theoretical Computer Science, 236, 5-19.
2. B. Selic, "The pragmatics of model-driven development," IEEE Software, vol. 20, no. 5, pp. 19–25, 2003
3. C. Atkinson, and T. Kuhne, "Model-driven development: a metamodeling foundation," IEEE Software, vol 20, no. 5, pp. 36–41, 2003
4. J. Bézivin, "In Search of a Basic Principle for Model Driven Engineering", European Journal for the Informatics Professional, vol. V, no. 2, 2004.
5. J-M. Favre, "Towards a basic theory to model model driven engineering," in the 3rd Workshop in Software Model Engineering (WiSME), 2004.
6. S. J. Mellor, K. Scott, A. Uhl, and D. Weise, MDA Distilled: Principles of Model-Driven Architecture, Addison Wesley, 2004
7. A. Kleppe, S. Warmer, W. Bast, MDA Explained. The Model Driven Architecture: Practice and Promise, Addison Wesley, 2003
8. C. Atkinson, and T. Kuhne, "Model-driven development: a metamodeling foundation," IEEE Software, vol. 20, no. 5, pp. 36-41, 2003.
9. OMG, "OMG, Model Driven Architecture (MDA)", ormsc/2001-07-01, 2001.
10. J. M. Neighbors, "The Draco approach to constructing software from reusable components," IEEE Transactions on Software Engineering, vol. SE-10, no. 5, pp. 564–574, 1984.
11. J. C. Cleaveland, "Building application generators", IEEE Software, vol. 5, no. 4, pp.25–33, 1988.
12. D. Jackson, "Alloy: A Lightweight Object Modeling Notation," ACM Transaction on Software Engineering and Methodology (TOSEM), vol. 11, no 2, pp. 256–290, 2002.
13. J-R. Abrial, B-Tool Reference Manual, Edinburgh Portable Compiler, 1991
14. V. Deursen, A. P. Klint, and J. Visser, "Domain-Specific Languages: An Annotated Bibliography," Sigplan Notices, vol. 35, no. 6, pp. 26-36, 2000.
15. F.F. Lidia, and A. Vallecillo-Moreno, "An introduction to UML profiles," UML and Model Engineering, vol 2, 2004.

16. O. Rahma and B. Coulette, "Applying Security Patterns for Component Based Applications Using UML Profile," in IEEE 15th International Conference on Computational Science and Engineering (CSE), pp. 186-193, IEEE, 2012.

17. B. Ebrahim and A. A. Ghorbani, "Towards an MDA-oriented UML profile for critical infrastructure modelling," in Proceedings of the 2006 International Conference on Privacy, Security and Trust, pp. 66, ACM, 2006,

18. S. Raul, F. Fondement, and A. Strohmeier, "Towards an MDA-oriented UML profile for distribution," in Proceedings of EDOC 2004, Eighth IEEE International Conference on Enterprise Distributed Object Computing, pp. 227-239, IEEE, 2004.

19. S. I. Wisniewski, L. T. Wiedermann, P. C. Stadzisz, and J. M. Simão, "Modeling of embedded software on MDA platform models," Journal of Computer Science & Technology, vol. 12, 2012.

20. S., Hassina, I. Bouacha, and M. S. Benselim, "Development of context–aware web services using the MDA approach," International Journal of Web Science, vol. 1, no. 3, pp. 224-241, 2012.

21. A. B. Djamel and M. Malki, "Development of semantic web services: model driven approach," in Proceedings of the 8th international conference on New technologies in distributed systems, ACM, 2008.

22. R. J. Machado, F. R. Wagner, and R. Kazman, "Introduction to special issue: model-based development methodologies," Innovations in Systems and Software Engineering, vol. 5, no. 1, pp. 1-3, 2009.

23. R. France, and B. Rumpe, "Model-driven development of complex software: A research roadmap," Future of Software Engineering, pp. 37-54, IEEE, 2007.

24. Object Management Group, "MDA Guide version 1.0.1. ", 2003, http://www.omg.org/mda/.

25. D. S. Frankel, Model Driven Architecture. Wiley 2003

Liviu Gabriel Cretu and Florin Dumitriu

PART I

MDE PRINCIPLES AND TECHNIQUES

CHAPTER 1

END TO END DEVELOPMENT ENGINEERING

ABDELGAFFAR HAMED AND ROBERT M. COLOMB

1.1 INTRODUCTION

The complexity of producing large-scale software systems is increasing due to the increased complexity of requirements. Technologies are volatile for many reasons but enhancing the quality of services is among clear reasons justified by software providers. For example, java platform versions and Google Chrome browser has adopted new browsers technology. The functionality of browsers is already crafted (i.e. Mozilla) but putting it into a new fashion is because of security, performance, reliability, and etc. On other hand, service-based system (SOA) has emerged as new engineering discipline encourages organizations to integrate their systems in a seamless manner. These highlight questions like

1. How to extend the traditional methods (Code-based) in a longlived architecture to deliver these new businesses?

This chapter was originally published under the Creative Commons Attribution License or equivalent. Hamed A, Colomb RM. End to End Development Engineering. Journal of Software Engineering and Applications 4,4 (2011); doi:10.4236/jsea.2011.44023.

2.   How to provide an effective integration with legacy systems?
3.   If a decision is made to change technology (acquiring new quality such as security and performance) is the design easily adaptable?

The trend now is proposing model-based engineering approach which means separating concerns where software development is driven by a family of high level languages [1]. To this end abstraction level is raised above 3GLs which increases re-using theme and put software artifact into a situation of core asset. More importantly formalizing of these artifacts (i.e. metamodels) leads to realize the benefit of high degree of automation. This means a machinery of specification (i.e. UML), synchronization and management of these models are essential. Thus, software not a program became like an information system itself. Thereby the crafting of code is becoming a manufacturing process not a personal skill.

Model Driven Architecture (MDA) is a new software development method following that trend. It raises abstraction level and maximizes re-use. Using MDA, we will be able to work with software artifacts as assets which from the software engineering perspective is a major success factor for reliable and fast development. The philosophy of MDA is to do more investment on software artifacts (models) to increase their efficiency, leading to systematic and more powerful mechanisms for software re-use.

MDA is an aspect of the more general discipline of software reuse. The synergistic relationship among MDA and the longer-established areas of Design pattern and software product line engineering (SPL) [2] has been studied as part of the present research [3,4].

The problem of producing a complete solution from specification through to implementation is still a long standing research aim, and because of the mapping gap from PIM to PSM, E2EDE has emerged. Most of previous work in MDA has been on infrastructure and components. Therefore the major question in this paper is how to write a program in MDA?

End to End development engineering (E2EDE) is a new trend to software engineering, proposed to answer that question, which uses MDA methodology and exploits some experience from Software Product Line (SPL) and lessons from Design Pattern (e.g. nonfunctional requirements) to automate the development from specification through to implementation. In doing so, we need to investigate the relationships among MDA, SPL, and design pattern and how MDA can fit on them. Therefore the contributions of the paper are the following:

1. We present E2EDE to automate the mapping process as realization to MDA which is intended to produce products without entirely writing code.
2. We discuss the relationship between MDA, SPL, and design pattern and how MDA can fit in the both longer established re-using approaches.
3. We share some lessons learned and challenges of MDA software engineering in practice.

Domain engineering is the key concept utilized from SPL which realizes breeding of a number of products that have similarity and some sort of variability in features. Design pattern in the history of software engineering has concerned with linking the design with nonfunctional requirements. Therefore, Nonfunctional requirements is borrowed as a concept.

The paper is organized as follows: Section 2 describes MDA as a major method used in E2EDE. In Section 3 we explain the problem through example of mappings from QVT specification. The proposed E2EDE methodology is discussed at Section 4. The concepts of E2EDE are validated by case study at Section 5. Sections 6 and 7 describe the relationship among MDA, Design Pattern and SPL. Section 8 draws on the principle of MDA and shows a case of strategic PSM. In Sections 9 and 10 we discuss MDA and E2EDE implementation aspects respectively. In Section 11 the realistic value of our approach with existing platforms is investigated. A conclusion is presented in Section 12.

1.2 MODEL DRIVEN ARCHITECTURE (MDA)

MDA is a new development paradigm initiated by the OMG aimed at software development driven by model [1]. In this case, a Platform Independent Model (PIM) is used to specify application behavior or logic by using MOF or a MOF-complaint modeling language [3]. This step represents a problem space in an application-oriented perspective. A Platform Specific Model (PSM) is used to realize a PIM. It represents a solution space from an implementation-oriented point of view. Therefore, a transformation from the problem space to the solution space is required. The automation of this process is the ultimate goal of MDA. Thereby, when we need to change the application, changes will be in only one part (PIM) without affecting implementation technologies (PSM). Conversely, when the platform such as SQL Server is changed retargeting a new platform for example new version (has enhanced feature), we need only to select the appropriate PSM and then regenerate the code not only without modifying PIM but also this time re-using most of the transformation. Productivity becomes higher and cost is reduced due to the increased reuse of models. In addition, maintenance becomes cheaper. It is worthwhile to observe here that MDA is working with models as assets that can be reused once the initial investment is made. MDA depends on a well established code-base.

1.2.1 MDA TRANSFORMATION PROCESS

The transformation from PIM to PSM is done by a maping function, which is a collection of mapping rules. In this case some or all of the content of the target model is defined. It is expected that when MDA automates this process, development efficiency and portability would significantly increase. In addition, the mapping function can be repeated many times (reused) for different applications using the same PIM and PSM metamodels. MDA also helps avoid risks of swamping the application with implementation detail which causes model divergence [5].

The steps of designing a system is to create a conceptual model by designers for application requirements and developing another implementation model to map the first into the second. But this might involve many sub activities. However, we can divide MDA into two major processes [1]:

1. Model to Model mappings: The mapping in this stage does not consider any specific characteristics or special cases that apply to technology or platform (called M2M). The result of this phase is still high level model but for code (PSM instances).

2. Bringing in a Particular Platform: The goal of this mapping (sometimes called M2T) is tailoring the conceptual model to specific technology. Different platforms have different features and constraints so step 1 will be refined to conform to features of one of the selected platform. The result in this phase is expected to be context dependant code expressed in a platform concrete syntax. In fact, we intended to use the word bringing to denote applying the principle of MDA in de-veloping standard PSM.

1.2.2 METAMODELING

The conceptual model of the design language such as UML data model (i.e. class diagram) is called a metamodel, which has concept like a class. A particular design in a design language is called model instance like student class in the student record system. This model instance can be visualized by using UML model instance (i.e. object diagram) but also MOF has similar model instances metamodel. A metamodel defines a schema for database called a repository. The population of this repository is the model instance. Formation rules of the metamodel are expressed as constraint on the repository [6]. A metamodel represents syntax of a modeling language. If the metamodel tells the designer how to create a model instance, it is said to be concrete syntax [6]. If it does not, it is said to be abstract syntax. Therefore, sometimes rendering conventions augmented with abstract syntax to generate concert syntax like MOF instance specification [7].

Model-based design that relies on a repository (tables or data structure) for storing a complex object (design), is the key art behind the MDA approach. For example QVT mappings are specified as patterns on schemas, or metamodel [8]. In this way, information contained in the models is separated from the algorithms defining tool behavior, instead of being hard-coded into a tool. The algorithmic part of tool communicates with models via an abstract program interface (API), which affords the facil-ity to create, modify and access the information in models [9]. Further, MDA tools can transform model instances into various forms. For example, the mappings from PIM to PSM takes PIM metamodel instances from the instance repository and turns it into corresponding instances updating the target repository, moving from problem space to solution space.

This mapping activity is done using standard language independent of the source and target. The metamodel of the mapping from end to another end can also be re-used as an asset.

1.2.3 QUERY, VIEWS, AND TRANSFORMATIONS (QVT)

Two kinds of transformation are recognized in MDA community:

- Horizontal, that does not change the abstraction level, for example from PIM to PIM which is used when a model is enhanced, filtered or specialized (mapping from analysis to design),
- Vertical, that changes the abstraction level, for example projection to the execution infrastructure. Four types of these transformations are categorized in [10].

There are tools to specify such mappings, such as query-view-transform QVT [8]. QVT is an OMG standard which helps us to specify rules for the transformation function. QVT uses the concept of predicate (expression evaluated to true or false) and pattern (set of expressions) in much similar way as prolog programming language.

The intended scenario of writing a program using MDA will be demonstrated first by an example then below in our case study where the mapping task is the major activity. Generally the application development is a process involves many transformations so vertical and horizontal or combination of them might be used.

1.3 MDA EXAMPLE AND MAPPING PROBLEM

We will use the QVT specification [8] example of object to relational mappings in order to understand where the problem is in this context. For sake of simplicity we focus on part of the mappings between PIM (object model) and PSM (relational model). This example shows the mappings take place between simplified UML2 metamodel in Figure 1, the PIM, and the PSM in Figure 2.

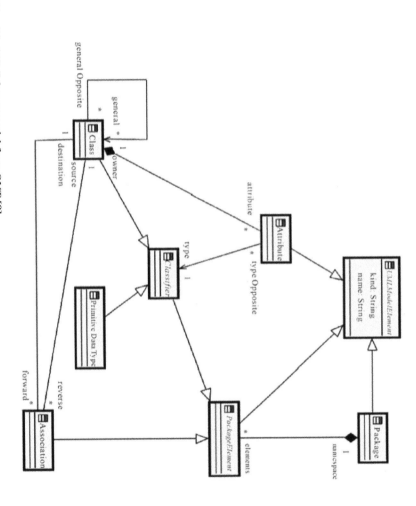

FIGURE 1: Simplified UML2 metamodel from QVT [8].

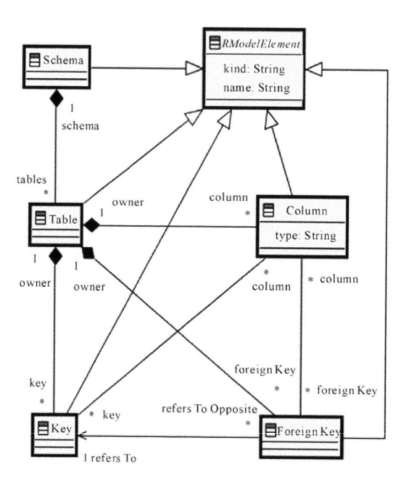

FIGURE 2: Simplified relational database model from QVT specification [8].

The mapping between conceptual models and relational schema is well established in the database. The general idea is that classes map to tables, packages map to schemas, attributes to columns, and associations to foreign keys. We will discuss part of this mapping informally then we will show simple QVT rules for that.

In Figures 3 and 4 examples we have a relation (use to specify rules of mapping source to target) named PackageToSchema, and ClassToTable. Both have two domains that will match elements in uml (our PIM) and rdbms (our PSM).The relation ClassToTable specifies the map of a class which has attribute name with value equal the variable "cn". All classes instances in uml repository will populate this variable one by one. For example if the model instance of our PIM is student record system, these will be person, lecturer, student, etc (M1). If the precondition is satisfied by this way the enforce clause is very similar to a checkonly clause. If there is an instance in the rdbms repository satisfying the pattern expression, then the enforce clause behaves as a predicate, with the value true. If no such instance exists, then the QVT engine will create one.

The mapping takes structural patterns in the M1 PIM model (problem domain) instance into in some cases quite different structural patterns in the M1 PSM model (implementation domain). The patterns are described in the M2 metamodel. Thereby that mapping is grasped as a part of the process of specifying and implementing the system. This process in most traditional software engineering methods is done manually. The ultimate goal of mapping is having a way to be able relate M0 instances of the PIM to M0 instances of the PSM. But the standarddocument of MDA [1] does not specify how to do that.

MOF specification has described how to create instances from MOF-based metamodel. When we talk about MOF we mean M2 level in the OMG hierarchy. Both create and destroy methods for objects and links are specified as MOF standard operations for creating and deleting dynamic objects [7]. So the objects created and destroyed by these methods are of kind M1 objects for M2 metaclasses. By this way an instance model will be created for M2 metamodel elements similar like having student, lecturer, and course, etc., instances. UML standard also specifies methods for creating instance model for M1 objects which are M0.Hence since like the instance model of record system is UML instance model then it should be able to create m0 objects using UML model instance inherited capabilities: create and destroy of objects and links.

The intended scenario for mapping is that an application using application terms have a facility to create objects which is PIM instance model. On other hand the implementation model that is PSM creates objects corresponding to that objects using PSM concepts and terms which represents a design vocabulary. To this end still in the MDA development (i.e. using MDA to solve problems) the question is how to do this process which requires finding concrete technical mapping methods.

A general method to approach this problem is needed whereby one could develop application without entirely writing code. Here the task for developer/modeler is a function of specification where application requirements, implementation and mapping metamodels are presented using design languages such as UML/MOF and mapping language such as QVT. In this case mapping and synchronization among models are performed by toolset.

1.4 PROPOSED E2EDE DESIGN & IMPLEMENTATION

This section demonstrates key points of E2EDE and explores most important aspects that should be addressed.

```
relationPackageToSchema /* map each package
toa schema */
    {
Domain uml p:Package {name=pn}
Domain rdbms s:Schema {name=pn}
        }
```

FIGURE 3: Mapping package to schema QVT rule.

1.4.1 INTRODUCTION

End to End development engineering (E2EDE) is a novel paradigm intended to automate software development from the specification end (i.e. object model) to the implementation end (i.e. relational model) using the MDA approach. The central issue is filling the mapping gap between PIM and PSM in MDA.

Theoretically E2EDE is inspired from an investigation of the synergistic relationship among MDA, SPL, and design patterns as we will see in Sections 6 and 7.The rationale behind establishing this relationship was from literature SPL and design patterns have long history of re-use software development. So they are longer established reuse methods. MDA is a more recent stream of re-use. E2EDE engineering is going to exploit this relationship to achieve its mapping goal. The key concept in SPL is variability which gives customization or configuration options. Variant feature is a place in the software artifact can be populated by at least one variant at a time from a set of variant. For example, if color is variant feature then Red is one variant. We conceive design decisions as variation points and the design choices as variants populating these points. This comes from the observation that PSM as a design artifact has different structures most properly lead to different architectural qualities. Therefore, to model

```
relationClassToTable /* map each persistent class
to a table */
{
Checkonly domain umlc:Class {
name=cn }
                    Enforce domain rdbmst:Table {
name=cn}
when { PackageToSchema(p, s); }
where { AttributeToColumn(t ,c); }   }
```

FIGURE 4: Mapping class to table QVT rule.

design decisions we need to represent variability explicitly in the PSM. The study of the design pattern approach highlights the importance of the relationship between design and requirements, specifically nonfunctional requirements, which is proposed to be modeled in the PIM. Still there is a research gap in these areas on how to map nonfunctional requirements with design decisions systematically. The problem has been looked at from one dimension, for example SPL has concerned only with variability without considering NFR such as [2,3,11, 12] while design pattern has recognized the impact of NFR dimension without variability in an explicit way [13-15].

However, the benefit here is PSM construction could be automated effectively because of consideration of design quality and management of single PSM. Hence, documenting variability in architecture and modeling nonfunctional requirements explicitly will become major activities during the development process. This section demonstrates key issues arising when we tackle E2EDE. Further, these issues have been applied to a selected case study to evaluate the possibility of the proposed engineering approach.

The ultimate goal of E2EDE is to provide a method of generating a solution from one specific source to a specific target like for example, from object-model to relational model. The advantages of E2EDE are reflected in the modeling support for the concepts in the domain and the ability to do more than general-purpose languages do, in addition to reduction of cost.

1.4.2 THE STEPS OF E2EDE PROCESS

In this section we will see the main steps of E2EDE. It will be detailed step by step and finally summarized as shown in Table 1.

1.4.2.1 MODELING VARIATION POINTS IN PSM (TASK A)

The key concept is to document variability in the PSM, which can be thought of as an abstract data type similar to the logical level in database systems. Usually, a solution is specified firstly at high abstraction level before rendered into a database technology. Variability in this PSM exposes different design decisions from the design space. The design decisions we mean in this context are architectural elements. Since it is possible to create different implementations from a generic specification, variability management concepts and techniques from SPL experiences are utilized to document design decision variants explicitly in the architecture. For example we will see in Section 5 two types of connection: Topic (indirect) and Queue (direct) for a messaging system. The variability difference is that in topic multiple subscribers receive a message while in queue only one subscriber is allowed to receive. This variability can be modeled as two different structures at PSM or formally as variants populating the *connectionType* variation point.

TABLE 1: The steps of E2EDE process.

Tasks	Technique	Specific Solution
A. Modeling Variation Points in PSM	variability from SPL	Profile For PSM
B. Analyzing Variability and categorized based on PSM /mapping, and functional/ non-functional	variability concepts + MDA concepts + design concepts	Guidelines and informal steps help categorizing different sorts.
C. Developing Profiles for variability &NFRs	UML-based extension mechanisms	MOF language
D. Modeling of Non-functional Requirements in PIM and classified into package/class level	nonfunctional requirements concepts	Profile for PIM + guidelines for classifying NFRs
E. Developing model-model mapping rules.	QVT language	QVT rules
F. Packaging mappings variability rules	opaque rule	QVT meta rules
G. Implement the system	metamodels	UML Package, Profile and relationship program metamodels.

Since standard UML does not have a variability concept, modeling variability in a PSM we need to use a profile to allow us to specify the variability ontology. A profile is a special domain language used as an extension mechan-ism to UML model elements while keeping their syntax and semantic intact.Proposed metamodels and profiles in the literature such as [2,12]can allow an architect to identify specific variation points, constraints and dependencies that indicate different relationships between variation points (VP) and variants (V), VP and VP, etc.

Because we are using design model (i.e. class diagram) the proposed profile here is different from these because there is no need for dependency and constraints concepts. They are built-in mechanisms whose semantics is specified with the mapping process and NFRs. Also, there is no need for open and closed concepts which gives the ability to add new variant or variation points because all are closed in this situation (MDA works above 3 GLs).

Therefore, developing a suitable variability MOF-profile is an essential part for the solution presented by E2EDE.In fact there are alternative ways to model variability and nonfunctional requirements concepts using a profile. The method we have chosen will help produce a working system.

The variability ontology needed includes the concepts *variant* indicated by <<V>> stereotype, *variation point* indicated by <<VP>>, and an ID tag attribute to identify each VP.

In Figure 5 the UML metaclass *class* is extended to represent variant and variation point. A tagged value extension mechanism is used to model identifier and type meta-attributes. Tagged values are additional meta-attributes assigned to a stereotype, specified as name-value pairs. They have a name and a type and can be used to attach arbitrary information to model elements.For instance, if we need to model *ConnectionType* (the two kinds of connections in messaging system) variation point we use the stereotype <<VP>> and for its variants Queue and Topic we use two <<V>> at class level. Then the tag for *ConnectionType* will be VPID =1 and *default* can take the value *Direct*. The effect tag of variant specifies design decision consequences like resource consumption.

1.4.2.2 VARIABILITY ANALYSIS (TASK B)

A taxonomy for variability has emerged from our analysis of variability in software architecture artifacts. They could be called Nonfunctional variability, Functional variability and Mapping variability. SPL has been focused mainly on functional variability. An extensive analysis of this

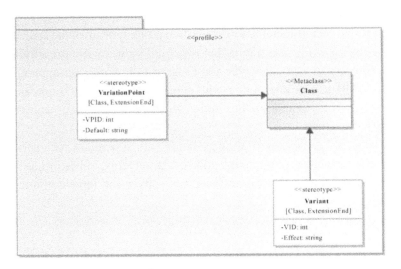

FIGURE 5: Variability MOF-profiles.

can be found in [16]. Although our proposed method includes this sort of variability, it highlights the influence of Nonfunctional variability in the design. Most of the issues discussed in Section 6.3 are of this kind. Mapping variability can be seen in the problem of mapping superclass/ subclass structures from object model into relational model. It is not like the others because the variation points are in the transformation, not in the PSM (i.e. the mappings are parameterized). In this case the mapping is from an object model as a source to the relational model as the target. The former specifies objects and relationships between them which may includes superclass-subclass relationship in a class diagram, while the latter specifies relations and their structure. The metamodels and mapping using QVT of these are well described in [8].The target does not include a structure corresponding to superclass-subclass in the source. To solve this deficiency four options are suggested for this mapping in the standard database literature [17].

Generally these options can be classified into single-relation and multiple-relation approaches named SR and MR respectively. In the SR approach a table for superclass attributes will be created with subclass attributes included as optional while in MR approach table for each subclass will be created. Two implementation techniques are available for both. SR can be implemented by introducing one type attribute indicating the subclass to which each tuple belongs (null values will introduced), or multiple boolean type attributes can be used (allowing overlapping subclasses). MR has as one option with super class attributes duplicated in each subclass table and another option to share a key among superclass and subclass tables.

For example, the option of one table for the superclass with subclass attributes included as optional is a good design in terms of performance for SQL navigation, at a cost of increased table space and increased integrity checking.

1.4.2.3 MODELING OF NON-FUNCTIONAL REQUIREMENTS (TASK D)

The E2EDE methodology considers NFRs as first class objects which allow a PIM metamodel to be more informative. The separation of concerns (i.e. PIM-PSM) of MDAeffectively supports their representation.

Functional requirements are functions that the developed software must be capable of performing, while nonfunctional requirements (NFRs) inform the design choices as to how functional requirements are going to be realized in software products [16]. There is no one agreed definition because of the extremely diverse nature of NFR. In fact, practices like in design pattern shows a single NFR can have different semantic interpretations (impact on implementation) within the same application. These can be called impact factors. For example in our case study, connection types, session types, and message types are impact factors affecting performance positively or negatively. There is confusion in term usage where a term sometimes refers to the nature of the requirement and sometimes refers to the design decisions. We will be using the term NFR to denote the nature of the requirement so a PIM metamodel is the place where we can define specific NFR types.

The difficulty of modeling and integrating explicitly NFRs (additional constraints) within the context of functional requirements is the fact that NFR affects the system as whole [18]. Non-functional requirements especially related to architecture are called quality attributes [4]. They affect design decisions where different quality of products can be distinguished. These are the decisions that drive the system architecture. The representation and categorization of non-functional requirements are still under research. More than one piece of information contributes negatively or positively to one NFR. Preliminary results show diversity in terminology and orientation [4]. In addition, there are dependency relationship among non-functional requirements. For example, in some cases maintainability requires portability. More importantly conflicts are found such as between performance and reliability as shown in our case study below.

The field of nonfunctional requirements as a component in requirements engineering is less developed than functional requirements[19], so there are only a few contributions such as [14,20,21].We are going to follow a simple approach that would be compatible with E2EDE. For example, Zuh and Ian [22] proposed a generic UML NFR Profile, but it is not suitable to work under MDA because the assumption was to treat NFR and design decision in one place. These are different (separate abstraction levels) according to E2EDE's principles. The 6-elements framework from SEI [21] follows a scenario-based approach that presents a good way to resolve the overlapping problem between NFRs. Our approach simply prioritizes NFRs to judge on design decisions, promoting automation.

Since the types of NFRs differ greatly among classes of application, a NFR Profile is needed as a domain specific language to allow system architecture to specify NFRs easily in a PIM metamodel. According to investigation in this track we have seen there is a need to prioritize NFRs so the toolset can tradeoff between NFRs or resolve conflicts. Most of the current contribution to NFR considers the human factor and does not take account of tool support. For example Zhu and Ian [22] proposed for the relationship between design decision and NFR: support, break, help and hurt. Daniel and Eric [14] follow the same trend. In order to reach our goal we need to identity NFRs so the identifier concept is used to discriminate NFR instances. The 6-elements framework suggested by [21] could be a useful tool for Non-functional analysis at earlier development phases.

Figure 6 shows the elements of the NFR profile (Task C) used by an architect to specify NFRs which is specializing a metaclass class with two tag attributes. Below in the anchor is an example of an instance model. It also shows NFRs can be at Package level, which represents global NFRs such as Application Type, while delivery mode is at class level. It also shows that NFRs can act as Packagelevel, which represents global NFRs such as Application Type, while delivery mode is at class level.

1.4.2.4 TRANSFORMATION OF INFORMATIVE PIM TO PSM (TASK E)

The notion of transformation is hardly a new concept in software engineering. Traditionally, most software engineering work is conceived of as mapping, like the transformation from software specification to software design. But what makes MDA different is considering mappings as first class objects in the effort to formalize this process by using standard languages such as QVT where mapping is from one metamodel to another metamodel. This approach is a prerequisite for the automation that MDA is seeking to achieve.

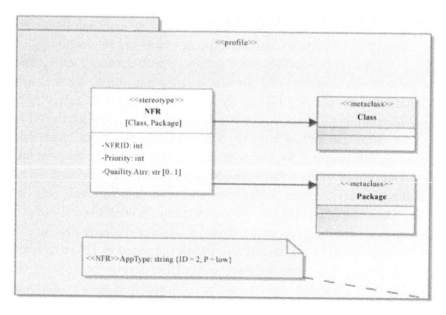

FIGURE 6: NFR UML profile.

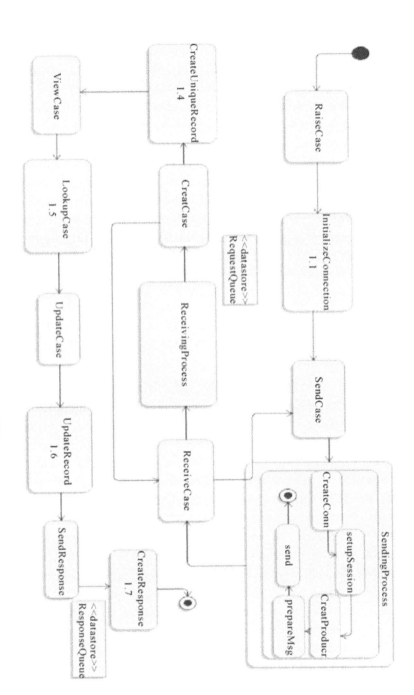

FIGURE 7: Behavioral mappings activity for helpdesk PIM to messaging system PSM.

The key concept of MDA mapping is to resolve a structure pattern instance from PIM into a PSM corresponding structure pattern(s) instance. For example, in case of mapping from object model (PIM) to the relational model (PSM), a class instance will map to a table instance.

Our work proposes NFRs as major design drivers feeding the mapping process. This feature facilitates the mapping task where it becomes easier to select the corresponding PSM structure. NFRs make the difference between two PSM configurations. For instance, as we will see later there are two types of messages, persistent and nonpersistent, in the messaging system. If performance impact factor(s) are most important, the nonpersistent variant is suitable while if reliability is a design issue, the persistent variant is the best option. The former architetture will expose performance quality while the latter will expose reliability based on the additional computation the application needs to maintain the message storing process.

1.4.2.5 MAPPINGS OF CLASS OPERATIONS

The class structure in UML includes methods or behavior. Because maintaining different views in one model is complex, UML supports capturing dynamic behavior of the system separately by a set of behavioral diagrams such as the activity diagram. This subsection is about highlighting mapping problem from PIM instances of the process model to PSM instances of its process model. In this case a metamodel does not have user-defined operations, the MOF specification has defined default methods: create object, destroy object, and create link in each MOF metaclass [7]. Firstly, these methods are abstract methods. Secondly, mappings of structural patterns are somehow straightforward but the relationship between PIM behavioral model and PSM behavior is nonlinear. So when mappings for example occurred for attributes which are going to be columns in the relational model, there might be a set of corresponding operations (1 to M relationship) in the PSM behavioral metamodel for a corresponding class' methods in PIM behavioral model. However, there is no uniquely determined method to do that. Recent attempt for example in this case was suggested by [6], one possible MDA program written for medium-sized problem involving organizing a swimming meet according to FINA rules (insert and update native call) utilizing OCL capability to construct SQL PSM.

However, we can use the hierarchy structure of UML activity diagram to show the implementation of PIM methods in PSM as workflow as in our case study in Figure 7: *Sendcase* mapped to *SendingProcess* where it is extended into five operations as described in 5.3.

We notice here future work is needed to find a method that realizes the operations mapping so we can see how to incorporate variability and NFR concepts. Generally the tasks comprise E2EDE process are shown in Table 1.

1.5 CASE STUDY

A set of applications has been analyzed to produce the PSM architecture used by this case study as an implementation end. This family of products which are mentioned in Table 2 has exposed commonality in most aspects under messaging system domain. This analysis step is in line with the principle of domain engineering where at least three products should expose commonalities to justify the investment in core asset architecture [23]. A Help desk system is one example from this set of products which is a major component in most current business web-based systems. The idea is to allow a user to raise a case for some aspect which needs a reply from some organization web site party. An employee should consult through the same web site a list of cases or a specific case that has been presented as a request in order to update it. Then the update is sent back to user, who may be offline, as response. A broker is an intermediate module used to exchange messages between the system and users. Users contacting the system are durable customers. The nonfunctional requirement for system performance is higher than reliability.

1.5.1 THE PROBLEM SPECIFICATION

The helpdesk software system is needed to service customer(s) and employee(s) at the same time. A customer will be required to insert

identification information such as user name and password after regis-
tration—both of which will be sent for validation to the web site system
which is located remotely somewhere on the internet. The customer as
well as the employee will then be able to perform one or more operations.

TABLE 2: Configuration for a set of products from PSM metamodel with profile.

Appliction domains	NFR Profile	Priority	Variation point (Design Decisions) <Message,connection,session,Ack>
1-Email System	App-size = normal	P1	
	Iscritical = yes	P2+P3>P1	<persistence,queue,transacted, AutoAck>
	Delivery = notUrgent	P3	
2-Chat	App-size = normal	P1>P2+P3	
	Iscritical = no	P2	<NonPersistence, Topic,nontransacted, DupAck>
	Delivery = medium	P3	
3-Forum	App-size = normal	P1>P2+P3	
	Iscritical = no	P2	<NonPersistence,Topic,nontransacted, AutoAck, >
	Delivery = medium	P3	
4-Mobile application	Reliability = high	P1=	
	Iscritical = yes	P2=	<persistence,queue, transacted, FastAck>
	Delivery = high	P3=	

The helpdesk must be able to provide the following services to the
customer:

1. A customer must be able to login using his account information.
2. A customer must be able to submit a case to any employee linked
   to organization, by writing a text message and submitting it to a
   broker.
3. A customer must be able to view their case history (feedback), status, and details.
4. A broker needs to maintain a queue in order to schedule cases and
   differentiate between different users' cases. They also must be able
   to create a message.

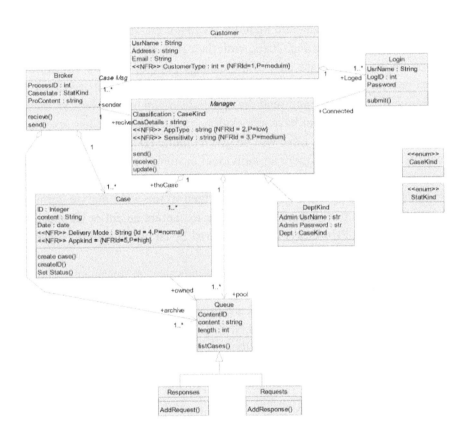

FIGURE 8: PIM: Helpdesk system with NFR documented.

5. An employee should be able view cases by individual case or list of cases and look for details.
6. An employee should be able to update a case.

This is the functionality needed to develop an application conceptual model (PIM) as we will see in Figure 8.

Figure 8 shows a class diagram for the helpdesk system. The basic structure of the class diagram includes six major classes: customer, login, broker, case, manager, and Queue with their responsibilities and relationships among them. In the case of the manager, one of the responsibilities is to provide access to a case in the response queue that has received a message from a broker and send the updated version back to broker; thus, Case, Queue, and broker have associations to manager. Case has association to the queue class. Case will be given unique ID and created so each case will represent uniquely an individual customer case which is stored in a queue either as a request if it came from the customer or response if it came from the system. The UI is specified in this PIM but we are not considering this part. It could be possible to capture an entire UI specification from this PIM that could be rendered by an outsourced third-party platform such as a browser.

We are using <<NFR>> stereotype to indicate non-functional requirements according to the NFR profile. Tag values are used to denote two pieces of information: ID to identify a NFR and priority (P) which assigns an integer number to indicate a priority level of NFR. These are the elements of the NFR specific-language used to model NFRs as described in 4.2.3 (Task D).

In the PIM shown in Figure 8 there are the following NFRs: Application sensitivity {High, low, medium}, AppKind{transactional,nontransactional}, CustomerType {normal, durable}, AppType {normal, critical}, and delivery Mode{normal,guaranteed}. (Task D). The interpretation of these NFRs will make sense when we link to design decisions as we will see later. We now have a helpdesk system conceptual model describing functionality as well as nonfunctional requirements.

The PSM in Figure 9 shows a messaging system which can be a realization of a PIM such as in Figure 8. It describes how data can communicate between two software entities: Producer instance and Consumer instance. A Session instance must be created between the two ends but to

do that a Connection instance must be created first with suitable parameters. Session has two types as does Connection, while Transact means the
underlying system should treat the data send as a transaction in database so
the system should guarantee correct update, consistency, and can rollback
a NonTransactional is to treat data not as a transaction. Consumer and data
instances can be synchronous (Synch) or Asynchronous (Asynch) which
refers to whether it is necessary or not for the consumer to attend at the
time of connection. Connection is Direct type or Indirect type transaction
in case of failure.

We can call Queue for the former which allows one receiver per send
action and Topic for the later that allows multiple receivers per send. Data
can be Persistence type which means using backing store, preserving it in
the case of any failure, or it can be NonPersistence. (Task B) We notice
this abstraction deals with concepts that are from implementation space
not like the PIM concepts that are from an application domain.

Figure 9 shows the capability to deal with different design decisions
configuration that are represented by variability (Task A, C). For example
Connection is denoted by <<VP>> stereotype which can take Direct or
Indirect variants. Likewise session denoted by <<VP>> with its two different variant kinds. The focus on the discussion will be only on variability
that is non-functional with respect to the PIM.

1.5.2 MAPPINGS (TASK E)

In order to explain how to apply this principle we will describe mappings
of this case manually, while it should be automated. The NFR in the PIM
of Figure 8 will guide the mapping process to configure a suitable PSM
from Figure 9 automatically. For instance, the two data variants: persistence or NonPersistence is selected according to the application need
for reliability or performance so delivery mode will determine that. The
current case study says Application Sensitivity is not high and a delivery
mode is normal hence these two NFRs are not reliability factors which
require maximizing performance. The delivery would use NonPersistence

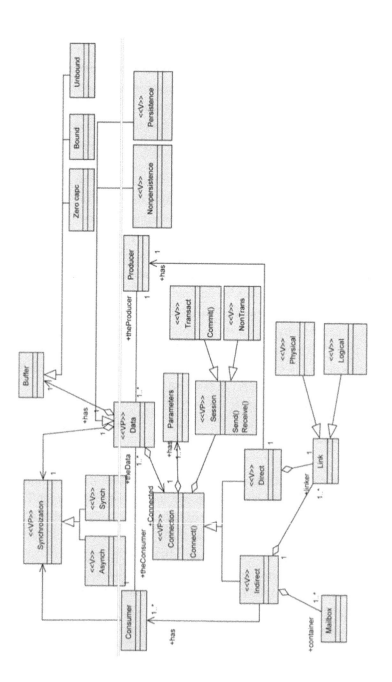

FIGURE 9: PSM of messaging system with variability in design decision.

option which does not necessarily insure message delivery by for example storing message until a receiver becomes available.

Similarly, the Session variation point has two variants: Transacted and Nontransacted. Because the AppType (i.e. size) NFR is normal application in the help desk PIM Nontransacted variant is the most suitable.

This factor affects performance directly for example when transacted variant is used performance is impacted negatively compared with the Nontransacted mode. This is because there is additional overhead for resource manipulation needed in the system for transaction mode.

Connection variation point has two connection variants: Direct and Indirect which means single receiver versus multiple receivers per message. They are selected based on AppKind and CustomerType Non-functional requirements. A Transactional application, for example banking transactions, requires usually direct connection such as for doing funds transfer. The same is true in our case study where direct connection is selected for request and response messages because CustomerType is single user. In contrast, mobile applications such as advertisements prefer broadcasting a message to group of receivers so indirect connection is the most suitable variant. In that case customer Type can be multiple users.

Generally in terms of performance indirect connection is contributing positively while direct connection is contributing negatively. The same message is forwarded to different subscribers which mean lower resource consumption.

Note that we need one of the variants to be set as default because the PIM and PSM are independent so that the default will be selected in case there is no corresponding NFR(s). For instance Figure 10 shows that the de-fault variant is selected ([2]) for ConnectionVP if there is no corresponding NFR addressed. We notice also two or more design decisions determined by single NFR such as Appkind can be used to decide both connection and session variants.

Table 2 shows informally part of mappings from Helpdesk system PIM to messaging system PSM with NFRs guidance. It also shows how application concepts turn into design concepts. For instance the Case from PIM metamodel which is a unit of work between customers and company holding the necessary information will be mapped into three objects: Message, Connection and Session.

Because we have two kinds of messages and so two different bodies of computations, we need to judge on suitable design by looking into NFRs presented in the PIM according to for example performance or reliability. NFRs can be extracted from system specification by different formats and meaning. For simplicity Iscritical (such as OCL style) is used instead of AppType. The mapping rules that can be used to implement the mappings specified in Table 1 are shown below.

Figure 10 like pseudo-code shows a sample of mappings rules to transform PIM instances with existence of priority consideration into PSM in-

```
PSMR= PSM repository holding instances
Pi=Priority
[1] CaseToData
        IF (Iscritical=Yes) and (delivery=guaranteed)
then
        If (P1[Is critical]>P2[delivery])
        Then store in PSMR ([Data,type=Persistence)])
        IF (Iscritical =NO) and (delivery=guranteed)
Then store in PSMR ([Data,type=NonPersistence)])
        IF (Iscritical =No) and (delivery=normal)
        Then store in PSMR ([Data,type=Persistence])


[2] CaseToConnection
Select connection.default-V          [Queue in this case]
Store in PSMR ([Connection.type=connection.default-V])


[3] CaseToSession
        IF (AppKind.value=transactional)
        Then store in PSMR ([session,type=transacted])
```

FIGURE 10: Part of informal mappings rules from helpdesk PIM to messaging system PSM.

stances. For example, [1] describes a conflict situation where if the application Iscritical and at the same time the delivery is guaranteed, the selection of design decision will depends on the highest priority. In this case persistence (factor of reliability) is chosen because P1 is greater than P2. Note here priority is used only in the case of NFR values causing a conflict.

We notice by this way an application could be configured at the two extremes: reliability and performance using suitable design decisions represented in the design artifact with NFRs guidance. It is also possible to configure an application in between these two extremes. Thus our method affords different products with architecture designs at different levels of quality-attributes. Inputs for mappings will be PIM metamodel (holds application instances), NFRsrepository (NFR instances), PSM metamodel, and Variability (design decision instances).

1.5.3 CLASS METHODS MAPPING

This activity is intended to realize the abstract operations expressed by one kind of behavior diagram for the helpdesk PIM metamodel. We can use an activity diagram to show the control flow and instances creation during the execution of the mappings from PIM to PSM at this stage. For example in the behavior instances model of Figure 8, the sendcase method in broker needs to map into the following sequence: createObject (connection), createObject (session), createObject (producer) as in the behavior instances model shown in Figure 7. It shows the control flow of mapping activity and relationship occurrences between source (helpdesk behavior model) and target (messaging system model). For example, raise case will be mapped to initialize Connection and sendcase will be mapped to sending process. We can determine PIM (source) and PSM (target) actions from this activity diagram. For example PSM activity are, initalizeConnetion, SendingProcess, ReceivingProcess, CreateUniqueRecord, lookupcase, UpdateRecord and createResponse (from 1.1 to 1.7). But still as we mentioned previously more investigation is needed in this place to map a PIM process model to PSM process model and understand this mapping completely.

1.6 MDA IN THE CONTEXT OF DESIGN PATTERN AND SPL

It is a claim in this paper that MDA is a re-use approach. In this section we see how MDA can fit in with other common re-use approaches such as design pattern and software product line (SPL).The investigation of this relationship is the reason behind approaching E2 EDE. Variability and Nonfunctional requirement concepts are borrowed as we have seen in section. MDA is a special case of design pattern techniques as we will argue in Section 6.1, while MDA and SPL have a synergistic relationship according to observations described in Section 6.2.

1.6.1 MDA AND DESIGN PATTERN

The design pattern concept goes back to Christopher Alexander [24]. His definition identified a relationship between three parts constituting a pattern: problem, solution and context. In software engineering, a design pattern is a general reusable solution to a commonly occurring problem in software design [25].

1.6.1.1 LIMITED TO DOMAINS WITH A WELL-ESTABLISHED CODE BASE

The nature of solution provided by MDA is more specific to the problem domain than the design pattern which is more general because there are many kinds of design patterns [26]. A general purpose pattern perspective in solving problems is more expensive in terms of the establishment of working environment than in MDA, which is characterized by its well-established specific backend. Typically, MDA is used to target platform(s) that have already been crafted. For instance, large scale software RDBMS (a complex proven solution) can be utilized automatically by tools which transform PSM relational model after mapping to the SQL language. In contrast, for a pattern to be executed generally involves establishing new tools. For instance, Yacoub, Xue and Ammar [27] proposed their own visual systematic tool.

1.6.1.2 SEPARATING CONCERNS ALLOWS APPLICATION LOGIC AND PLATFORM TO BE VARIABLE AND ENCOURAGES RE-USE

It is observed that design pattern tends to integrate the behavior aspects with implementation aspects which result in risks of platform changing or volatility. Further, some implementation details become suppressed as consequence of behavioral variation as in the publish-subscribe pattern which does not say anything about remote objects design [15]. If this pattern is used in a distributed environment it becomes necessary to distinguish local from remote objects which is not available as a design decision at design time.

1.6.1.3 END OF PATTERN LIFE CYCLE

Design Pattern follows a life-cycle as patterns become more mature and quality increases [28]. MDA produces high quality patterns because PSMs are end of the pattern life cycle. Although the nonfunctional requirement emerged first in the design pattern approach, MDA gives a wide opportunity to represent NFR explicitly. It is the critical requirement that discriminates between pattern architecture designs. In fact, it is still a research question how to graft design pattern with recognition of NFRs. In Buschmann [15] we can observe the role of NFRs in balancing design forces.

1.6.2 MDA AND SOFTWARE PRODUCT LINE (SPL)

Software product line engineering is a paradigm to develop software applications (software-intensive systems and software products) using common platforms and mass customization [2]. The intended goal is to avoid reinventing the same solution for different applications in order to achieve shorter development time and high quality products (i.e. Nokia mobile applications). There are two distinct development processes adopted by SPL: domain engineering and application engineering. The former is concerned with design for reuse by seeking communalties and variability in the software product line. As a result a reference architecture called product line architecture (PLA) is established. The aim of the latter is to drive applications by exploiting the variability of the software product line.

1.6.2.1 DEFINING VARIATION POINTS AND VARIANTS

The central concept in SPL is the explicit representation of variability. Variability is a variable item of the real world or a variable property of such an item [16].A variant identifies a single option of a variation point and can be associated with other artifacts corresponding to a particular option (dependency relationship). For example, payment method as a variation point can be realized by variants: payment by credit card or payment by cash, etc. It is necessary in SPL to identify variability by defining variation points and variants, which is used by a selection process to produce different products.

There are two types of variability: Variability in time, which is different versions of the artifact at different times (i.e. performance), while variability in space refers to an artifact in different shapes at same time. For example "*system access by*" variation point in a home security system can have two variants: web browser and mobile phone. Variability in space is the central challenge faced by SPL, so management of variability is the main issue in this engineering approach [16].

A set of closely related objects, packaged together with a set of defined interfaces, forms a component [28]. Usually a component-based approach is used to realize SPL concepts. SPL tightly couples application and implementation models together.MDA as an approach reduces the SPL to abstract computational processes. It separates the application from implementation by creating PIM and PSM abstraction levels.

1.6.3 MDA IN THE CONTEXT OF THE SOFTWARE PRODUCT LINE

Both software product line engineering (SPL) and model driven architecture (MDA) are emerging as effective paradigms for developing a family of applications in a cost effective way [3]. SPL through its feature-based models provides a capability to capture variability in intensive systems, while the effectiveness of MDA is primarily due to potential for automation it offers for variability in technology. Generally MDA can fit into SPL as an effective software development method. For instance MDA can tackle implementation variability within a specific platform. So the synergistic relationship between the two approaches has been studied recently [4,20,29]. The basic differences between the two approaches are as follows:

1.6.3.1 MDA DECOUPLES IMPLEMENTATION MODEL FROM APPLICATION MODEL

The PSM is constructed as an API to specify the implementation aspects for an intended target such as relational database model. Similarly a PIM model is built which specifies the business logic. This will add value by enabling MDA to tackle technology variability which allows the same PIM to be rendered into different platforms or PSMs.

Although components raise the reuse level a little bit, they still suffer from the software evolution problem. For example, any small interface changes will entail finding everywhere the interface is used, changing it to reflect the new interface, testing new code, reintegrating and retesting the system as whole. Therefore, a small change in the interface can cause enormous changes by following each code part that refers to this component interface. In contrast, the PSM, an intermediate subsystem, abstracts this tedious task by concentrating the changes in one place. Also, MDA avoids the problem of features explosion that tends to complicate maintenance [9]. In addition, keeping a mapping function separate avoids swamping the source model (application) with implementation details and reduces the problem of model divergence because the target (implementation) is generated [29].

Furthermore, MDA increases architecture longevity (ageing) compared to the fact that sometimes PLE suffers from architecture lifespan which may reach end of life [22]. In this case evolving architecture will be expensive or risky. MDA's potentiality comes where evolving the architecture becomes much cheaper because each of PSMs and PIMs are adapted separately and they do not carry any volatility risks (technology variability).

1.6.3.2 MDA IS INTENDED TO AUTOMATE THE CRAFT OF CODE

The potential of MDA is due to the capability of automation it offers. It is recognized that if we will be able to formalize the model to the extent that it has no ambiguity and the model is machine readable (executable) then the code in principle can be mechanically generated. MOF is a powerful metamodeling language that realizes this trend by allowing tools to interoperate and accurately modeling the conceptual model of a design language such as UML. Crafting code becomes a model driven process wherein a transformation from source model (PIM) to a target model (PSM) can be automated by for example QVT tools. Eventually the PSM can automatically mapped into text (code). MDA works best if the scale of PSM objects is the same as that of PIM. The mapping function is kept separate so that it can generalize some concepts and it can be repeated many times (repeated design decisions) showing a big picture of reuse. The mapping function can be automated at the instance level because it is an algorithmic process in which generic transformation rules are established at the type level. The general feature of automation is the synchronization between the two ends.

1.6.3.3 HIGHER ABSTRACTION AND SYSTEMATIC DEVELOPMENT METHODOLOGY

The main goal of MDA is to raise the abstraction level higher than traditional middleware and 3 GL/4 GLs programming languages. This means taking advantage of software-platform independence that enables a specification to execute on a variety of software platform with a stable software architecture design. The granularity of code re-use will increase to the level of a PSM (ADT) instead of components as in SPL. The PSM is scoped to this level of code reuse. For example relational database PSM is an abstraction for the family of relational databases above any specific technology. Also, there is a difference between MDA and SPL in defining interfaces to components and frameworks via an API. In MDA, the interface is not concrete but it is meta-interface exported by marking models [29]. The mappings are externalized and generalized, which can be reused in similar problems.

MDA is standards-based development method which is specified entirely by a nonprofit organization, OMG, since 2001 [1]. It involves algorithmic mapping processes from model to model (PIM-PSM) and from model to text (PSM-code). The mapping process is rule-driven in which transformation rules are expressed by a standard language (e.g. QVT). However, different viewpoints could be constructed for different abstraction levels. Formal mapping functions will often fill the gap between any two different abstraction levels (consider compilers). Further, having MOF as metalanguage and other well-established OMG standards (i.e. XMI), it promises industrial-scale systematic re-use and integration capability.

1.7 HOW DESIGN PATTERN AND SPL CONTRIBUTE TO E2E2D ENGINEERING

The survey of the relationship among MDA, SPL, and Design Patterns has shown a synergistic relationship. MDA improves each approach by supporting these quailties: automation, proper management of technology changes or volatility, high granularity of reuse and more important a capability of integration.

Design Pattern is not an end to end concept because it is an abstraction for software implementation.

Design pattern could be used to construct the architecture in E2EDE. It adds value by acting as a proven solution and a documented experience.

SPL is an end to end concept but in addition to the problem of coupling application and implementation together, it does not tackle the variability in the implementation part. In contrast, E2EDE is mainly addressing this challenge. In addition, there is no concrete link as in E2EDE between higher level models and lower detailed models.

SPL engineering gives another insight for E2EDE: the concept of explicit variability representation and management. Introducing variability explicitly in the PSM helps mainly in its construction. This means a PIM can become informed about variation points that are documented explicitly therefore it becomes possible to automate the design decision process. A UML profile for specifying PLA [3] can fill the gap between PSM and the PLA core assets artifact.

Metamodeling and MDA are an alternative technique successfully used to organize SPL and feature model concepts as demonstrated by Muthig and Atkinson [11]. Furthermore, unlike orthogonal models, the variability model and original model would not be separated, which increases readability.

1.8 STRATEGIC MESSAGING SYSTEM PSM

The philosophy of MDA is to do more investment on metamodels so as to hopefully obtain payoff at production time by producing larger number of products. It can be conceived as the same scale as where database systems and X11 [20] are considered viable.

We have looked at PSM in Figure 9 in the previous section as a specific implementation for helpdesk system. In fact this PSM was built from a general messaging system perspective. The concepts in this PSM form an ontology. There are many messaging systems which commit to that ontology. Examples are: Chat system, Email system, instant messaging system, media streaming system, mobile applications, etc.

As we argued before re-use is a major trend in the software development community. Important are not only reusable components but also strategic reusable assets like models and transforms.

Table 2 shows a simple configuration for four products as a picture of the benefits of re-using the messaging system PSM. Further, it is obvious that the rationale of this specific architecture design does not exhaust the E2EDE approach. An architect can reason about different architecture designs.

In Table 3 we see there are number of NFRs common to this set of applications, which are re-used to make a design decisions. They are App-size (i.e. Application size), Iscritical and Delivery. Both App-size and Iscritical are a kind of Package level NFRs while Delivery is a class level NFR because it is about an object class inside the system. Design decisions are: message (data), connection and session, and Acknowledgement mechanisms. In the example of email system two reliability factors are higher than the other; App-size has lower value than for delivery and apply-size, therefore message (data) delivery is persistence with Queue type connection and transacted session. The Acknowledgement will be given normal value which is AutoAck. All these values makes reliability higher than performance because of the overhead processing (i.e. store) which what is said by NFRs. The inverse of this situation typically is in Chat and Forum application where P1 of application size put into highest priority than data delivery and Iscritical so the configuretion of parameters is set to increase performance. The mobile application comes in the middle between performance and reliability more oriented to reliability. Note that this is an arbitrary configuration but any other scenarios are possible. The point is by that we can see an example of NFRs and variability reusing among products in messaging systems.

TABLE 3: Part of mappings from helpdesk system to messaging system.

PIM	Relevant NFR	PSM Variation Points
1. Case	Data needed between producer and consumer and let the system works so it is functional. But there is a quality on its processing based on priority and type.	1.1 Message 1.2 connection
1.1. Data [message]	Apptype{normal,critical}or sensitivity {low, high} and delivery mode	1.1.1 persistence or 1.1.2 nonpersistence
1.2. connection	customerType and AppKind{transactional, nontrnsact}	1.2.1 queue or 1.2.2 topic
1.2.x.1. session	AppKind and delivery mode	1.2.3 transacted 1.2.4 Nontransacted
1.3. broker	User or customerType	1.3.1 Consumer::Asynch or 1.3.2 consumer::Synch

1.9 HOW MDA WORKS

MDA is new trend in software development. This section sketches key points about MDA implementation. The history of software engineering shows that a software design model is a complex object that needs to be maintained during a project life cycle and refined over a long period. CASE tool (computer-aided software engineering) is used to allow easy model creation, editing, rendering etc. In this case, a tool designer utilizes information system technology to keep this complex object in a database called a repository. A repository consists of a schema which stores model instances [6]. In fact this repository does not need the complete commercial database machinery. There are recently emerging MOF-standards like XMI [30] used as a mechanism not only for persistence purpose but also as a mechanism for exchanging models between tools which it was difficult before in a classic CASE tool (i.e. magic draw, rational rose). Many recent MOF-based toolsets support in addition to efficient access methods, both system and userdefined API serialization mechanisms in which developers can render a model using an XMI concrete syntax for different purposes. There are many tools with different features and capabilities working in this context, extensively studied in [31]. EMF [32] an open platform adopting MDA principles provides a Java code-generation facility to achieve interoperability between applications based on a MOF metamodeling framework.

1.10 E2EDE IMPLEMENTATION

The implementation of E2EDE need to be considered as there is some limitation in current MDA tools. Our approach in this space is to separate working on the model view from the implementation view the same way UML gives a different views for different purposes such class diagram and activity diagram.

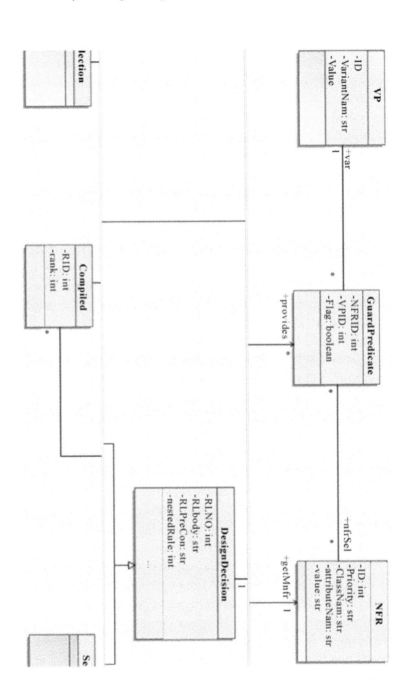

The proposed profiles are useful in terms of readability and explicit showing of the NFRs and VPs but for implementation it needs suitable representation to fit the MDA computation environment.

There are three reasons underlying the solution suggested in this section: source, target and mapping metamodels. Firstly, current tools have a limitation of recognizing a profile instances in a model annotated by a profile elements such as MediniQVT [33]. (Tag values are not visible to QVT pattern expressions.) Therefore we suggest a representation for profiles to resolve this issue. Secondly, if we look practically to the mapping the metalevels concept breaks down when we compare two systems. For instances, if we used UML as PIM metamodel and MOF as PSM metamodel, the mapping is from instances of M0 objects to instances of M1 objects. The same is true more generally when we use Profile instances that are at level higher than instances level of the metamodel. In our specific case, profile instances are at M1 level while the metamodel instances needed by QVT engine are at M0 level. However, OWL-Full [34] can be suggested as an alternative technology to UML which could resolve this solution. OWL has an OWL metaclass class which is itself a class, so we can build a profile mechanism by declaring subclasses of OWL class.

Finally there is a need for linking a single VP with a set of NFRs and mapping variability should be considered. (Task G) Figure 11 describes the relationship between VP, NFR and a Design Decision. A design decision is one of two kinds: *selection* which denotes the normal variability exists on PSM, and *compiled* which represents the mapping variability highlighted in the previous sections. This sort of design decision groups related rules that have some common property which is modeled by the attribute rank. An instance of compiled design decision is associated with an instance of NFR because NFR(s) is the reason behind this grouping.

For example, consider how the mapping variability discussed in Section 4.2.2 could be represented. Also, more information details about design decisions can be added, for instance to compiled subclasses, like the effects and cost of effect etc. However, an instance of a design decision is an opaque rule specifying the creation of valid PSM instances when its precondition is satisfied as shown in the following. A program manipulating this metamodel should differentiate between three modes: default, application of a rule, and conflict resolution. A conflict mode needs to refer to NFR's priority. Seduocode based in QVT relation language is shown in Figure 12 .This part showing application of Task F.

Figure 12 demonstrates statements describe two disjoint types of connection that will only be created as PSM instances when certain Preconditions are satisfied. The function of the Guard Predicate class is to collect VP related NFRs which has multiplicity one to many. This means a pattern structure in PIM will be linked with one variant through one or more NFRs. For instance, in the two examples we have two sets of NFR related to Direct and Indirect variants respectively: {important, transactional}, {normal, Nontransactional}. Note that variants in PSM are disjoint and covering because they are alterna-tive design elements. NFR and VP are imported from corresponding packages.

The metamodel in Figure 13 is a lightweight UML2.0 metamodel used as an example by the QVT specification. We use this as a base for presentation purposes (Profile). The full work makes use of UML.

The extension or adaptation to this existing metamodel was special NFR (SNFR) metaclass, general NFR (GNFR) metaclass and NFR metaclass. Working with this case study shows that there are two kinds of NFR: package level (general) and class level (special).

1-RLPrecod = CustomerType =important,
AppKind=transactional
Enforce domain MSGPSM co:Conection { type='Direct',
name=con}

2-RLPrecod = CustomerType =normal,
AppKind=Nontransactional

Enforce domain MSGPSM co:Conection { type='Indirect',
name=con}

FIGURE 12: Opaque rules for mapping variability rules.

An extension to the same UML simple metamodel could be done for variability model using an extension to the metaclass class to represent variation point, variant and QuailityAttribute. The same extension is found in the literature such as [2,3,12] but there are two problems with this. Firstly, it does not model mapping variability and for example the conflict cases that arise when we link NFRs with variants. Secondly, it is impossible to use the UML toolset to do that modification because it is at the level of UML metamodel. Here the proposed approach generally involves Profiles, packages and model manipulation.

The meaning of variability in PSM is somehow different from traditional variability in SPL. In E2EDE, variants are disjoint and covering which represents only alternative design decisions. These decisions can be overlapped and not covering in SPL. Variants in E2EDE exist on a PSM artifact to represent Nonfunctional while SPL traditionally represents only functional variability. There is no dependency such as between VP-VP because it is already inherited from the UML design language.

1.10.1 PACKAGES (TASK G)

PSM variability needs to be represented in a way access-ible and without ambiguity to the relationship programs. The relationship program has end to end functionality. It is intended to link a PSM variant with the relevant NFR(s). The traditional mechanism in literature used to model variability is through a subclass structure of the UML class model like [12]. This is suitable for humans but if the system is scaled up, it would be difficult for a human to comprehend that system. The second problem is that some times in these large system names of classes, properties, and association etc, can be ambiguous. Therefore we need a representation mechanism that allows the program to find model elements. MOF and UML support a Package mechanism which has a capability to make names of members unique within the package that owns them. Further it is has a facility to disambiguate names where necessary by adding the package name as prefix. So both human and programs could easily access model elements without ambiguity. Further a package may need to import or merge another package.

Therefore, the semantic operations of incorporating a subclass (variant) in the model will be through legal standard package operations. In UML2 infrastructure a package [35] is defined to group elements, and provides a namespace for the grouped elements. A package merge is used as basic re-use mechanism that allows extension by new features. For instance, UML2.1.2 superstructure builds on the Infrastructure library by re-use of the kernel package. It is defined in UML2.1.2 infrastructure as a direct relationship between two packages that indicates the contents of the two packages are to be combined. Conceptually this means there is a resulting element combining the characteristics of both source and target.

Since we modeled VP and V using the generalization concept, a subclass is always an extension for superclass i.e. by adding new structural features. A package merge has these capabilities. Therefore, a PSM super-subclass structure will be modeled using packages.

The second value of using a package is that it is a powerful mechanism for embedding an entire metamodel (sub architecture) to represent a variant that could be reused in the main model (namespace). It is effective due to its capability to represent PSM implementation variability that can scale up as practically used by OMG as a basic building block to develop and reuse a variety of infrastructure and superstructure constructs. Further the capability of package operations (i.e. import, merge, etc) allows one to build complex structures by combining simple constructs using a systematic rule. This feature in the programming languages concepts is recognized as orthogonality [36].

So now we have the representation of variability in PSM using the package mechanism. In addition, we have NFRs represented in PIM metamodel which has representation in Figure 13. They were two kinds: package level NFRs and class level NFRs. To this end we need a relationship program using NFRs to select the suitable variant(s). This will be modeled using model manipulation tools. But in order for this relationship program to work we represented elements of the problem in way easier for the programs to find and manipulate (Package).

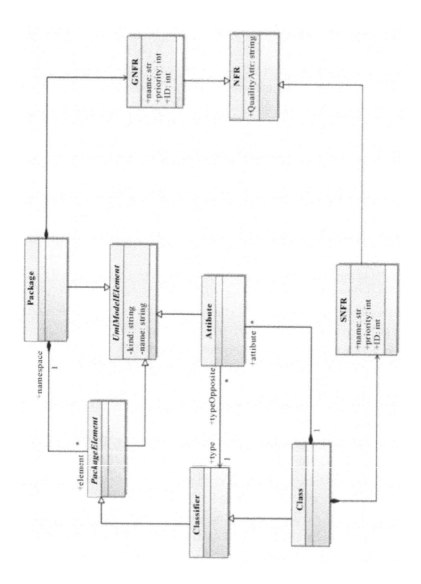

FIGURE 13: Simple UML2.0 metamodel extention from QVT specification as Profile implementation.

1.11 LESSONS & REALISTIC OF E2EDE

The key point from the step toward strategic PSM like the one presented in section 8 is since there are a group of different products complaint with a standard interface, they are sharing an abstract data type (ADT). It becomes easy for example to replace one by another, for example Dell laptops standard architecture is the reason behind a wide set of products. Another example from our community is the service-oriented architecture where its standard interface leads to proliferation of applications and what is known as Agility. This scenario even could be applied to situation where there is no standard specification. Here we need a reengineering process to fill the gap but this time with the lowest reengineering cost, with assumption that the different products have largely similar functionality. Typically any drift from common functionality would be resolved as a mapping from the PIM to the PSM. Any further changes made necessary by use of a particular platform should be relatively minor. Typically it is the case of messaging system PSM there is no standard specification but E2EDE encourage reaching agreements on messaging design vocabulary. Our investigation shows us there is similarity even if sometimes there are differences in naming.

One could see the advantage of what we are taking about if we look at Advanced Message Queuing Protocol (AMQP) [37] practice when it standardized message format (known as a wire-level protocol) which is proprietary in JMS [38]. Any tool conforming to this data format can interoperate with any other compliant tool regardless of implementation language. Both JMS and Microsoft's MSMQ [39] comprise alternative candidate platforms for our messaging system PSM. Both have similar capabilities but have differences in performance and integration features plus others. Our messaging PSM is developed from the standard of JMS which is recognized as the best-known standard in the asynchronous messaging world [40]. As we mentioned, a complete ontology of messaging systems needs to be established by a standards body so one could take the advantage of replacing one messaging platform by another. This standard will establish a vendor-neutral protocol by studying different practices of messaging paradigms such publish/ subscribe, point-to-point, request-response, etc.

The standard would specify message format, Brokers behaveior scenarios, and others.

1.12 CONCLUSIONS

MDA is about mapping PIM instances to PSM instances automatically using a standard mapping language such as QVT as a new trend of developing applications. The MDA standard specification does not show in details how to do the mappings from PIM metamodel (application-space) to PSM metamodel (implementation-space). This situation raises a question: how to develop End to End applications which is the ultimate goal of MDA.

In the view of that question we have proposed E2EDE, a novel software development approach which bridges the mapping gap between PIM (functional specification) and PSM (implementation specification) using the MDA method.

E2EDE approach is based on documenting variability in architecture artifact design on the PSM by utilizing the variability notion in the software product line approach. Our variability analysis has shown taxonomy for variability including mapping variability.

NFRs is proposed to be documented in PIM to make the PIM more informative thereby guiding the mapping process to select from among design alternatives in order to automatically produce a suitable implementation or PSM instance model. In this scenario the mapping process is modeled in a configurable way to drive an architecture that can lead to considerable cost-saving. We have shown that this study has contributed to NFRs knowledge by identifying two kinds of NFRs: Package level and class level. The former have more re-use potential.

E2EDE contributes to the MDA domain by finding concrete mapping methods for generating high quality applications within specific but big enough domains through building explicit links between design decisions and NFRs.

E2EDE implementation models were developed and it was discovered that a profile is good at presentation level but not suitable for implementation level. Generally, we followed Profiles, Packages, and model manipulation approach where metamodels were developed for source, target and relationship program.

We have investigated the realistic application of E2EDE and found that there different examples of messaging systems without a standard. For use of E2EDE, having a standard PSM would be an advantage. It increases the reuse theme (PIM with NFRs can be like variant feature) and achieves interoperability. The best situation would be gained if PSM is built by standards bodies such as ISO or the OMG.

Finally, throughout this paper we have seen how MDA can fit in with SPL and Design pattern under the reuse umbrella which helps explore the research issues that are arose such as Non-functional requirements when we tackle E2EDE engineering. A case study was presented to show the possibility of success under this approach. A strategic PSM for messaging systems is developed as another potentially valuable product. In addition, the lessons and the realistic application of the approach are investigated.

REFERENCES

1. "MDA Guide Version 1.0.1," 2001. http://www.omg.org/cgi-bin/doc?omg/03-06-01.
2. K. Pohl, G.Böckle and F. J. van der Linden, "Software Product Line Engineering: Foundations, Principles and Techniques," Springer, Berlin, 2005, pp. 53-72.
3. H. Min and S. D. Kim, "A Technique to Represent Product Line Core Assets in MDA/PIM for Automation," Proceedings Rapid Integration of Software Engineering Techniques Second International Workshop (RISE 2005), Minneapolis, Vol. 3943, 2006, pp. 66-80.
4. M. Matinlassi, "Quality-Driven Software Architecture Model Transformation," PhD Dissertation, VTT Technical Research Centre of Finland, 2006. www.vtt.fi/inf/pdf/publications/2006/P608.pdf
5. S. J. Mellor, K. Scott, A. Uhl and D. Weise, "MDA Distilled: Principles of Model-Driven Architecture," Addison Wesley, New York, 2004.
6. R. M, Colomb "Metamodelling and Model-Driven Architecture," In Publishing.
7. "MOF 2.0 Core Final Adopted Specification," 2004. http://www.omg.org/cgi-bin/doc?ptc/03-10-04.
8. "OMG MOF QVT Final Adopted Specification," 2005. http://www.omg.org/docs/ptc/05-11-01.pdf
9. S. Jarzabek, "Effective Software Maintenance and Evolution: A Reuse-Based Approach," Auerbach Publications, Boca Raton, 2007, pp. 68-106. doi:10.1201/9781420013115
10. D. Ramljak, J. Puksec, D. Huljenic, M. Koncar and D. Simic, "Building Enterprise Information System Using Model Driven Architecture on J2EE Platform," Proceed-

ings IEEE the 7th International Cconference on Telecommunications, Zagreb, June 2003, Vol. 2, pp. 521-526.

11. D. Muthig and C. Atkinson, "Model-Driven Product Line Architectures," Second International Conference on Software Product Lines, San Diego, Vol. 2379, August 2002, pp. 79-90.

12. B. Korherr, "A UML2 Profile for Variability Models and Their Dependency to Business Processes," Proceedings of IEEE Conference Database and Expert Systems Applications, Regensburg, September 2007, pp. 829-834.

13. L. Chung "Representing and Using Non-Functional Requirements: A Process-Oriented Approach," PhD Thesis. University of Toronto, Toronto, 1993.

14. D. Gross and E. Yu, "From Non-Functional Requirements to Design through Patterns," Requirements Engineering, Vol. 6, No. 1, 2001, pp. 18-36. doi:10.1007/s007660170013

15. F. Buschmann, K. Henney and D. C. Schmidt, "Pattern Oriented Software Architecture on Patterns and Pattern Languages," John Wiley & Sons, England, Vol. 5, 2007, pp. 67-74.

16. M. Svahnberg, J. Van Gurp and J. Bosch, "A Taxonomy of Variability Realization Techniques," ACM SoftwarePractice & Experience, Vol. 35, No. 8, July 2005, pp. 705-754.

17. R. Elmasri and S. B. Navathe, "Fundamentals of Database Systems," 5th Editon, Addison-Wesley, Reading, 2007, pp. 232-234.

18. I. Dubielewicz, B. Hnatkowska, Z. Huzar and L. Tuzinkiewicz, "Feasibility Analysis of MDA-Based Database Design," IEEE International Conference on Dependability of Computer Systems, Washington, May 2006, pp. 19-26. doi:10.1109/DEPCOS-RELCOMEX.2006.26

19. M. Glinz, "On Non-Functional Requirements," Proceedings of the 15th IEEE International Requirements Engineering Conference, Delhi, October 2007, pp. 21-26.

20. Wikipedia, "X Window System (Computer Science)," 2008. http://en.wikipedia.org/wiki/X_window_system.

21. L. Bass, P. Clements and R. Kazman, "Software Architecture in Practice," 2nd Edition. Addison-Wesley, Massachusetts, 2003, pp. 75-88.

22. L. Zhu and I. Gorton, "UML Profiles for Design Decisions and Nonfunctional Requirements," IEEE Second Workshop on Sharing and Resuing Architectural Knowledge, Minneapolis, May 2007, pp. 4954.

23. F. J. V. Linden, K. Schmid and E. Rommes, "Software Product Lines in Action: The Best Industrial Practice in Product Line Engineering," Springer, Berlin Heidelberg, 2007, pp. 43-45.

24. C. Alexander, S. Ishikawa, M. Silverstein, M. Jacobson, I. Fiksdahl-King and S. Angel, "A Pattern Language," Oxford University Press, New York, 1977.

25. Wikipedia, "Design Patterns (Computer Science)," 2008. http://en.wikipedia.org/wiki/Design_pattern_%28computer_science%29

26. E. Gamma, R. Helm, R. Johnson and J. Vlissides, "Design Patterns: Elements of Reusable Object-Oriented Software," Addison-Wesley, New York, 1995, pp. 79315.

27. M. Yacoub, H. Xue and H. Ammar, "Automating the Development of Pattern-Oriented Designs for Application Specific Software Systems," Proceedings IEEE the

3rd Symposium on Application-Specific Systems and Software Engineering Technology, Washington DC, March 2000, pp. 163-170.

28. S. M. Yacoub, "Pattern-Oriented Analysis and Design (POAD): A Methodology for Software Development," PhD Thesis, West Virginia University, Morgantown, December 1999.

29. S. J. Mellor, K. Scott, A. Uhl and D. Weise, "MDA Distilled: Principles of Model-Driven Architecture," Addison Wesley, New York, 2004.

30. "OMG MOF XMI Final Adopted Specification," July 2010. http://www.omg.org/technology/documents/formal/xmi.htm.

31. P. Konemann, "The Gap between Design Decisions and Model Transformations," September 2009. http://www2.imm.dtu.dk/.../the_gap_between_design_decisions_and_model_transformations.pdf

32. D. Steinberg, F. Budinsky, M. Paternostro and E. Merks, "EMF: Eclipse Modeling Framework," 2nd Edition, Addison-Wesley Professional, Singapore, December 26 2008.

33. "IKV++ technologies ag.MediniQVT," 2007. http://projects.ikv.de/qvt/

34. "W3C OWL Web Ontology Language," August 2010. http://www.w3.org/TR/owl-ref/

35. "OMG (2007b) OMG Unified Modeling Language (OMG UML), Superstructure, V2.1.2," OMG Document Number: Formal/2007-11-02.

36. W. R. Sebesta "Concepts of Programming Languages," 5th Edition, Addison Wesley, Boston, 2005.

37. "Microsoft Messaging Queue," August 2010. http://www.microsoft.com/windowsserver2008/en/us/ technologies.aspx.

38. "Advanced Message Queuing Protocol (AMQP)," 2010. http://www.amqp.org/confluence/display/AMQP/Advanced+Message+Queuing+Protocol

39. "Java Messaging System Standard," 2010. http://java.sun.com/products/jms/

40. S. Vinoski, "Advanced Message Queuing Protocol," IEEE Internet Computing, Vol. 10, No. 6, 2006, pp. 87-89. doi:10.1109/MIC.2006.116

CHAPTER 2

MODEL-DRIVEN ENGINEERING FOR SOFTWARE PRODUCT LINES

JEAN-MARC JÉZÉQUEL

2.1 INTRODUCTION

Software is nowadays a critical asset for many organizations: many aspects of our daily lives indeed depend on complex software-intensive systems, from banking and communications to transportation and medicine. Constant market evolution triggered an exponential growth in the complexity and variability of modern software solutions. Due to the increasing demand of highly customized products and services, software organizations now have to produce many complex variants accounting not only for differences in software functionalities but also for differences in hardware (e.g., graphic cards, display capacities, and input devices), operating systems, localization, user preferences, look and feel, and so forth. Of course, since they do not want to develop each variant from scratch and independently, they have a strong motivation to investigate new ways of reusing common parts to create new software systems from existing software assets.

Software Product Lines (SPL) [1], or software product families [2, 3], are emerging as a paradigm shift towards modeling and developing software system families rather than individual systems. SPL engineering embraces the ideas of mass customization and software reuse. It focuses on the means of efficiently producing and maintaining multiple related software products (such as cellular phones [4]), exploiting what they have in common and managing what varies among them [5].

Several definitions of the software product line concept can be found in the research literature. Northrop defines it as "a set of software-intensive systems sharing a common, managed set of features that satisfy the specific needs of a particular market segment or mission and are developed from a common set of core assets in a prescribed way" [6]. Bosch provides a different definition [7]: "A SPL consists of a product line architecture and a set of reusable components designed for incorporation into the product line architecture. In addition, the PL consists of the software products developed using the mentioned reusable assets". In spite of the similarities, these definitions provide different perspectives of the concept: market-driven, as seen by Northrop, and technology-oriented for Bosch.

SPL engineering is a process focusing on capturing the commonalities (assumptions true for each family member) and variability (assumptions about how individual family members differ) between several software products [8]. Instead of describing a single software system, a SPL model describes a set of products in the same domain. This is accomplished by distinguishing between elements common to all SPL members, and those that may vary from one product to another. Reuse of core assets, which form the basis of the product line, is key to productivity and quality gains. These core assets extend beyond simple code reuse and may include the architecture, software components, domain models, requirements statements, documentation, test plans, or test cases.

The SPL engineering process consists of two major steps.

1. Domain Engineering, or development for reuse, focuses on core assets development.
2. Application Engineering, or development with reuse, addresses the development of the final products using core assets and following customer requirements.

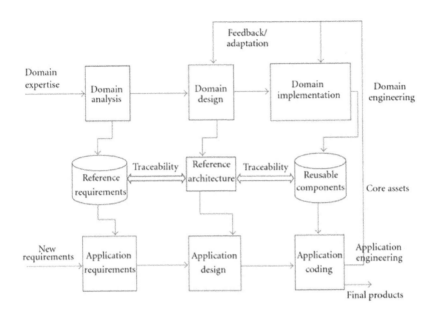

FIGURE 1: Product line engineering process [6].

Figure 1 graphically represents the general SPL engineering process, as it can be found in the research literature [6]. As illustrated, the two phases are intertwined: application engineering consumes assets produced during domain engineering, while feedback from it facilitates the construction of new assets or improvement of existing ones.

Domain Engineering consists of collecting, organizing, and storing past experiences in building systems in the form of reusable assets and providing an adequate means for reusing them for building new systems [9]. It starts with a domain analysis phase to identify commonalities and variability among SPL members. During domain design, the product line architecture is defined in terms of software components and is implemented during the last phase.

Application Engineering, also known as product derivation, consists of building the actual systems from the core assets.

Central to both processes is the management of variability across the product line [3]. In common language use, the term variability refers to the ability or the tendency to change. Variability management is thus seen as the key feature that distinguishes SPL engineering from other software development approaches [10]. Variability management is thus growingly seen as the cornerstone of SPL development, covering the entire development life cycle, from requirements elicitation [11] to product derivation [12] to product testing [13, 14].

A traditional way used by scientists to master the increasing complexity and variability of real-world phenomena is to resort to modeling. Modeling is not just about expressing a solution at a higher abstraction level than code [15]. This limited view on modeling has been useful in the past (assembly languages abstracting away from machine code, 3GL abstracting over assembly languages, etc.) and it is still useful today to get, for example, a holistic view on a large C++ program. But modeling goes well beyond that. In engineering, one wants to break down a complex system into as many models as needed in order to address all the relevant concerns in such a way that they become understandable enough. These models may be expressed with a general purpose modeling language such as the UML [16], or with Domain Specific Languages when it is more appropriate. Each of these models can be seen as the abstraction of an aspect of reality for handling a given concern. The provision of effective means for handling such concerns makes it possible to effectively manage variability in product-lines.

Modeling variability allows a company to capture and select which version of which variant of any particular aspect is wanted in the system [10]. To do it cheaply, quickly, and safely, redoing by hand the tedious weaving of every aspect is not an option; some form of automation is needed to leverage the modeling of variability [17, 18]. Model-Driven Engineering (MDE) makes it possible to automate this weaving process [19]. This requires that models are no longer informal, and that the weaving process is itself described as a program (which is as a matter of facts an executable metamodel [20]) manipulating these models to produce, for example, a detailed design that can ultimately be transformed to code, or to test suites [21], or other software artifacts.

MDE has started to be used by organizations to effectively manage software product lines. An entire SPL can be expressed and created from a single configurable model. Models can explicitly show both the common and varying parts of the SPL design. Using MDE technology, SPLs can be planned, specified, processed, and maintained on a higher abstraction level.

In recent years, several variability modeling techniques have been developed, aiming to explicitly and effectively represent SPL variability, and to leverage these models for a variety of engineering purposes. The purpose of this paper is to survey several classification dimensions of variability modeling, and explore how do they fit with other artifact production purposes.

The remainder of the paper is organized as follows. Section 2 gives an historical perspective on the emergence of variability modeling. In Section 3, we define several dimensions of variability modeling and then illustrate them with an overview of representative variability modeling methods. Note that this section does not have any goal of exhaustivity; for a systematic literature review, we refer the reader to [22]. Here we only subjectively select a set of approaches that we feel are representative of the possible ways of modeling variability in SPL. Going from contemplative to productive, in Section 4 we present some MDE tools leveraging variability models for a range of product line engineering activities. Section 5 concludes the paper and discusses further readings in the field.

2.2 THE EMERGENCE OF VARIABILITY MODELING

2.2.1 DEFINITIONS OF VARIABILITY

The basic vision underlying SPL can probably be traced back to Parnas seminal article [23] on the Design and Development of Program Families. Central to the SPL paradigm is the modeling and management of variability, the commonalities and differences in the applications in terms of requirements, architecture, components, and test artifacts [24]. Software variation management is often split into two dimensions [24].

- Variability in time, referring to the existence of different versions of an artifact that are valid at different times;
- Variability in space, referring to the existence of an artifact in different shapes at the same time.

Variability in time is primarily concerned with managing program variation over time and includes revision control system and the larger field of software configuration management [25]. The goal of SPL engineering is mainly to deal with variability in space [26, 27].

Weiss and Lai [28] defined variability in SPL as "an assumption about how members of a family may differ from each other". From a software perspective [29], variability can be seen as the "the ability of a software system or artifact to be efficiently extended, changed, customized, or configured for use in a particular context".

Variability has also been defined in many other different ways in a product line context. According to Bachmann and Clements [30] "variability means the ability of a core asset to adapt to usages in different product contexts that are within the product line scope". For Pohl et al. [24] it is the "variability that is modeled to enable the development of customized applications by reusing predefined, adjustable artifacts". A more goal-oriented definition of variability is also given by Bachmann and Clements [30] as a way to "maximize the return on investment for building and maintaining products over a specified period of time or number of products".

2.2.2 CLASSIFICATIONS OF VARIABILITY

Several possible classifications have been proposed. Halmans and Pohl [3] distinguish between essential and technical variability, especially at requirements level. Essential variability corresponds to the customer's viewpoint, defining what to implement, while technical variability relates to product family engineering, defining how to implement it. A classification based on the dimensions of variability is proposed by Pohl et al. [24]. Beyond variability in time and variability in space as discussed above, Pohl et al. claim that variability is important to different stakeholders and thus has different levels of visibility: external variability is visible to the customers while internal variability, that of domain artifacts, is hidden from them. Other classification proposals come from Meekel et al. [31] (feature, hardware platform, performances, and attributes variability) or Bachmann and Bass [32] who discuss about variability at the architectural level.

The management of variability can also be described through a process oriented point of view [29]:

1. identification of variability determines where variability is needed in the product line (list the features that may vary between products),
2. constraining variability provides just enough flexibility for current and future system needs,
3. implementing variability selects a suitable variability realization technique based on the previously determined constraints,
4. managing variability requires constant feature maintenance and re-population of variant features.

2.2.3 MODELING VARIABILITY

Central to the modeling of variability is the notion of feature, originally defined by Kang et al. as "a prominent or distinctive user-visible aspect, quality or characteristic of a software system or systems" [33]. Customers and engineers refer to product characteristics in terms of what features a product has or delivers, so it is natural to express any commonality and variability between products also in terms of features [34]. Hence Czarnecki and Eisenecker adapted this definition to the SPL domain as "a system property relevant to some stakeholder used to capture commonalities or discriminate among systems in a family" [35].

A feature can play different roles during the SPL engineering process. During domain engineering, they are units of evolution that adapt the system family to optional user requirements [36]. During application engineering, "the product is defined by selecting a group of features, for which a carefully coordinated and complicated mixture of parts of different components are involved" [37].

Based on this notion of feature, Kang et al. proposed to use a feature model [33] to model the variability in a SPL. A feature model consists of a feature diagram and other associated information: constraints and dependency rules. Feature diagrams provide a graphical tree-like notation depicting the hierarchical organization of high-level product functionalities represented as features. The root of the tree refers to the complete system and is progressively decomposed into more refined features (tree nodes). Relations between nodes (features) are materialized by decomposition edges and textual constraints. Variability can be expressed in several ways. Presence or absence of a feature from a product is modeled using mandatory or optional features. Features are graphically represented as rectangles while some graphical elements (e.g., unfilled circle) are used to describe the variability (e.g., a feature may be optional).

Features can be organized into feature groups. Boolean operators exclusive alternative (XOR), inclusive alternative (OR), or inclusive (AND) are used to select one, several, or all the features from a feature group. Dependencies between features can be modeled using textual constraints: requires (presence of a feature imposes the presence of another), mutex (presence of a feature automatically excludes another).

For the last 25 years, there have been a lot of contributions from research and industry in this area. The initial proposal of Kang et al. was part of the Feature Oriented Domain Analysis (FODA) methodology [33]. Its main purpose was to capture commonalities and variabilities at requirements level. Feature Diagrams proved themselves very useful as a concise way to describe allowed variabilities between products of the same family, to represent feature dependencies, to guide feature selection as to allow the construction of specific products [38].

This notation has the advantage of being clear and easy to understand. However it lacks expressiveness to model relations between variants or to explicitly represent variation points. Consequently, several extensions were added to Kang et al.'s original notation, in particular for people wanting to extend Feature Diagrams beyond the requirement level.

2.2.4 *MANAGING VARIABILITY INTO THE CODE*

Several authors have also focused on proposing mechanisms to implement and manage variability especially at design or code level. Jacobson et al. [39] and Bachmann and Clements [30] propose to use mechanisms, like, inheritance, extensions and extension points, parameterization, templates and macros, configuration and module interconnection languages, generation of derived components, and compiler directives for this purpose.

For example, the contribution of [40] is to propose a method to reify the variants of an object-oriented software system into language-level objects; and to show that newly available compilation technology makes this proposal attractive with respect to performance (memory footprint and execution time) by inferring which classes are needed for a specific configuration and optimizing the generated code accordingly. This approach opens the possibility of leveraging the good modeling capabilities of object-oriented languages to deal with fully dynamic software configuration, while being able to produce space and time efficient executable when the program contains enough static configuration information.

Creational Design Patterns [41] are used to provide the necessary flexibility for describing and selecting relevant configurations within an object-oriented implementation, and thus benefitting from a better security implied by static typing, that is checked by the compiler. With this design framework, the actual configuration management can be programmed within the target language; it boils down to only create the class instances relevant to a given configuration [42]. However some care has to be taken for programming the creation of these objects to ensure that the design is flexible enough. In simple cases, an Abstract Factory is used to define an interface for creating variants. The factory features one Factory Method (encapsulating the procedure for creating an object) for each of the variability dimensions. The Factory Methods are parameterized to let them create various kinds of products (i.e., variants of a type), depending on the dynamic configuration selected at runtime. These Factory Methods are abstractly defined in the abstract factory, and given concrete implementations in its subclasses, called concrete factories.

In this approach, product derivation can be seen as an application of ideas circulating in the "Partial Evaluation" community for years. Actually, it can be seen as taking benefit of the fact that the type of configurable parts have bounded static variations (i.e., the sets of possible types are known at compile time). Thus the Partial Evaluation community trick known as The Trick (see [42]) can be applied to specialize the general program at compile time, and thus obtain specific products only embedding the code they really need.

More generally along these lines, Svahnberg et al. [29] present a taxonomy of different ways to implement variation points, which they refer to as "variability realization techniques".

2.2.5 BRIDGING THE GAP BETWEEN REQUIREMENT AND CODE: FEATURE MODELING EXTENSIONS

To bridge the gap between variability modeling at the level of requirements as originally found in Feature Models, and variability realization techniques as surveyed by Svahnberg et al. [29], many researchers proposed to extend Feature Models to encompass a wider spectrum of assets.

A first extension of FODA is the Feature Oriented Reuse Method (FORM) [43] developed by Kang et al. in 1998. It proposes a four-layer decomposition structure, corresponding to different stakeholder viewpoints. There are small differences in the notation compared to FODA: feature names appear in boxes, three new types of feature relations introduced (composed-of, generalization/specialization, implemented-by).

Griss et al. propose FeatuRSEB [44], a combination of FODA and the Reuse-Driven Software Engineering Business (RSEB) method. The novelties proposed are introduction of UML-like notational constructs for creating Feature Diagrams, explicit representation of variation points, and variants (white and black diamonds), explicit graphical representation for feature constraints and dependencies. Van Gurp et al. [45] slightly extend FeatuRSEB by introducing binding times (annotation to indicate when features can be selected) and external features (capabilities offered by the target platform).

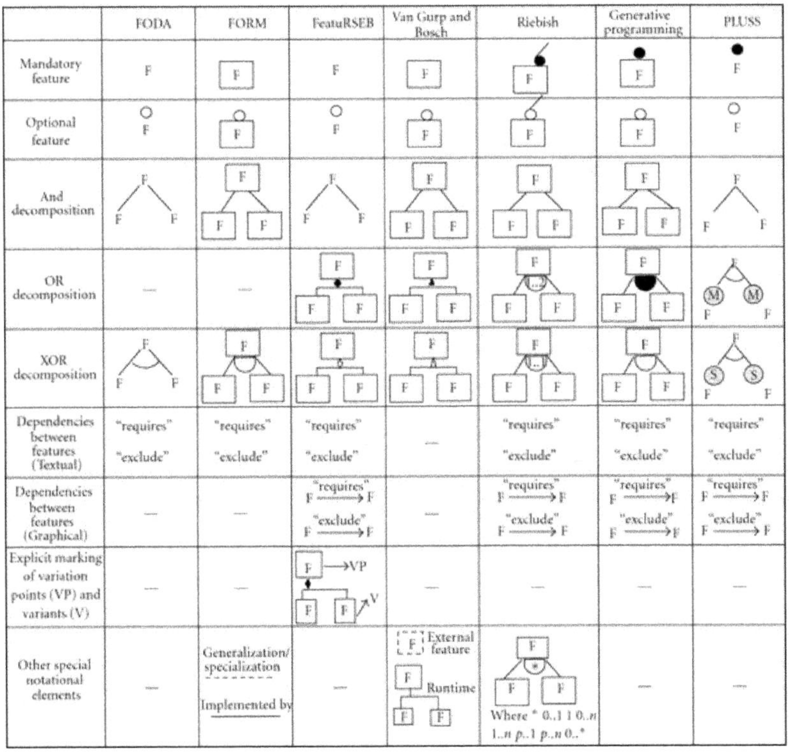

FIGURE 2: Feature Diagram Dialects—synthesis of variability modeling concepts.

Riebisch proposed to explicitly represent cardinalities in Feature Diagram and thus extends them with UML multiplicities [46]. Group cardinalities are introduced and denote the minimum and maximum number of features that can be selected from a feature group. There are two other changes: first a feature is allowed to have multiple parents and second, it is no longer features that are optional or mandatory, but edges.

Czarnecki and Eisenecker adapted Feature Diagrams in the context of Generative Programming [35] by adding an OR feature decomposition and defining a graphical representation of features dependencies. More recently, this notation was extended with new concepts: staged configuration (used for product derivation) and group and feature cardinalities [47].

Product Line Use Case modeling for System and Software engineering (PLUSS) [48] is another approach based on FeatuRSEB [44] that combines Feature Diagrams and Use Cases. The originality of this approach is that the decomposition operator is made explicit to compose feature: two new types of nodes are introduced: single adapters (represent XOR-decomposition) and multiple adapters (OR decomposition).

Many other extensions to feature modeling have been proposed to increase their expressiveness. Deursen and Klint in [49] defines an abstract syntax and semantics for Feature Diagrams. Batory [50] introduces propositional constraints defined between features. Ferber et al. [51] defines a separate view to represent feature dependencies and interactions.

Figure 2 from [52] provides a synthesis of the concepts used to capture variability and how they are graphically represented by the feature modeling languages described in this section. The figure shows what each feature modeling dialect is able to represent, as well as its limitations.

Despite their popularity and widespread use, all these Feature Models variants only provide a hierarchical structuring of high-level product functionalities [53], with very little connection with the actual software products. Since there is no indication of what the concrete representations of the features are, Feature Models only allow the SPL engineer to make a simple configuration of products through a feature selection. It is thus clear that more than a simple Feature Model is required for performing product derivation.

These limitations generated the need for other more expressive mechanisms for representing variability and linking it to the base assets.

2.3 AN OVERVIEW ON REPRESENTATIVE VARIABILITY MODELING METHODS

2.3.1 INTRODUCTION

Since SPLs revolve around the ideas of capturing commonalities and variations, a SPL can be fully modeled as

- an assests model that models a set of core assets, that is, reusable components used for the development of new products;
- a variability model that represent the commonality and variability between product line members.

Since standard languages are generally not developed to explicitly represent all types of variability, SPL models are frequently expressed by extending or annotating standard languages (models). The annotated models are unions of all specific models in a model family and contain all necessary variability concepts.

In MDE, the structure of a domain is explicitly captured in a metamodel. So it is clear that we need two different metamodels (i.e., two different sets of concepts) to handle both aspects of SPLs, but we also need to somehow connect these two sets of concepts to manipulate models of SPLs. Consequently, as noted by [54], there are two categories of techniques to handle variability: amalgamated and separated. The amalgamated approach proposes to connect the asset model and the variability model at metamodel level, that is, to augment the asset metamodel with variability concepts, while the separated approach proposes to connect them at model level, that is, the two modeling languages remain independent and the connection is made across model elements of either metamodels.

In turn, each of these two main styles of approaches decomposes into several threads that we are going to overview in the next subsections, taking into account issues such as addressing behavioral variability or handling variability at several stages in the software lifecycle (requirements time, design time, deployment time, and runtime) Table 1 summarizes the classification proposed in [52]. It outlines what does happen at metamodel and model level for the identified classes and subclasses of variability modeling techniques.

TABLE 1: Classification of variability modeling techniques.

Technique name	Metamodel level		Model level	
Unique model (combined) for product line assets and PL variability				
Annotating the base model by means of extensions	AMM + V		PLM (conforms to AMM + V)	
Combine a general, reusable variability metamodel with base metamodels	AMM	VMM	PLM (conforms to (AMM o VMM))	
Separate (distinct) assets model and variability model				
Connect Feature Diagrams to model fragments	AMM	VMM	AM	VM (FDM)
Orthogonal Variability Modeling (OVM)	AMM	VMM	AM	VM (OVM)
ConIPF Variability Modeling Framework (COVAMOF)	AMM	VMM (CVV)	AM	VM (CVV)
Decision model based approaches	AMM	VMM (DMM)	AM	VM (DM)
Combine a common variability language with different base modeling languages	AMM	VMM (CVL)	AM	VM (CVL)

AMM: assets metamodel, AM: assets model, VMM: variability meta-model, VM: variability model, AMM + V: assets metamodel with variability, PLM: product line model, CVL: common variability language, FDM: feature diagram model, and DMM: decision metamodel, DM: decision model.

2.3.2 AMALGAMATED APPROACH

Techniques using an amalgamated approach extend a language or a general purpose metamodel with specific concepts that allow designers to describe variability. Their core characteristic is the mix of variability and product line assets concepts into a unique model. Concepts regarding variability and those that describe the assets metamodel are combined into a new language, that may either have a new, mixed syntax, or one based on that of the base model extended by the syntax of the variability language. This applies at both metamodel and model level. We further distinguish 3 subcategories: ad hoc extensions to existing languages, generic extensions that can be woven into any language, and finally ad hoc languages.

2.3.2.1 ANNOTATE A BASE MODEL BY MEANS OF EXTENSIONS

Clauss [55, 56], first proposed to apply variability extensions to UML Class Diagrams, leveraging the UML of extension mechanism that allows designers to describe generic models. Clauss uses such generic models in which he explicitly defines variability at particular points called hot spots. The extensions proposed are based on the notions of variation points and variants: variation points help locate variability; each variant denotes a concrete way to realize that variability.

Variation points and variants are explicitly marked with the stereotypes *<<Variation Point>>*, respectively *<<Variant>>*, specified for the Generalizable Element UML metaclass. Therefore the variation point notion can be applied to classes, components, packages, collaborations, and associations. The *<<Variation Point>>* stereotype can be used together with several tagged values to specify the binding time (development, installation, or runtime) and the multiplicity of variants associated to a variation point. A variation point is connected to its variants through generalization/ parameterization relations. It also has a unique name used to clearly associate it to its variants. Concerning variants, it is possible to capture dependencies between them using the *<<mutex>>* or *<<require>>* stereotypes. It is also possible to specify evolutionary constraints between elements using the *<<evolution>>* stereotype. Optional model elements can be identified with the *<<optional>>* stereotype. Presence conditions, similar with those used for variants, and tagged values for the binding time, can also be used with optional elements.

A second approach belonging to this category proposes to extend UML to specify product line variability for UML class and sequence diagrams [16, 57]. It defines a set of stereotypes, tagged values, and structural constraints and gather them in a UML profile for product lines [12].

Class diagrams are first extended with the concept of optionality. The *<<optional>>* stereotype marks model elements that can be omitted in some products. It is applied to the Classifier, Package, and Feature metaclasses from UML. As for the previous approach, the variation point concept is used. It is are modeled using UML inheritance and stereotypes: a variation point is defined by an abstract class and a set of subclasses which represent its variants. The abstract class is tagged with the *<<variation>>* stereotype while the subclasses with *<<variant>>*. The UML profile also contains constraints which specify structural rules applicable to all models tagged with a specific stereotype.

For sequence diagrams, variability is introduced through three concepts: optionality, variation, and virtuality. The *<<optional Lifeline>>* and *<<optional Interaction>>* stereotypes identify optional objects and interactions in a sequence diagram. Variation refers to the existence of several possible interaction variants and is specified using the *<<variation>>* and *<<variant>>* stereotypes, which extend the Interaction metaclass. Finally, virtuality means that parts of a sequence diagram can be redefined for individual products by another sequence diagram. The *<<virtual>>* stereotype is used for this.

The work of Gomaa and Shin [58, 59] on multiple view product line modeling using UML also falls into this category. It promotes the use of different perspectives for a better understanding of the product line. The used views are use case model view for functional SPL requirements; static model view for static structural SPL aspects; collaboration model view to capture the sequence of messages passed between objects; state chart model view to address dynamic SPL aspects.

A multiple-view model is modified at specific locations, different for each view. To represent SPL variability in the Use Case model view, Use Cases are stereotyped as either kernel, optional or variant, while extend and include relations allow a Use Case to extend or include another Use Case at a variation point. In the class diagrams, abstract classes and hot spots provide ways for variation points. For the collaboration and state chart models, concepts from single-system development such as alternative branches, message sequences, and state transitions are used. Of course, when a view is modified at a variation point, the other views also need to be modified in order to maintain consistency.

Initially defined for Use Cases, the stereotypes mentioned above were also applied to other views. For the static model view, additional stereotypes are introduced: *<<control>>* (provide overall coordination), (details of application logic), *<<entity>>* (encapsulate data), and *<<inter face>>*

(interface to external environment). Variation is also expressed using classical UML concepts like abstract classes and inheritance.

Finally, de Oliveira Jr. et al. [60] present a UML-based process for variability management that allows the identification, representation, and delimitation of variabilities. In the variability identification and definition phases of the process, a series of stereotypes can be used to explicitly identify variation points, mark mandatory and optional elements, and identify exclusive or inclusive variants of a variation point. Dependency relations between variants are also supported. These extensions are applied to UML class and Use Case diagrams. For each stereotype, the set of UML relations on which it can be applied is provided.

In addition to stereotypes, UML notes are used to support variability representation. For a variation point, they define the type of relationship with its variants ({} for optional, {or} and {xor} for alternative and exclusive alternative); its name and multiplicity (minimum number of variants to be chosen for it); the binding time (design, implementation, compiling, linking or runtime); whether or not it supports new variants to be added. This information is established during the variability delimitation process.

Table 2 (from [52]) recalls the stereotypes and extensions introduced by each method discussed above, while Table 3 presents which type of UML diagrams are supported.

2.3.2.2 COMBINE A GENERAL, REUSABLE VARIABILITY METAMODEL WITH DIFFERENT DOMAIN METAMODELS

In the previous approaches, authors extended the UML metamodel for modeling variability in multiple UML diagrams like Class or Sequence diagrams. Morin et al. [61, 62] propose a more generic solution that can be applied to any kind of metamodel and that is fully supported by a tool. They propose a reusable variability metamodel describing variability concepts and their relations independently from any domain metamodel. Using Aspect-Oriented Modeling (AOM) techniques, variability can be woven into a given base metamodel, allowing its integration into a wide variety of metamodels in a semiautomatic way.

TABLE 2: Annotating UML with stereotypes—synthesis.

Variability	Clauss	Ziadi and Jézéquel	Gomaa	Oliveira et al.
Variation point	<<variation Point>>	<<variation>>		<<variation Point>>
Variant <<alternative—XOR>>	<<variant>>	<<variant>>	<<variant>>	<<alternative—OR>>
Dependencies <<require>>	<<mutex>>		<<require>>	<<mutex>>
Optional elements <<optionalInteraction>> <<optionalLifeline>>	<<optional>>	<<optional>>	<<optional>>	<<optional>>
Mandatory elements			<<kernel>>	<<mandatory>>
Other concepts <<algorithm>> <<entity>> <<interface>>	<<evolution>>	<<virtual>> Generic/specific constraints	<<control>>	UML notes

TABLE 3: Annotating UML with stereotypes—supported diagrams.

Method name	Class	Use cases	Sequence	State charts
Clauss	Yes	No	No	No
Ziadi and Jézéquel	Yes	No	Yes	No
Gomaa	Yes	Yes	Yes	Yes
Oliveira et al.	Yes	Yes	No	No

A key point of this method is the definition of a general variability metamodel, based on the work of Schobbens et al. [36, 38] on feature modeling. The abstract syntax proposed in [38] serves as the basis for the variability metamodel defined by Morin et al. [61]. In this meta-model, the central metaclass PointOfVariability can be woven with any base metamodel element on which variants are needed. VariabilityOfElement is a subclass of the PointOfVariability metaclass that allows actual domain concepts to vary. Boolean operators inspired from feature diagrams are used to actually represent variability: and, xor, or, opt. The cardinality operator $Vp(i,j)$ provides a greater degree of flexibility. Operators can either be homogeneous (apply only to elements of the same type) or heterogeneous (apply to elements of different types).

The process of creating the new metamodel that integrates concepts from both variability and base metamodels is easy: new metaclasses are created to connect the base metamodel with the variability aspect. The base metamodel is just extended, none of its elements are removed. This allows an easy translation of models encoded in the variability-woven metamodel into the original one and the reuse of already developed tools such as model editors or checkers. Once the weaving of variability is done to obtain an extended metamodel, product line models can be created. These are models with variability, conforming to the variability extended metamodel.

2.3.2.3 AD HOC LANGUAGE SUPPORTING VARIABILITY: CLAFER

Contrary to previous approaches, Clafer [63] (Class, Feature, and Reference) is a standalone, lightweight modeling language with first-class support for feature modeling. More precisely, the language integrates feature modeling (i.e., a formalism to model variability, see below) into class modeling, so that variability can be naturally expressed in class models.

Clafer has a minimalistic syntax and semantics (very few underlying concepts), trying to unify existing notations (such as feature, class, and metamodels), both syntactically and semantically. It supports the most common constructions from domain modeling, modeling requirements, and structural modeling. Clafer models are expressive, yet analyzable with state-of-the-art tools, such as SAT/SMT-solvers and Alloy Analyzer. Currently, Clafer relies on Alloy (which uses SAT-solvers) to do analyses.

2.3.3 SEPARATED APPROACHES

Techniques in this category have separate representations for the variability and for the assets model. Elements from the variability model relate to asset model elements by referencing them one way or another. The key characteristic of such methods is the clear separation of concerns they provide. This separation applies at both metamodel and model level, with the following advantages: each asset model may have more than one variability model; designers can focus on the product line itself and not on its variability, which is addressed separately. It also opens the way for a standardized Common Variability Language (CVL) as discussed below.

Istoan [52] further identifies three subcategories of methods which share the same principle but differ in the type of variability model they use.

2.3.3.1 CONNECT FEATURE DIAGRAMS TO MODEL FRAGMENTS

Since Feature Diagrams only concentrate on a specific aspect of SPL modeling, there is a need to combine them with other product representations, that is, to associate model fragments to features. Various model fragment types can be associated to features. The feature diagram defines the product line variability, with each feature having an associated implementation. Concerning our classification, we make a clear distinction between assets and variability related concepts at metamodel level. This situation extends to model level: separate assets and variability models do coexist. For this category of methods, the assets model typically consists of a set of software artefact/asset fragments, while the variability model is a Feature Diagram.

Perrouin et al. [64] address specific and unforeseen customer requirements in product derivation by combining automated model composition with flexible product derivation approaches [65]. Their contribution are two metamodels defined to support the approach: a generic feature metamodel that supports a wide variety of existing FD dialects (used in the preconfiguration process), and a subset of UML used to define the assets metamodel (transformed during the customization step).

Their generic feature metamodel leverages Schobbens et al.'s pivot abstract syntax [36] that subsumes many of the existent FD dialects. In their proposal, Feature Diagram is the central metaclass and contains a list of features (Feature metaclass), with is a special one that is considered as the root node. Variability is represented using boolean operators. All classical feature diagram operators are provided: or, and, xor, opt, and card. They are subtypes of the abstract Operator metaclass. Decomposition edges represent relations between features. Feature dependencies like mutex or require can also be represented.

In the feature diagram metamodel, the Feature meta-class is connected using a composite association to a class called Model that defines the core assets involved in feature realization. This relation specifies that a feature may be implemented by several model fragments. Initially exploited with class diagrams [65], the metamodel allows any kind of assets to be associated with features.

Czarnecki and Antkiewicz [66] proposes a general template-based approach for mapping feature models to concrete representations using structural or behavioural models. They use a model representing a superimposition of all variants, whose elements relate to corresponding features through annotations. The approach is general and works for any model whose metamodel is expressed in MOF.

The idea promoted by Czarnecki and Antkiewicz is to separate the representation of a model family (product line model) into a feature model (defines feature hierarchies, constraints, possible configurations) and a model template (contains the union of model elements in all valid template instances). Elements of a model template can be annotated. These annotations are defined in terms of features from the feature model, and can be evaluated according to a particular feature configuration. Possible annotations are presence conditions (PCs) and metaexpressions (MEs). PCs are attached to a model element to indicate whether it should be present in a template instance. Typical PCs are boolean formulas over a set of variables, each variable corresponding to a feature from the FD. Complex PCs can be expressed using XPath. MEs are used to compute attributes of model elements. When a PC is not explicitly assigned to an element of a model template, an implicit presence condition (IPC) is assumed. IPCs reduce the necessary annotation effort for the user. Czarnecki and Antkiewicz define a set of choices of IPCs that can be used for UML class and activity diagrams, based on the element's type.

General guidelines for applying this method for a particular target notation are provided. They require to decide first the form of PCs and MEs,

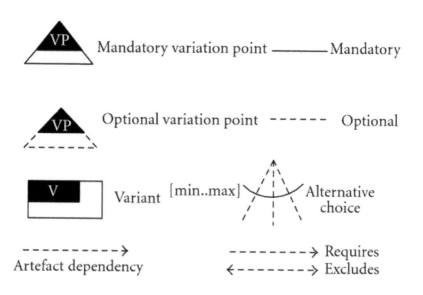

FIGURE 3: OVM method: synthesis of concepts.

attach IPCs to model elements not explicitly annotated, decide on the type of the annotation mechanism used (e.g., UML stereotypes), and on how to render the annotations (labels, icons, or colouring).

There exist other methods belonging to this category, which we briefly mention below. Laguna and González-Baixauli [67] separate SPL variability aspects using goal models and UML diagrams, while keeping features at the core of the representation. They combine previous approaches with the UML package merge implementation to provide a set of mapping rules from features to class diagram fragments. Apel et al. [68] introduce superimposition as a technique to merge code fragments belonging to different features. They extend the approach and analyse whether UML class, state, and sequence diagrams can be decomposed into features and then recomposed using superimposition to create complete models corresponding to SPL products.

2.3.3.2 ORTHOGONAL VARIABILITY MODELING

With Orthogonal Variability Modeling, the assets model and the variability model are kept separate. The variability model relates to different parts of the assets model using artifact dependencies. The differentiating factor from the previous category is the type of variability model used: an orthogonal variability model (OVM). There is also a difference regarding the assets model which is a compact software development artifact and no longer a set of model fragments.

Pohl et al. [24] propose the OVM concept, that is, later refined in [69]; a model that defines the variability of a SPL separately and then relates it to other development artifacts like Use Cases, component, and test models. OVM provides a view on variability across all development artifacts.

The central concepts used in OVM are variation points (VP) and variants (V). A VP documents a variable item and a V its possible instances. Both VPs and Vs can be either optional or mandatory. Optional variants of the same VP are grouped together by an alternative choice. An optional variant may be part of at most one alternative group. To determine how many Vs may be chosen in an alternative choice, the cardinality notation [min..max] is used. OVM also supports the documentation of Vs belonging to different VPs. Simple constraints between nodes (mutex or require) can be graphically represented and can be applied to relations between Vs, but also to VP-V and VP-VP relations.

Modeling VPs, Vs and how they are connected is just a first step of the OVM process. The variability model can be related to software artifacts specified by other models. Pohl et al. document these relations using traceability links between the variability model and the other development artifacts. A special type of relationship called artifact dependency [24] which relates a V or a VP to a development artifact serves this purpose. A synthesis of OVM concepts together with their graphical representation is shown in Figure 3.

These concepts are captured and formalized slightly differently in [69]; while Pohl et al. [24] group them into a metamodel which defines what a well-formed OVM diagram is, Metzger et al. [69] formalize OVM's abstract syntax using a mathematical notation: an OVM is defined as a tuple of the form (VP, V, VG, Parent, Min, Max, Opt, Req, and Excl).

OVM is a general approach that can be used to document variability in several software artifacts. Requirements variability is handled by relating the OVM to textual requirements or Use Cases. Architectural variability is documented in the development view by relating OVM to component, class, or object diagrams; in the process view by connecting OVM models to state machines, activity, or sequence diagrams; and in the code view by relating OVM to deployment diagrams.

2.3.3.3 CONIPF VARIABILITY MODELING FRAMEWORK (COVAMOF)

The COVAMOF method [70, 71] is yet another orthogonal variability method that differs in the type of variability model, that is, used. Sinnema et al. [70] identify four requirements which they considered essential for a variability modeling technique, and that they wanted to support in COVAMOF:

1. uniform and first class representation of variation points at all abstraction levels;

2. hierarchical organization of variability representation;
3. first-class representation of dependencies, even complex ones;
4. explicit modeling of interactions between dependencies.

COVAMOF was hence designed to uniformly model variability in all abstraction layers of a SPL. The COVAMOF framework addresses variability in a dedicated view called COVAMOF Variability View (CVV). Variability is represented as variation points and dependencies and provides means to explicitly model simple and complex relations between dependencies.

Variation points in the CVV reflect the variation points of the product family and are associated with product family artifacts. Five types of variation points are defined in CVV: optional, alternative, optional variant, variant, and value. A variation point also contains a description, some information about its state, the rationale of the binding, the realization mechanism, and the associated binding time. The state can be either opened (new variants can be added) or closed (not possible to add new variants). If a variation point does not have a realization mechanism associated in the PL artifacts, it will be realized by a variation point on a lower level. This is done using a realization relation which defines how variation points in one abstraction layer realize variation points in a higher layer.

Dependencies are associated with one or more variation points in the CVV and are used to restrict the selection of associated variants. A dependency has several properties: type, description, validation time, and type of associations to variation points. These associations to variation points are classified according to the impact that variant selection has on the validity of the dependency: predictable (impact can be determined before the actual variant binding), directional (specifies whether variants selection should have positive or negatively effect), and unknown. Three different types of dependencies are possible: logical, numerical, and nominal, which express the validity of the dependency in different ways. CVV also explicitly defines dependency interactions which specify how two or more dependencies mutually interact.

The main entities of the CVV metamodel are presented in Figure 4, while Figure 5 (from [52]) summarize the main concepts introduced by COVAMOF and their graphical representation.

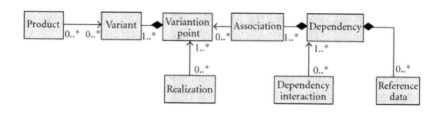

FIGURE 4: The COVAMOF meta-model.

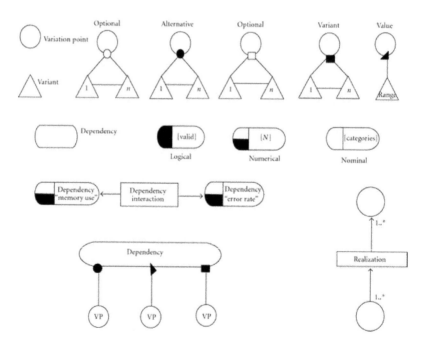

FIGURE 5: Summary of COVAMOF concepts.

2.3.3.4 DECISION MODEL BASED APPROACHES

This class of approaches keeps the same general characteristics as all other in this category. They differ in using decision models as variability model. Decision-oriented approaches were designed to guide the product derivation process based on decision models. Research literature offers several definitions of the term. Weiss and Lai [28] define it as "the document defining the decisions that must be made to specify a member of a domain". For Bayer et al. [72] it is a model that "captures variability in a product line in terms of open decisions and possible resolutions". A decision model is basically a table where each row represents a decision and each column a property of a decision.

Decision modeling in SPL was initially introduced as a part of the Synthesis Project by Campbell et al. [73]. Decisions were defined as "actions which can be taken by application engineers to resolve the variations for a work product of a system". Decision-oriented approaches treat decisions as first-class citizens for modeling variability. They describe the variation points in a PL and define the set of choices available at a certain point in time when deriving a product.

A representative approach in this category is DOPLER (Decision-Oriented Product Line Engineering for effective Reuse) from Dhungana et al. [74]. It aims at supporting the modeling of variability for industrial SPL with a focus on automating the derivation of customer-specific products. It is a flexible and extensible decision-oriented variability modeling language. DOPLER was designed to support the modeling of both problem space variability (stakeholder needs) using decision models, and solution space variability (architecture and components of technical solution) using asset models and also to assure traceability between them.

A core concept used by DOPLER is the decision. It is specified by a unique name and has a type, which defines the range of values which can be assigned to a decision. Available decision types in DOPLER are boolean, string, number, and enumeration. Decisions can be annotated using decision attributes to capture further information (description, question) for the modeler or user. As the value range determined by the basic decision type is often too broad, validity conditions can be used to restrict it.

Visibility conditions specify when a particular decision becomes relevant to the user and thus define hierarchical dependencies between decisions. Decisions are usually not independent of each other and cannot be made in isolation. Dependencies between them can be specified using decision effects. In DOPLER decisions are directly connected to assets, which represent the available artifacts of the product line. A collection of assets is defined in an asset model. Assets can have a type (defined for specific domains) and several attributes. Relations between assets are specified using asset dependencies. Assets are linked to decisions using inclusion conditions which describe the context in which a particular asset is required in a particular product. One inclusion condition can refer to multiple decisions.

These concepts are gathered and formalized by Dhungana et al. in a specific metamodel (see Figure 6). It is generic and can be adapted to different domains by defining concrete asset types, asset type attributes, and relationships between assets.

Along the same lines as DOPLER, Xabier Mansell and Sellier [75] propose a decision modeling process based on which the European Software Engineering Institute Spain and IKV++ Technologies AG Germany developed the VManage method [76]. It offers an XML-based solution to formally specify a PL decision model and use it for automatic product derivation. Each decision from the decision model has a set of properties: name, description, type, default value, validity, and dependencies. The different types of decisions are specified using an XML schema. There are two possible kinds of decisions: unrestricted and restricted. Furthermore, VManage supports collections of decisions (instances of a decision or set of decisions). A metamodel that supports the approach and defines the general elements that form a decision model is available in [75].

Another proposal comes from Schmid and John [77] and is an extension of the original Synthesis approach. It adds binding times, set-typed relations, selector types, mapping selector types to specific notations, using multiplicity to allow the selection of subsets of possible resolutions, clear separation of constraints on the presence and value of decisions. The KobrA approach [78] integrates product line engineering and component-based software design. KobrA decision models are described using a tabular notation. A clear distinction is made between simple and high level decisions. For simple decision, references are given to the involved assets

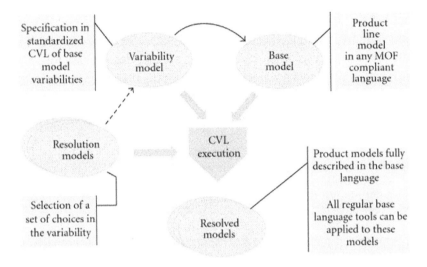

FIGURE 6: DOLPER meta-model.

and variation points. In the case of high-level decisions, references are given to the other decisions that are affected by resolving it. The decision model thus forms a hierarchy.

2.3.3.5 COMBINE A COMMON VARIABILITY LANGUAGE WITH DIFFERENT BASE LANGUAGES

Methods in this category propose a generic language or model that subsumes variability related concepts. The same general variability model can be combined with different base models, extending them with variability. Regarding our classification, at metamodel level there is a separate generic variability metamodel and an assets metamodel (AMM). The AMM is actually the metamodel of the base language on which the common variability language is applied. At model level, variability model elements relate to assets model elements by referencing and using substitutions.

We discuss in more detail the Common Variability Language (CVL) as proposed for standardization at the OMG. It is based on several previous works, notably by Haugen et al. [54, 79]. CVL models specify both variabilities and their resolution. By executing a CVL model, a base SPL model is transformed into a specific product model as illustrated in Figure 7.

The Variability Model and the Resolution Models are defined in CVL while the Base Model and Resolved Models can be defined in any MOF-defined language (see Figure 8).

- The Base Model represents an instance of an arbitrary MOF metamodel, such as UML, on which variability is specified using CVL. From the standpoint of CVL the base model is just a collection of objects and links between them.
- The Foundation Layer comprises means to define abstract variability with proper constraints, how to resolve the variability to define products, and how to realize the products to produce products defined in the base language.
- The Compositional Layer on top of the foundation layer includes ways to combine models in the foundation layer such that variability definitions can be reused, resolutions may have cascading effects, and several different

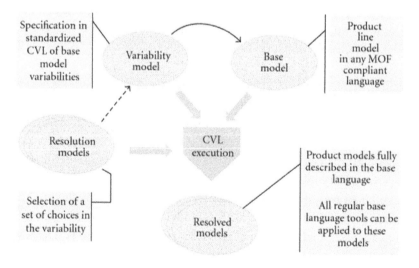

FIGURE 7: Using CVL.

base models (defined in different base languages) can be described. The configurable unit module provides the constructs that are needed for the modularization and encapsulation of variability as configurable units, that is, component-like structures that may be configured through an exposed variability interface.

Let us now detail the Foundation Layer, which is made of the variability realization model, the variability abstraction model, and Constraints and Resolutions, as shown in Figure 8.

Variability Realization
The variability realization model provides constructs for specifying variation points on the base model. A variation point is an item that defines one step in the process of how the base model is modified to reach the specified product. This module is the part of CVL that impacts the base model. The variation points refer to base model elements via base model handles.

The realization layer makes it possible to derive the products from the CVL description by transforming a base model in some MOF defined lan-

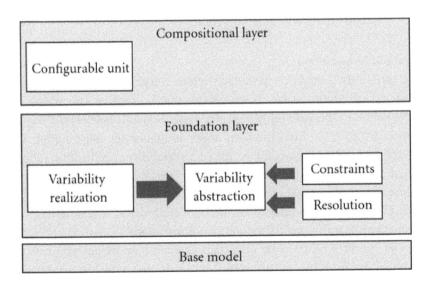

FIGURE 8: The Structure of CVL.

guage to another product model in that same language. Every construct of the realization layer defines a Variation Point of the base model representing a small modification of the base model into the product model. There are several kinds of variation points.

1. Existence is an indication that the existence of a particular object or link in the base model is in question.
2. Substitution is an indication that a single object, an entire model fragment, or the object at the end of a link, may be substituted for another. Object substitution involves two objects and means redirecting all links in which one is involved to the other and then deleting the former. Fragment substitution involves identifying a placement fragment in the base model via boundary element, thereby creating a conceptual "hole" to be filled by a replacement fragment of a compatible type.
3. Value assignment is an indication that a value may be assigned to a particular slot of some base model object.
4. Opaque variation point is an indication that a domain specific (user defined) variability is associated with the object(s) where the semantic of domain specific variability is specified explicitly using a suitable transformation language.

Variability Abstraction

The variability abstraction module provides constructs for specifying and resolving variability in an abstract level, that is, without specifying the exact nature of the variability w.r.t. the base model. It isolates the logical component of CVL from the parts that manipulate the base model. The central concept in this module is that of a variability specification (abbreviated as VSpec), which is an indication of variability in the base model. VSpec are similar to features in feature modeling, to the point that the concrete syntax of the variability abstraction is similar to a feature diagram where the variability specifications are shown as trees.

The specifics of the variability, that is, what base model elements are involved and how they are affected, is not specified, which is what makes VSpecs abstract. The effect on the base model may be indicated by binding VSpecs to variation points which refer to the base model. VSpecs may be arranged as trees, where the parent-child relationship organizes the resolution space by imposing structure and logic on permissible resolutions.

There are three kinds of VSpecs provided in the base layer: choices, variables, and variability classifiers.

1. A choice is a VSpec whose resolution requires a yes/no decision. Nothing is known about the nature of the choice in the level of a VSpec tree, beyond what is suggested by its name. For example, the fact that there is a choice X in the tree indicates that in the resolution process there will be a need to decide yes or no about X, and that this decision may have some effect on the base model, the nature of which is unknown. It could decide for instance whether or not a given element will be deleted, a given substitution will be performed, a link will be redirected, and so forth.

2. A variable is a kind of VSpec whose resolution involves providing a value of a specified type. This value is meant to be used in the base model, but similar to choices, it is unknown in this level exactly where and how.

3. A variability classifier (abbreviated as VClassifier) is a kind of VSpec whose resolution means creating instances and then providing per-instance resolutions for the VSpecs in its subtree. Like choices and variables, it is unknown at this level what the effect of each instance will be. Each VClassifier has an instance multiplicity which indicates how many instances of it may be created under its parent in permissible resolutions.

VSpecs are organized in a Tree Structure. The subtree under a node represents subordinate VSpecs in the sense that the resolution of a node imposes certain constraints on the resolutions of the nodes in its subtree:

1. A negative resolution implies a negative resolution for its subchoices and no resolutions for all other child VSpecs.

2. Each choice has a field isImpliedByParent which, when True, indicates that if its parent is resolved positively then it must be decided positively. A resolution for a nonchoice VSpec is always considered positive for this definition. The general rule is as fol-

lows: if a parent is resolved positively, that is, it is either a positive choice decision or any variable resolution or any instance, then its subchoices with isImpliedByParent = True must be resolved positively, its sub-variables must be resolved, that is, given a value, and its subclassifiers must be instantiated according to their instance multiplicity.

Each VSpec may also have a group multiplicity indicating how many total positive resolutions there may be under it in case it is resolved positively, where positive resolution means the same as above, that is, a positive choice decision or any variable value assignment or any instance of a VClassifier.

Constraints

Additional constraints can be used to express intricate relationships between VSpecs that cannot be directly captured by hierarchical relations in a VSpec tree. To this end CVL introduces a basic constraint language, a restricted subset of The Object Constraint Language (OCL), that is, amenable to formal processing and practical constraint solving.

Resolutions

VSpecs are resolved by VSpec resolutions, thus three kinds of VSpec resolutions mirror the three kinds of VSpecs. Choice resolutions resolve choices, variable value assignments resolve variables, and VInstances resolve VClassifiers. Each VSPpec resolution resolves exactly one VSpec of the appropriate kind. In the absence of classifiers each VSpec is resolved by at most one VSpec resolution.

Compositional Layer

The abstraction and realization modules of the foundation layer provide constructs for specifying logically organized variation points on a base model but do not provide means for grouping such specifications into units configurable as wholes. Base models on which variability will be specified with CVL may exhibit complex structures of modularization, composition, and encapsulation. For example a UML design for a real system will typically contain many packages, components, and classes organized in hierarchies, possibly deep ones. For scalability purposes, CVL must therefore itself accommodate such structures so that product line designs, that is, base models plus CVL variability defined against them, may continue to exhibit the same structures supported by the base models. Variability Encapsulation is helpful to the following.

1. Accommodate the modular specification of large, complex systems with variability.
2. Accommodate the construction of libraries of reusable assets (components with variability in them) which are used in multiple projects of a given organization after configuring their variability. In this mode of work the system overall architecture does not contain variability but is constructed from configured components taken from a pool of reusable assets with variability.
3. Accommodate configuration dependencies between units over base models of different domains, that is, different metamodels. For example, the configuration of a unit of requirements may trigger the configuration of a UML unit designed to fulfill those requirements.

2.4 EXPLOITATION OF VARIABILITY MODELS

2.4.1 USING MDE TO PROCESS VARIABILITY MODELS

Models have been used for long as descriptive artifacts, and proved themselves very helpful for formalizing, sharing, and communicating ideas. Modeling variability in SPL is thus already very useful by itself, as highlighted by the popularity of feature modeling languages and their supporting tools (Pure::Variants [80], RequiLine, Gears [81], etc.).

In many cases we can however go beyond that, that is, we want to be able to perform computations on Variability Models, for a variety of purposes, such as validation of the consistency of models, automatic composition or decomposition of variability models, production of new artifacts (e.g., tests), and of course concrete product derivation. These usages of variability models require that they are no longer informal, and that the language used to describe them has a well-defined abstract syntax (i.e., metamodel) and semantics, as it is the case for the Variability Modeling Languages surveyed in the previous section.

From the methods that extend UML, those of Ziadi and Jézéquel [12], Gomaa and Shin [59], and de Oliveira Jr. et al. [60] provide formalizations of their approaches in the form of metamodel extensions. Conversely, Pohl et al. [24] use an explicit ad hoc metamodel, as well as Sinnema et al. who regroup the concepts used by the COVAMOF framework in a well defined metamodel described in [70, 71]. The concepts introduced in DOPLER are also gathered in a specific metamodel detailed in [74]. Morin et al. [62] also propose an explicit variability metamodel, to be woven into other metamodels as discussed before.

Once variability is actually modeled, based on a well-defined metamodel, standard Language Engineering tools can be leveraged. This tools fall into two categories:

1. endomorphic tools, processing variability models on their own, for either validation (self consistency) or composition/decomposition
2. exomorphic tools, generating other artifacts from variability models, such as concrete software products or test cases.

On the concrete side, one can rely on, for example, well-tooled Eclipse standards such as E-MOF to describe these metamodels, and then readily benefit from a set of tools such as reflexive editors, or XML serialization of models, and also from a standard way of accessing models from Java, that is used in for example, [54].

This toolset can easily be complemented with operational semantics tools such as Kermeta [15, 20], a Kernel Metamodeling language and environment, to obtain a complete environment for such Variability Modeling languages, including checkers, interpreters, compilers, and so forth. Kermeta has indeed been designed to easily extend metamodels with many different concerns (such as static semantics, dynamic semantics, model transformations, connection to concrete syntax, etc.) expressed in heterogeneous languages, using an aspect-oriented paradigm. Kermeta is used for example, to support Perrouin et al.'s approach [64], to support product derivation in [12], and to weave variability into metamodels [62].

Another example is *fmp2rsm*, a tool supporting Czarnecki and Antkiewicz template based approach [66]. It is delivered as an Eclipse plug-in integrating the Feature Modeling Plug-in (FMP) with Rational Software Modeler (RSM), a UML modeling tool from IBM.

The use of such an MDE environment thus makes it quite straightforward to build a wide range of tools able to process Variability Models in several different ways that are described in the following sections.

2.4.2 AUTOMATED ANALYSIS OF FEATURE MODELS

Feature models may have interesting properties that can be automatically extracted by automated techniques and reported to an SPL engineer [82]. In particular, a feature model might represent no valid configuration, typically due to the presence of incompatible cross-tree constraints, or a feature model might have dead features, that is, features not present in any valid configuration.

The automatic analysis of feature models is thus an active area of research that is concerned with extracting information from feature models using automated mechanisms. Since the introduction of feature models, the literature has contributed with a number of algorithms to support the analysis process. Mannion [83] was the first to identify the use of propositional logic techniques to reason about properties of a feature model. Several other proposals [84–88] have been made to formalize Feature Models, but the most complete proposal, called Free Feature Diagrams, probably comes from Schobbens et al. [36].

The following steps are typically performed to encode a feature model as a propositional formula defined over a set of Boolean variables, where each variable corresponds to a feature:

1. each feature of the feature model corresponds to a variable of the propositional formula,
2. each relationship of the model is mapped into one or more formulas depending on the type of relationship (Xor- and Or-groups),
3. the resulting formula is the conjunction of all the resulting formulas of step 2,

4. plus additional propositional constraints.

Batory [50] established the relationship that exists between feature model, propositional logic, and grammar. Batory also suggested to use logic truth maintenance system (LTMS) to infer some choices during the configuration process. Schobbens et al. [36] have formalized some operations and their complexity. Benavides et al. [89] presented a structured literature review of the existing proposals for the automated analysis of feature models. Example analyses include consistency check or dead feature detections [90], interactive guidance during configuration [91, 92], or fixing models and configurations [93–95]. It should be noted that most of the reasoning operations (e.g., satisfiability) are difficult computational problem and are NP-complete [36].

On the technical side, various kinds of automated support have been proposed:

1. propositional logic: SAT (for satisfiability) solvers or Binary Decision Diagram (BDD) take a propositional formula as input and allow reasoning about the formula (validity, models, etc.),
2. constraint programming: a constraint satisfaction problem (CSP) consists of a set of variables, a set of finite domains for those variables, and a set of constraints restricting the values of the variables. A CSP is solved by finding states (values for variables) in which all constraints are satisfied. In contrast to propositional formulas, CSP solvers can deal not only with binary values (true or false) but also with numerical values such as integers or intervals,
3. description logic (DL): DLs are a family of knowledge representation languages enabling the reasoning within knowledge domains by using specific logic reasoners. A problem described in terms of description logic is usually composed by a set of concepts (i.e., classes), a set of roles (e.g., properties or relationships), and set of individuals (i.e., instances). A description logic reasoner is a software package that takes as input a problem described in DL and provides facilities for consistency and correctness checking and other reasoning operations.

Benavides et al. [89] report that CSP solvers or DL solvers are mostly used for extensions of feature models (e.g., feature models with feature attributes), whereas propositional logic quite well fits basic feature models, as well as the core of the OMG's CVL proposal.

2.4.3 MULTIVIEWS AND COMPOSITIONAL APPROACHES

At the code level, when features are implemented separately in distinct modules (files, classes, packages, plug-ins, etc.), they can easily be composed in different combinations to generate variants. Voelter and Groher [96] call this kind of variability positive variability, since variable elements are added together. Many techniques have been proposed to realize compositional approaches (frameworks, mixin layers, aspects [97], stepwise refinement [98], etc.). In model-based SPL engineering, the idea is that multiple models or fragments, each corresponding to a feature, are composed to obtain an integrated model from a feature model configuration. Aspect-oriented modeling techniques have been applied in the context of SPL engineering [62, 99, 100]. Apel et al. [68] propose to revisit superimposition technique and analyze its feasibility as a model composition technique. Perrouin et al. propose a flexible, tool-supported derivation process in which a product model is generated by merging UML class diagram fragments [64].

Acher et al. [101] point out that quite often however, there is a need to compose and decompose variability models at the abstract modeling level, because variability exists across very different concerns of an SPL [59]: from functionality (e.g., particular function may only exist in some services or can be highly parameterized), deployment technology (e.g., operating system, hardware, libraries required, and dependency on middleware), specificities of data format (e.g., image format), to nonfunctional property (like security, performance or adaptability), and so forth.

Acher et al. [102] coined the term multiple feature models to characterize a set of feature models, possibly interrelated, that are combined together to model the variability of a system. These multiple feature models can either come from the problem domain (e.g., variability of independent services that are by nature modular entities, when independent suppliers describe the variability of their different products, etc.) or as an engineering artifact to modularize the variability description of a large system into different criteria (or concerns).

More specifically, Acher et al. [103] have identified some important issues when dealing with multiple feature models, for example, for representing SPL based on Service-Oriented Architectures.

Consistency Checking of Multiple: Feature Models variability must be dealt with both within and across services. Within services, there are complex relationships between services' concerns. Across services, interactions between services (e.g., a feature of one service may exclude another feature of another service) have to be managed when services are combined to form workflows.

- Grouping Feature Models: For each category of activity to be performed in the workflow, there are several candidate services provided by different suppliers. Grouping similar services helps in finding the relevant service and in maintaining the service directory.
- Updating Feature Models: When concerns are interrelated within a service by constraints, some features of some concerns may become dead or mandatory. Hence for each concern of service the variability information needs to be updated so that each feature model is a correct representation of the set of configurations.
- Reasoning Locally about Some Specific Parts of the Feature Models: need to reason about some specific parts of the two services.
- Multiple Perspectives Support: Ideally, different experts should focus on different, specific dimension (e.g., security) and the details that are out of the scope of their expertise should be hidden. Dedicated decomposition facilities should be applied to feature models.
- Multistage and Multistep Process: The design of a product within a SPL is usually not realized in one step or by a unique stakeholder. For example, the specific requirements of an application are obtained by configuring the feature model, that is, by gradually removing the variability until only those features that are part of the final product remain. At each step of the process, it should be possible to reiterate the reasoning tasks mentioned above (consistency checking of FMs, update of FMs, etc).

On these issues, the contributions of [102] can be summarized in two main points:

1. a set of composition and decomposition operators to support Separation of Concerns in feature modeling. The operators are formally defined (using propositional logic), fully automated, guaranteeing properties in terms of sets of configurations, and can be combined together or with other operators, for example, to realize complex reasoning tasks;
2. a domain-specific, textual language, called FAMILIAR, that provides an operational solution for using the different operators and managing multiple feature models on a large scale.

Instead of merging multiple feature models as in [102], another approach is to reference those multiple feature models, as proposed by Hartmann et al. [104]. This approach introduces the Supplier Independent Feature Model (SIFM) in order to select products among the set of products described by several Supplier Specific Feature Models (SSFM).

The overall idea is that any feature of SIFM, say feature F, is then related to the features F of SSFMs using cross-tree constraints. Additional constraints between SSFMs are expressed so that features F of SSFMs cannot be selected at the same time. By defining such constraints between SIFM and SSFMs, Hartmann et al. [104] allow users to build a multiple SPL thanks to several suppliers' SPLs. The SIFM is designed as follows. First, the root feature SIFM has two subfeatures: the feature Suppliers and the common root feature of SSFMs. Then, the feature Suppliers contains as many subfeatures as there are suppliers and those features are mutually exclusive (only one supplier must be selected). The SIFM contains the super-set of the features from all the suppliers and constraints are specified to inter relate features of SIFM and SSFMs. In addition, cross-tree constraints between features are specified in such a way that each child feature F is related to the corresponding features F in each appropriate SSFM.

This approach has the advantage to be realizable by current feature modeling tools and techniques. However, it leads to reasoning on a large set of features (i.e., all the features of SIFM and SSFMs) related by a large number of constraints. The number of variables to be generated may become an issue in terms of computational or space complexity and hinder some automated analysis operations of feature models.

In the context of feature-based configuration, several other works proposed techniques to separate the configuration process into different steps or stages [92, 105]. Hubaux et al. [106] provide view mechanisms to decompose a large feature model. However they do not propose a comprehensive solution when dealing with cross-tree constraints. They also consider that the root feature should always be included, which is a limitation not imposed in [102].

2.4.4 PRODUCT DERIVATION

The product derivation process can be defined as a process of constructing products from Software Product lines, based on the modeling of variability and the choices made by the product configurator [107].

Feature Diagrams are mostly used for product configuration during product derivation. A feature configuration corresponds to an individual product, but lacks details on how the selected features are combined into the actual software product. Many works have thus started about 15 years ago to investigate the modeling and derivation of functional [3, 108, 109] and static [55, 110] aspects of SPL, with however much less emphasis on modeling and derivation of behavior [12, 58, 72, 78, 111], be it interaction-based (focusing on the global interactions between actors and components, e.g.; UML sequence diagrams) or state-based (concentrating on the internal states of individual components, e.g., UML StateCharts).

Product derivation methods slightly differ depending on whether the variability modeling follows an Amalgamated Approach or a Separated Approach, as defined in Sections 3.2 and 3.3.

2.4.4.1 PRODUCT DERIVATION IN AMALGAMATED APPROACHES

Ziadi et al. [12] propose an algebraic specification of UML sequence diagrams as reference expressions, extended with variability operators (optionality, choice, etc.). Generic and specific constraints then guide the derivation process. Behavioral product derivation is formalized using Reference Expressions for Sequence Diagrams (RESD), that are expressions on basic Sequence Diagrams (bSDs) composed by interaction operators to provide the so-called Combined Sequence Diagrams of UML2. A RESD is an expression of the form:

<RESD>::=<PRIMARY>("alt"<RESD>| "seq"<RESD>)*

<PRIMARY>::=|<IDENTIFIER >|"("<RESD>")" |"loop" "("<RESD>")"

where IDENTIFIER refers to a Basic Sequence Diagram and $E_\varnothing$ is the empty Sequence Diagram (without any interaction). As introduced in Section 3.2.1, variability is introduced through three concepts: optionality, variation, and virtuality that are also formalized as algebraic operators to extend RESDs with variability mechanisms. The optional expression (OpE) is specified in the following form:

OpE::= "optional" <IDENTIFIER>"["<RESD>"]"

A Variation expression (VaE) is defined as

VaE::= "variation" <IDENTIFIER>"["<RESD>"," <RESD> ("," <RESD>)*"]"

A virtual expression specifies a virtual SD. It is defined by a name and a reference expression:

ViE::= "virtual" <IDENTIFIER> "[" <RESD>"]"

SDs for Product Lines (RESD-PL) can now be defined as: <RESD-PL>::=<PRIMARY-PL>("alt" <RESD-PL> | "seq"<RESD-PL>)*

<PRIMARY-PL>::= $E_\varnothing$| <IDENTIFIER> | "("<RESD-PL>")" |"loop" "("<RESD-PL>")" | VaE | OpE |ViE

The first step towards product behaviors derivation is to derive the corresponding product expressions from PL-RESD. Derivation needs some decisions (or choices) associated to these variability expressions to be made to produce a product specific RESD. A decision model is made of the following

1. The presence or absence of optional expressions.
2. The choice of a variant expression for variation expressions.
3. The refinement of virtual expressions.

An Instance of a Decision Model (noted hereafter IDM) for a product P is a set of pairs (name$_i$, Res), where name$_i$ designates a name of an optional, variation, or virtual part in the PL-RESD and Res is its decision resolution related to the product P. Decision resolutions are defined as follows.

1. The resolution of an optional part is either TRUE or FALSE.
2. For a variation part with E$_1$, E$_2$, E$_3$ ... as expression variants, the resolution is i if E$_i$ is the selected expression.
3. The resolution of a virtual part is a refinement expression E.

The derivation [[PLE]]$_{DMi}$ can then be seen as a model specialization through the interpretation of a RESD-PL PLE in the DMi context, where DMi is the instance of the decision model related to a specific product. For each algebraic variability construction, the interpretation in a specific context is quite straightforward.

1. Interpreting an optional expression means deciding on its presence or not in the product expression. This is defined as

[[**optional** *name* [E]]]$_{DMi}$

$$= \begin{cases} E & \text{if } (name, TRUE) \in DMi \\ E_\phi & \text{if } (name, FALSE) \in DMi \end{cases} \tag{1}$$

2. Interpreting a variation expression means choosing one expression variant among its possible variants. This is defined as:

$$[[\textbf{variation } name\ [E_1, E_2, \dots]]]_{DMi}$$

$$= \{E_j \quad if\ (name, j)\ \in DMi$$

$$(2)$$

3. Interpreting virtual expressions means replacing the virtual expression by another expression:

$$[[\textbf{virtual } name\ [E]]]_{DMi}$$

$$= \begin{cases} E & if\ (name, E')\ \in DMi \\ E & otherwise \end{cases} \qquad (3)$$

The derived product expressions are expressions without any variability left, that is, expressions only involving basic SDs and interaction operators: alt, seq, and loop. Since the empty expression ($E_\varnothing$) is a neutral element for the sequential and the alternative composition, and idempotent for the loop, derived RESD can be further simplified using algebraic rewriting rules:

1. $E\ seq\ E_\varnothing = E\ E_\varnothing;\ seq\ E = E$
2. $E\ alt\ E_\varnothing = E;\ E_\varnothing\ alt\ E = E$
3. $loop\ (E_\varnothing) = E_\varnothing$

The second part of the derivation process proposed in [12] is to leverage StateCharts synthesis from these scenarios [112], from which direct implementations can easily be obtained [113].

Along the same general lines, Gomaa and Shin [59] define product derivation as a tailoring process involving selection of the appropriate components and setting of the parameter values for individual components to include in the product line member.

For Morin et al. [62], product derivation starts by computing a feature diagram from the product line model. Then, for a selected group of features, the derive operation (implemented in a generic way in the base metamodel) is called. Alternatively, Perrouin et al. [64] first configure the feature model, based on the user's feature selection, and then compose the model fragments associated to the selected features.

2.4.4.2 PRODUCT DERIVATION IN SEPARATED APPROACHES

As introduced in Section 3.3.1, the idea of [66] was to separate the representation of a model family (product line model) into a feature model (defining feature hierarchies, constraints, and possible configurations) and a model template (containing the union of model elements in all valid template instances). Model template elements (structural or behavioral) can be annotated with presence conditions (PCs) and metaexpressions (MEs). To derive an individual product (an instance of a model family), the configurator must first specify a valid feature configuration. Based on it, the model template is instantiated automatically. To improve the effectiveness of template instantiation, the process can be specialized by introducing additional steps: patch application and simplification. The complete template instantiation algorithm can be summarized as follows: an initial evaluation of MEs and explicit PCs, followed by computing implicit PCs and information required for patch application; then elements whose PCs are false are removed and patches are applied; the process ends with a simplification phase.

In [47], Czarnecki et al. also propose a staged configuration approach where feature models are stepwise specialized and instantiated according to the stakeholder interests at each development stage. Specialization and configuration are distinguished: specialization is defined as the process in which variabilities in feature models are removed (i.e., a specialized feature model has fewer variabilities than its parent feature model, a fully specialized feature model has no variability while a configuration is an instantiation of a feature model). The concept of multilevel staged configuration is also introduced, referring to a sequential process in which a feature model is configured and specialized by stakeholders in the development stages.

Hubaux et al. propose a formalization of this kind of multistage configuration [105]. They notably propose the formalism of feature configuration workflow in order to configure a large feature model in different steps, possibly carried out by different stakeholders.

For OVM, Pohl et al. [24] dedicate several chapters of their book to explain how product line variability can be exploited to develop different applications.

In [71] Sinnema et al. discuss in detail the entire COVAMOF Derivation Process. It is realized in four steps: product definition (the engineer creates a new Product entity in the CVV), product configuration (the engineer binds variation points to new values or variants based on customer requirements), product realization (execute the effectuation actions for each of the variants that are selected for the Product entity) and product testing (determine whether the product meets both the functional and the nonfunctional requirements), and the last three steps can occur in one or more iterations.

The goal of DOPLER [74] is to guide stakeholders through product derivation and to automatically generate product configurations. Based on the decision values set by a user, the assets required for composing the product are automatically determined and product configurations can be generated. In [114] Rabiser et al. extend the DOPLER metamodel to provide additional means to support, control and manage derivation: guidance, tasks, roles, users, and property.

Haugen et al. [54] use two transformations to derive products. A Resolution Transformation takes a variation model and a resolution model as input and produces a resolved variation model. Then a Variability Transformation takes the resolved variation model and a domain-specific model as input and produces a new, resolved domain-specific base model.

Beyond coming with a metamodel and a set of well-formedness rules expressed in OCL, the proposed OMG standard for CVL also explicitly addresses the derivation process, that is seen as the dynamic semantics of CVL (i.e., deriving products is done by "executing" CVL on a given resolution model). Semantically, the aim of deriving a resolved model from a base model and a variability model (for a given resolution model) is to reduce the solution space cardinality (the set of all possible resolved models for a given base model and a given variability model). This derivation is thus obtained by considering a variability model as a program parameterized by the resolution model and operating on the base model, to provide a resolved model. Initially, the resolved model is equal to the base model. Then the execution of each statement of the variability model adds new constraints on the solution space, hence progressively reducing its cardinality, eventually down to 1 to get a fully resolved model, or to 0 if there are inconsistencies in the CVL model.

Since the CVL semantics is defined operationally for each statement as adding new constraints on the solution space, it boils down to giving the pre- and postcondition of the execution of each Variation Point metaclass of a CVL model. These constraints are defined using OCL pre and post conditions on an abstract eval operation, woven into each relevant class of the CVL metamodel. On the implementation side, Kermeta can readily be used to get an interpretor for deriving products from a product line, as implemented in [115].

2.4.5 TEST GENERATION

Testing is an important mechanism both to identify defects and assure that completed products work as specified. This is a common practice in single-system development, and continues to hold in Software Product Lines. However, in the early days of SPL research, very few SPL processes addressed the testing of end-product by taking advantage of the specific features of a product line (commonality and variabilities). It was indeed clear that classical testing approaches could not directly be applied on each product since, due to the potentially huge number of products, the testing task would be far too long and expensive [116]. Hence there was a need for testing methods, adapted to the product line context, that allow reducing the testing cost [117].

For example, the early approach presented in [14, 118] is based on the automation of the generation of application system tests, for any chosen product, from the system requirements of a Product Line [119]. These PL requirements are modeled using enhanced UML use cases which are the basis for the test generation. Product-specific test objectives, test scenarios, and test cases are successively generated through an automated process. The key idea of the approach is to describe functional variation points at requirement level to automatically generate the behaviors specific to any chosen product. With such a strategy, the designer may apply any method to produce the domain models of the product line and then instantiate a given product: the test cases check that the expected functionalities have correctly been implemented. The approach is adaptive and provides automated test generation for a new product as well as guided test generation support to validate the evolution of a given product.

More recently the SPL testing field has attracted the attention of many more researchers, which results in a large number of publications regarding general and specific issues. da Mota Silveira Neto et al. [120] present a systematic mapping study, performed in order to map out the SPL testing field, through synthesizing evidence to suggest important implications for practice, as well as identifying research trends, open issues, and areas for improvement. Their goal was to identify, evaluate, and synthesize state-of-the-art testing practices in order to present what has been achieved so far in this discipline.

They identified four main test strategies that have been applied to software product lines.

1. Incremental testing of product lines: the first product is tested individually and the following products are tested using regression testing techniques. Regression testing focuses on ensuring that everything used to work still works, that is, the product features previously tested are retested through a regression technique.
2. Opportunistic reuse of test assets: this strategy is applied to reuse application test assets. Assets for one application are developed. Then, the application derived from the product line use the assets developed for the first application. This form of reuse is not performed systematically, which means that there is no method that supports the activity of selecting the test assets.
3. Design test assets for reuse: test assets are created as early as possible in domain engineering. Domain test aims at testing common parts and preparing for testing variable parts. In application engineering, these test assets are reused, extended and refined to test

specific applications. General approaches to achieve core assets reuse are: repository, core assets certification, and partial integration. The SPL principle design for reuse is fully addressed by this strategy, which can enable the overall goals of reducing cost, shortening time-to-market, and increasing quality.

4. Division of responsibilities: this strategy relates to select testing levels to be applied in both domain and application engineering, depending upon the objective of each phase, that is, whether thinking about developing for or with reuse. This division can be clearly seen when the assets are unit tested in domain engineering and, when instantiated in application engineering, integration, system, and acceptance testing are performed.

Specific testing activities are often split among the two types of activities: domain engineering and application engineering. Alternatively, the testing activities can be grouped into core asset and product development. From the set of studies they overview, around four adopt (or advocate the use of) the V-model as an approach to represent testing throughout the software development life cycle. However, there is no consensus on the correct set of testing levels for each SPL phase.

From the amount of studies analyzed in [120], only a few addressed testing nonfunctional requirements. They point out that during architecture design, static analysis can be used to give an early indication of problems with non-functional requirements. One important point that should be considered when testing quality attributes is the presence of trade-offs among them, for example, the trade-off between modularity and testability. This leads to natural pairings of quality attributes and their associated tests. When a variation point represents a variation in a quality attribute, the static analysis should be sufficiently complete to investigate different outcomes. da Mota Silveira Neto et al.. highlight that investigations towards making explicit which techniques currently applied for single-system development can be adopted in SPL are needed, since studies do not address such an issue.

Their mapping study has also outlined a number of areas in which additional investigation would be useful, specially regarding evaluation and validation research. In general, SPL testing lack evidence, in many aspects. Regression test selection techniques, test automation and architecture-based regression testing are points for future research as well as techniques that address the relationships between variability and testing and techniques to handle traceability among test and development artifacts.

2.5 CONCLUSIONS

SPL engineering is a process focusing on capturing the commonalities (assumptions true for each family member) and variability (assumptions about how individual family members differ) between several software products. Models have been used for long as descriptive artifacts, and proved themselves very helpful for formalizing, sharing, and communicating ideas. Modeling variability in SPL has thus already proven itself very useful, as highlighted by the popularity of feature modeling languages and their supporting tools.

In many cases we have shown that we could go beyond that, to be able to perform computations on Variability Models, for a variety of purposes, such as validation of the consistency of models, automatic composition, or decomposition of variability models, production of new artifacts (e.g., tests), and of course concrete product derivation. These usages of variability models require that they are no longer informal, and that the language used to describe them has a well-defined abstract syntax (i.e., metamodel) and semantics. Model-Driven Engineering (MDE) makes it possible to easily implement a set of tools to process variability models, either endomorphic tools, processing variability models on their own, for validation (self consistency) or composition/decomposition purposes, or exomorphic tools, that is, generating other artifacts from variability models, such as concrete software products or test cases.

The goal of this paper was not to present an exhaustive survey on variability modeling methods and related tools, but to organize the plethora of existing approaches into several classification dimensions, and provide representative examples of Model-Driven Engineering tools and algorithms exploiting them. The reader interested in more systematic literature reviews can check [22, 120–122].

The recent outburst of variability modeling methods that we are wit-
nessing is somehow resembling the blossoming of so many general purpose modeling languages of the early 90's, that were ultimately unified by
the OMG into the UML.

Maybe it is also time for variability modeling methods to be unified
into something well accepted by the community. It might be the case that
the OMG is again playing this unifying role with the Common variability
Language (CVL), that we introduced in this paper.

REFERENCES

1. L. M. Northrop, "A framework for software product line practice," in Proceedings
    of the Workshop on Object-Oriented Technology, pp. 365–376, Springer, London,
    UK, 1999.
2. F. van der Linden, "Software product families in Europe: the esaps & cafe projects,"
    IEEE Software, vol. 19, no. 4, pp. 41–49, 2002.
3. G. Halmans and K. Pohl, "Communicating the variability of a software product fam-
    ily to customers," Software and System Modeling, vol. 2, no. 1, pp. 15–36, 2003.
4. A. Maccari and A. Heie, "Managing infinite variability in mobile terminal software:
    research articles," Software: Practice and Experience, vol. 35, no. 6, pp. 513–537,
    2005.
5. Software Product Line Conference—Hall of Fame, http://splc.net/fame.html.
6. L. M. Northrop, "SEI's software product line tenets," IEEE Software, vol. 19, no. 4,
    pp. 32–40, 2002.
7. J. Bosch, Design and Use of Software Architectures: Adopting and Evolving a Prod-
    uct-Line Approach, ACM Press, Addison-Wesley, New York, NY, USA, 2000.
8. J. Coplien, D. Hoffman, and D. Weiss, "Commonality and variability in software
    engineering," IEEE Software, vol. 15, no. 6, pp. 37–45, 1998. View at Scopus
9. G. Perrouin, Architecting software systems using model transformation and archi-
    tectural frameworks [Ph.D. thesis], University of Luxembourg (LASSY)/University
    of Namur (PReCISE), 2007.
10. J. Bosch, G. Florijn, D. Greefhorst, J. Kuusela, J. Henk Obbink, and K. Pohl, "Vari-
    ability issues in software product lines," in Proceedings of the 4th International
    Workshop on Software Product-Family Engineering (PFE'01), pp. 13–21, Springer,
    London, UK, 2002.
11. P. Heymans and J. C. Trigaux, "Modelling variability requirements in software prod-
    uct lines: a comparative survey," Tech. Rep., FUNDP Namur, 2003.
12. T. Ziadi and J. M. Jézéquel, "Product line engineering with the UML: deriving prod-
    ucts," in Software Product Lines, pp. 557–586, Springer, New York, NY, USA, 2006.
13. C. Nebut, S. Pickin, Y. le Traon, and J. M. Jézéquel, "Automated requirements-based
    generation of test cases for product families," in Proceedings of the 18th IEEE Inter-
    national Conference on Automated Software Engineering (ASE'03), 2003.

14. C. Nebut, Y. le Traon, and J. M. Jézéquel, "System testing of product families: from requirements to test cases," in Software Product Lines, pp. 447–478, Springer, New York, NY, USA, 2006.

15. J. M. Jézéquel, "Model driven design and aspect weaving," Journal of Software and Systems Modeling, vol. 7, no. 2, pp. 209–218, 2008.

16. T. Ziadi, L. Héelouët, and J. M. Jézéquel, "Towards a UML profile for software product lines," in Software Product-Family Engineering, vol. 3014 of Lecture Notes in Computer Science, pp. 129–139, 2003.

17. D. Batory, R. E. Lopez-Herrejon, and J. P. Martin, "Generating product-lines of product-families," in Proceedings of the Automated Software Engineering (ASE'02), pp. 81–92, IEEE, 2002.

18. K. Czarnecki, T. Bednasch, P. Unger, and U. Eisenecker, Generative Programming for Embedded Software: An Industrial Experience Report, Lecture Notes in Computer Science, 2002.

19. J. Bzivin, N. Farcet, J. M. Jézéquel, B. Langlois, and D. Pollet, "Reective model driven engineering," in Proceedings of UML 2003, G. Booch, P. Stevens, and J. Whittle, Eds., vol. 2863 of Lecture Notes in Computer Science, pp. 175–189, Springer, San Francisco, Calif, USA, 2003.

20. P. A. Muller, F. Fleurey, and J. M. Jézéquel, "Weaving executability into objecto-riented meta-languages," in Proceedings of the 8th International Conference on Model Driven Engineering Languages and Systems (MoDELS/UML'05), Lecture Notes in Computer Science, pp. 264–278, Springer, Montego Bay, Jamaica, 2005.

21. S. Pickin, C. Jard, T. Jéron, J. M. Jézéquel, and Y. le Traon, "Test synthesis from UML models of distributed software," IEEE Transactions on Software Engineering, vol. 33, no. 4, pp. 252–268, 2007.

22. L. Chen, M. Ali Babar, and N. Ali, "Variability management in software product lines: a systematic review," in Software Product Line Conference, pp. 81–90, Carnegie Mellon University, Pittsburgh, Pa, USA, 2009.

23. D. L. Parnas, "On the design and development of program families," IEEE Transactions on Software Engineering, vol. 2, no. 1, pp. 1–9, 1976.

24. K. Pohl, G. Böckle, and F. J. van der Linden, Software Product Line Engineering: Foundations, Principles and Techniques, Springer, New York, NY, USA, 2005.

25. J. Estublier, "Software configuration management: a roadmap," in Proceedings of the Conference on the Future of Software Engineering (ICSE), pp. 279–289, 2000.

26. M. Erwig, "A language for software variation research," in Proceedings of the 9th International Conference on Generative Programming and Component Engineering (GPCE'10), pp. 3–12, ACM, New York, NY, USA, October 2010.

27. M. Erwig and E. Walkingshaw, "The choice calculus: a representation for software variation," ACM Transactions on Software Engineering and Methodology, vol. 21, no. 1, 2011.

28. D. M. Weiss and C. T. R. Lai, Software Product-Line Engineering: A Family-Based Software Development Process, Addison-Wesley, Longman, Boston, Mass, USA, 1999.

29. M. Svahnberg, J. van Gurp, and J. Bosch, "A taxonomy of variability realization techniques: research articles," Software Practice and Experience, vol. 35, no. 8, pp. 705–754, 2005.

30. F. Bachmann and P. Clements, "Variability in software product lines," Tech. Rep. cmu/sei-2005-tr-012, Software Engineering Institute, Pittsburgh, Pa, USA, 2005.

31. J. Meekel, T. B. Horton, and C. Mellone, "Architecting for domain variability," in Proceedings of the 2nd International ESPRIT ARES Workshop on Development and Evolution of Software Architectures for Product Families, pp. 205–213, 1998.

32. F. Bachmann and L. Bass, "Managing variability in software architectures," SIG-SOFT Software Engineering Notes, vol. 26, no. 3, pp. 126–132, 2001.

33. K. C. Kang, S. G. Cohen, J. A. Hess, W. E. Novak, and A. S. Peterson, "Featureoriented domain analysis (foda) feasibility study," Tech. Rep., Carnegie-Mellon University Software Engineering Institute, 1990.

34. I. Jacobson, Object-Oriented Software Engineering: A Use Case Driven Approach, Addison Wesley Longman, Redwood City, Calif, USA, 2004.

35. K. Czarnecki and U. W. Eisenecker, Generative Programming: Methods, Tools, and Applications, ACM Press, Addison-Wesley, New York, NY, USA, 2000.

36. P. Y. Schobbens, P. Heymans, J. C. Trigaux, and Y. Bontemps, "Generic semantics of feature diagrams," Computer Networks, vol. 51, no. 2, pp. 456–479, 2007.

37. M. L. Griss, "Implementing product-line features with component reuse," in Proceedings of the 6th International Conerence on Software Reuse (ICSR-6), pp. 137–152, Springer, London, UK, 2000.

38. P. Y. Schobbens, P. Heymans, and J. C. Trigaux, "Feature diagrams: a survey and a formal semantics," in Proceedings of the 14th IEEE International Requirements Engineering Conference (RE'06), pp. 136–145, IEEE Computer Society, Washington, DC, USA, 2006.

39. I. Jacobson, M. Griss, and P. Jonsson, Software Reuse: Architecture, Process and Organization for Business sucCess, ACM Press/Addison-Wesley, New York, NY, USA, 1997.

40. J. M. Jézéquel, "Reifying configuration management for object-oriented software," in International Conference on Software Engineering, ICSE'20, Kyoto, Japan, April 1998.

41. E. Gamma, R. Helm, R. Johnson, and J. Vlissides, Design Patterns: Elements of Reusable Object-Oriented Software, Addison-Wesley, 1995.

42. J. M. Jézéquel, "Reifying variants in configuration management," ACM Transaction on Software Engineering and Methodology, vol. 8, no. 3, pp. 284–295, 1999.

43. K. C. Kang, S. Kim, J. Lee, K. Kim, E. Shin, and M. Huh, "Form: a feature-oriented reuse method with domain-specific reference architectures," Annuals of Software Engineering, vol. 5, no. 1, pp. 143–168, 1998.

44. M. L. Griss, J. Favaro, and M. d'Alessandro, "Integrating feature modeling with the rseb," in Proceedings of the 5th International Conference on Software Reuse (ICSR'98), p. 76, IEEE Computer Society, Washington, DC, USA, 1998.

45. J. van Gurp, J. Bosch, and M. Svahnberg, "On the notion of variability in software product lines," in Proceedings of the Working IEEE/IFIP Conference on Software Architecure (WICSA'01), pp. 45–54, IEEE Computer Society, August 2001.

46. M. Riebisch, "Towards a more precise definition of feature models," in Modelling Variability for Object-Oriented Product Lines, pp. 64–76, 2003.

47. K. Czarnecki, S. Helsen, and U. W. Eisenecker, "Formalizing cardinality-based feature models and their specialization," Software Process Improvement and Practice, vol. 10, no. 1, pp. 7–29, 2005.
48. M. Eriksson, J. Börstler, and K. Borg, "The pluss approach—domain modeling with features, use cases and use case realizations," in Software Product Lines (SPLC), Lecture Notes in Computer Science, pp. 33–44, 2005.
49. A. Deursen and P. Klint, "Domain-specific language design requires feature descriptions," Journal of Computing and Information Technology, vol. 10, p. 2002, 2001.
50. D. S. Batory, "Feature models, grammars, and propositional formulas," in Proceedings of the 9th international conference on Software Product Lines (SPLC'05), pp. 7–20, 2005.
51. S. Ferber, J. Haag, and J. Savolainen, "Feature interaction and dependencies: modeling features for reengineering a legacy product line," in Software Product Lines (SPLC), Lecture Notes in Computer Science, pp. 235–256, 2002.
52. P. Istoan, Méthodologie pour la dérivation des modèles comportementaux des produits dans les lignes de développement logiciel [Ph.D. thesis], Université de Rennes 1, University of Luxembourg (LASSY), 2013.
53. A. Classen, P. Heymans, and P. Y. Schobbens, "What's in a feature: a requirements engineering perspective," in Proceedings of 11th International Conference on Fundamental Approaches to Software Engineering, pp. 16–30, Springer, 2008.
54. O. Haugen, B. Moller-Pedersen, J. Oldevik, G. K. Olsen, and A. Svendsen, "Adding standardized variability to domain specific languages," in Proceedings of the 12th International Software Product Line Conference (SPLC'08), pp. 139–148, Limerick, UK, September 2008.
55. M. Clauss, "Generic modeling using UML extensions for variability," in Proceedings of OOPSLA Workshop on Domain-specific Visual Languages, pp. 11–18, 2001.
56. M. Clauss and I. Jena, "Modeling variability with UML," in Proceedings of the GCSE Young Researchers Workshop, 2001.
57. T. Ziadi, L. Hélouët, and J. M. Jézéquel, "Modeling behaviors in product lines," in Proceedings of the International Workshop on Requirements Engineering for Product Lines (REPL'02), pp. 33–38, 2002.
58. H. Gomaa, Designing Software Product Lines with UML: From Use Cases to Pattern-Based Software Architectures, Addison Wesley, Longman, Redwood City, Calif, USA, 2004.
59. H. Gomaa and M. E. Shin, "Multiple-view modelling and meta-modelling of software product lines," IET Software, vol. 2, no. 2, pp. 94–122, 2008.
60. E. A. de Oliveira Jr., I. M. de Souza Gimenes, E. H. Moriya Huzita, and J. C. Maldonado, "A variability management process for software product lines," in Proceedings of the Centre for Advanced Studies on Collaborative Research Conference (CASCON '05), pp. 225–241, 2005.
61. B. Morin, J. Klein, O. Barais, and J. M. Jézéquel, "A generic weaver for supporting product lines," in Proceedings of the 13th International Workshop on Early Aspects (EA'08), pp. 11–18, ACM, New York, NY, USA, 2008.
62. B. Morin, G. Perrouin, P. Lahire, O. Barais, G. Vanwormhoudt, and J. M. Jézéquel, "Weaving variability into domain metamodels," in Proceedings of the 12th Interna-

tional Conference on Model Driven Engineering Languages and Systems (MODELS'09), pp. 690–705, 2009.

63. K. Bak, K. Czarnecki, and A. Wasowski, "Feature and meta-models in clafer: mixed, specialized, and coupled," in Software Language Engineering, B. Malloy, S. Staab, and M. van den Brand, Eds., vol. 6563 of Lecture Notes in Computer Science, pp. 102–122, Springer, Berlin, Germany, 2011.

64. G. Perrouin, J. Klein, N. Guel, and J. M. Jézéquel, "Reconciling automation and exibility in product derivation," in Proceedings of the 12th International Software Product Line Conference (SPLC'08), pp. 339–348, IEEE Computer Society, Washington, DC, USA, 2008.

65. G. Perrouin, "Coherent integration of variability mechanisms at the requirements elicitation and analysis levels," in Proceedingd of the Workshop on Managing Variability for Software Product Lines: Working with Variability Mechanisms at 10th Software Product Line Conference, August 2006.

66. K. Czarnecki and M. Antkiewicz, "Mapping features to models: a template approach based on superimposed variants," in Proceedings of the 4th International Conference on Generative Programming and Component Enginering (GPCE'05), pp. 422–437, Springer, 2005.

67. M. A. Laguna and B. González-Baixauli, "Product line requirements: multiparadigm variability models," in Proceedings of the 11th Workshop on Requirements Engineering WER, 2008.

68. S. Apel, F. Janda, S. Trujillo, and C. Kästner, "Model superimposition in software product lines," in Proceedings of the 2nd International Conference on Theory and Practice of Model Transformations (ICMT'09), pp. 4–19, Springer, Berlin, Germany, 2009.

69. A. Metzger, K. Pohl, P. Heymans, P. Y. Schobbens, and G. Saval, "Disambiguating the documentation of variability in software product lines: a separation of concerns, formalization and automated analysis," in Proceedings of the 15th IEEE International Requirements Engineering Conference (RE'07), pp. 243–253, New Delhi, India, 2007.

70. M. Sinnema, S. Deelstra, J. Nijhuis, and J. Bosch, "COVAMOF: a framework for modeling variability in software product families," in Proceedings of the 3rd Software Product Line Conference (SPLC'04), pp. 197–213.

71. M. Sinnema, S. Deelstra, and P. Hoekstra, "The COVAMOF derivation process," in Proceedings of the 9th International Conference on Reuse of Off-the-Shelf Components (ICSR'06), pp. 101–114, 2006.

72. J. Bayer, O. Flege, and C. Gacek, "Creating product line architectures," in IW-SAPF, pp. 210–216, 2000.

73. G. Campbell, N. Burkhard, J. Facemire, and J. O'Connor, "Synthesis guidebook," Tech. Rep. SPC-91122-MC, Software Productivity Consortium, Herndon, Va, USA, 1991.

74. D. Dhungana, P. Grünbacher, and R. Rabiser, "The DOPLER meta-tool for decision-oriented variability modeling: a multiple case study," Automated Software Engineering, vol. 18, no. 1, pp. 77–114, 2011.

75. J. Xabier Mansell and D. Sellier, "Decision model and exible component definition based on xml technology," in Software Product Family Engineering (PFE), Lecture Notes in Computer Science, pp. 466–472, 2004.

76. European Software Engineering Institute Spain and IKV++ Technologies AG Germany, "Master: model-driven architecture instrumentation, enhancement and rene-ment," Tech. Rep. IST-2001-34600, IST, 2002.

77. K. Schmid and I. John, "A customizable approach to full lifecycle variability management," Science of Computer Programming, vol. 53, no. 3, pp. 259–284, 2004.

78. C. Atkinson, J. Bayer, and D. Muthig, "Component-based product line development: the KobrA approach," in Proceedings of the 1st Conference on Software Product Lines: Experience and Research Directions: Experience and Research Directions, pp. 289–309, Kluwer Academic, Norwell, Mass, USA, 2000.

79. F. Fleurey, O. Haugen, B. Moller-Pedersen, G. Olsen, A. Svendsen, and Z. Xiaorui, "A generic language and tool for variability modeling," Tech. Rep., SINTEF, 2009.

80. D. Beuche, "Modeling and building software product lines with pure: variants," in Proceedings of the 12th International Software Product Line Conference (SPLC'08), p. 358, Limerick, Ireland, September 2008.

81. C. W. Krueger, "The biglever software gears unified software product line engineering framework," in Proceedings of the 12th International Software Product Line Conference (SPLC'08), p. 353, Limerick, UK, September 2008.

82. M. Acher, P. Collet, P. Lahire, and R. France, "Slicing feature models," in Proceedings of the 26th IEEE/ACM International Conference on Automated Software Engineering (ASE'11), pp. 424–427, January 2011.

83. M. Mannion, "Using first-order logic for product line model validation," in Proceedings of the 2nd International Conference on Software Product Lines (SPLC 2), pp. 176–187, Springer, London, UK, 2002.

84. T. Asikainen, T. Männistö, and T. Soininen, "A unified conceptual foundation for feature modelling," in Proceedings of the 10th International Software Product Line Conference (SPLC'06), pp. 31–40, IEEE Computer Society, August 2006. View at Scopus

85. D. Fey, R. Fajta, and A. Boros, "Feature modeling: a meta-model to enhance usability and usefulness," in Proceedings of the 2nd International Conference on Software Product Lines (SPLC 2), pp. 198–216, Springer, London, UK, 2002.

86. V. Vranic, "Reconciling feature modeling: a feature modeling metamodel," in Proceedings of the 5th Net.ObjectDays, pp. 122–137, Springer, 2004.

87. M. O. Reiser, R. T. Kolagari, and M. Weber, "Unified feature modeling as a basis for managing complex system families," in Proceedings of the 1st International Workshop on Variability Modelling of Software-Intensive Systems (VaMoS'07), pp. 79–86, 2007.

88. K. Czarnecki and A. Wasowski, "Feature diagrams and logics: there and back again," in Proceedings of the 11th International Software Product Line Conference (SPLC'07), pp. 23–34, Kyoto, Japan, September 2007.

89. D. Benavides, S. Segura, and A. Ruiz-Cortés, "Automated analysis of feature models 20 years later: a literature review," Information Systems, vol. 35, no. 6, pp. 615–636, 2010.

90. M. Mendonca, A. Wasowski, and K. Czarnecki, "SAT-based analysis of feature models is easy," in Proceedings of the 13th International Software Product Line Conference (SPLC'09), pp. 231–241, IEEE, 2009.

91. T. T. Tun and P. Heymans, "Concerns and their separation in feature diagram languages—an informal survey," in Proceedings of the Workshop on Scalable Modelling Techniques for Software Product Lines (SCALE@SPLC'09), pp. 107–110, 2009.

92. M. Mendonca and D. Cowan, "Decision-making coordination and efficient reasoning techniques for feature-based configuration," Science of Computer Programming, vol. 75, no. 5, pp. 311–332, 2010.

93. P. Trinidad, D. Benavides, A. Durán, A. Ruiz-Cortés, and M. Toro, "Automated error analysis for the agilization of feature modeling," Journal of Systems and Software, vol. 81, no. 6, pp. 883–896, 2008.

94. J. White, D. Benavides, D. C. Schmidt, P. Trinidad, and A. Ruiz-Cortés, "Automated diagnosis of product-line configuration errors in feature models," in Proceedings of the 12th International Software Product Line Conference (SPLC'08), pp. 225–234, IEEE, Limerick, UK, September 2008.

95. M. Janota, SAT solving in interactive configuration [Ph.D. thesis], Department of Computer Science at University College Dublin, 2010.

96. M. Voelter and I. Groher, "Product line implementation using aspect-oriented and model-driven software development," in Proceedings of the 11th International Software Product Line Conference (SPLC'07), pp. 233–242, 2007.

97. M. Mezini and K. Ostermann, "Variability management with feature-oriented programming and aspects," SIGSOFT Software Engineering Notes, vol. 29, no. 6, pp. 127–136, 2004.

98. D. Batory, J. N. Sarvela, and A. Rauschmayer, "Scaling step-wise refinement," IEEE Transactions on Software Engineering, vol. 30, no. 6, pp. 355–371, 2004.

99. P. Lahire, B. Morin, G. Vanwormhoudt, A. Gaignard, O. Barais, and J. M. Jézéquel, "Introducing variability into aspect-oriented modeling approaches," in Proceedings of 10th ACM/IEEE International Conference on Model Driven Engineering Languages and Systems (MoDELS'07), Lecture Notes in Computer Science, pp. 498–513, Springer, 2007.

100. B. Morin, F. Fleurey, N. Bencomo et al., "An aspect-oriented and model-driven approach for managing dynamic variability," in Proceedings of the 11th International Conference on Model Driven Engineering Languages and Systems (MoDELS'08), vol. 5301 of Lecture Notes in Computer Science, pp. 782–796, 2008.

101. M. Acher, P. Collet, P. Lahire, A. Gaignard, R. France, and J. Montagnat, "Composing multiple variability artifacts to assemble coherent workows," Software Quality Journal, p. 40, 2011, Special issue on Quality Engineering for Software Product Lines.

102. M. Acher, P. Collet, P. Lahire, and R. France, "Decomposing feature models: Language, environment, and applications," in Proceedings of the Automated Software Engineering (ASE'11), IEEE/ACM, Lawrence, Kansas, USA, November 2011, short paper: demonstration track.

103. M. Acher, P. Collet, P. Lahire, and R. France, "Separation of concerns in feature modeling: support and applications," in Proceedings of the 11th International Con-

ference on Aspect-Oriented Software Development (AOSD'12), Hasso-Plattner-Institut Potsdam, ACM, Potsdam, Germany, March 2012.

104. H. Hartmann, T. Trew, and A. Matsinger, "Supplier independent feature modelling," in Proceedings of the 13th International Software Product Line Conference (SPLC'09), pp. 191–200, IEEE, 2009.

105. A. Hubaux, A. Classen, and P. Heymans, "Formal modelling of feature configuration workows," in Proceedings of the 13th International Software Product Line Conference (SPLC'09), pp. 221–230, IEEE, 2009.

106. A. Hubaux, A. Classen, M. Mendonça, and P. Heymans, "A preliminary review on the application of feature diagrams in practice," in Proceedings of the International Workshop on Variability Modelling of Software-Intensive Systems (VaMoS'10), pp. 53–59, 2010.

107. S. Deelstra, M. Sinnema, and J. Bosch, Experiences in Software Product Families: Problems and Issues During Product Derivation, Lecture Notes in Computer Science, 2004.

108. A. Bertolino, A. Fantechi, S. Gnesi, G. Lami, and A. Maccari, "Use case description of requirements for product lines," in Proceedings of the International Workshop on Requirement Engineering for Product Line (REPL'02), pp. 12–18, September 2002.

109. T. von der Massen and H. Lichter, "Requiline: a requirements engineering tool for software product lines," in Software Product-Family Engineering, Lecture Notes in Computer Science, pp. 168–180, 2004.

110. T. Ziadi and J. M. Jézéquel, "Product line engineering with the UML: products derivation," in Families Research Book, Lecture Notes in Computer Science, chapter WP4, Springer, New York, NY, USA, 2004.

111. S. Robak, R. Franczyk, and K. Politowicz, "Extending the UML for modeling variability for system families," International Journal of Applied Mathematics Computer Sciences, vol. 12, no. 2, pp. 285–298, 2002.

112. T. Ziadi, L. Hélouët, and J. M. Jézéquel, "Revisiting statechart synthesis with an algebraic approach," in Proceedings of the 26th International Conference on Software Engineering (ICSE'04), pp. 242–251, ACM, Edinburgh, UK, May 2004.

113. F. Chauvel and J. M. Jézéquel, "Code generation from UML models with semantic variation points," in Proceedings of MOD-ELS/UML'2005, S. Kent L. Briand, Ed., vol. 3713 of Lecture Notes in Computer Science, Springer, Montego Bay, Jamaica, 2005.

114. R. Rabiser, P. Grunbacher, and D. Dhungana, "Supporting product derivation by adapting and augmenting variability models," in Proceedings of the 11th International Software Product Line Conference (SPLC'07), pp. 141–150, IEEE Computer Society, Kyoto, Japan, 2007.

115. M. Gouyette, O. Barais, J. le Noir et al., "Movida studio: a modeling environment to create viewpoints and manage variability in views," in IDM-7éme journées sur l'Ingénierie Dirigée par les ModèLes-2011, I. Ober, Ed., vol. 1, pp. 141–145, Polytech, Université Lille 1, Service Reprographie de Polytech, Lille, France, 2011.

116. J. D. McGregor, "Building reusable testing assets for a software product line," in Proceedings of the 12th International Software Product Line Conference (SPLC'08), p. 378, Limerick, UK, September 2006.

117. J. D. McGregor, "Testing a software product line," in PSSE, pp. 104–140, 2007.

118. C. Nebut, Y. le Traon, F. Fleurey, and J. M. Jézéquell, "A requirement-based approach to test product families," in Proceedings of the 5th Workshop on Product Families Engineering (PFE'05), vol. 3014 of Lecture Notes in Computer Science, Springer, 2003.

119. C. Nebut, F. Fleurey, Y. le Traon, and J. M. Jézéquel, "Requirements by contracts allow automated system testing," in Proceedings of the 14th International Symposium on Software Reliability Engineering (ISSRE'03), pp. 85–96, IEEE, 2003.

120. P. A. da Mota Silveira Neto, I. D. Carmo MacHado, J. D. McGregor, E. S. de Almeida, and S. R. de Lemos Meira, "A systematic mapping study of software product lines testing," Information and Software Technology, vol. 53, no. 5, pp. 407–423, 2011.

121. S. Mujtaba, K. Petersen, R. Feldt, and M. Mattsson, "Software product line variability: a systematic mapping study," 2008.

122. M. Sinnema and S. Deelstra, "Classifying variability modeling techniques," Information and Software Technology, vol. 49, no. 7, pp. 717–739, 2007.

CHAPTER 3

A QUALITY MODEL FOR CONCEPTUAL MODELS OF MDD ENVIRONMENTS

BEATRIZ MARÍN, GIOVANNI GIACHETTI, OSCAR PASTOR, AND ALAIN ABRAN

3.1 INTRODUCTION

Historically, software production methods and tools have a unique goal: to produce high-quality software. Since the goal of Model-Driven Development (MDD) methods is no different, MDD methods have emerged to take advantage of the benefits of using of models [1] to produce high-quality software. Model-Driven Technologies [2] attempt to separate business logic from platform technology in order to allow automatic generation of software through well-defined model transformations. In a software production process based on MDD technology, the conceptual models are key inputs in the process of code generation. Thus, the conceptual models must provide a holistic view of all the components of the final application (including the structure of the system, the behavior, the interaction between the users and the system, and the interaction among the components of the

Marín B, Giachetti G, Pastor O, and Abran A. A Quality Model for Conceptual Models of MDD Environments. Advances in Software Engineering 2010 (2010); http://dx.doi.org/10.1155/2010/307391.

system) in order to be able to automatically generate the final application. Therefore, the evaluation of the quality of conceptual models is essential since this directly affects the quality of the generated software products.

To evaluate the quality of conceptual models, many proposals have been developed following different perspectives [3]. There are proposals that are based on theory [4], experience [5], the observation of defects in the conceptual models in order to induce quality characteristics [6], the evaluation of the quality characteristics defined in the ISO 9126 standard [7] in conceptual models by means of measures [8], a synthesis approach [9], and so forth. Taking into account the advantages and disadvantages of each development perspective for quality frameworks [3], defect detection is considered as a suitable approach because it provides a high level of empirical validity provided by the variety of conceptual models that are observed. However, it is interesting to note that this approach is not broadly used in the software engineering discipline, even though defect detection is the most common quality evaluation approach used by other disciplines such as health care [10].

To develop an effective quality assurance technique, it is necessary to know what kind of defects may occur in conceptual models related to MDD approaches. Currently, there are some approaches that detect defects in conceptual models (such as [11, 12]), which are mostly focused on the detection of defects that come from either the data perspective (data models) or the process perspective (process models). However, defect detection has not been clearly accomplished from the interaction perspective (interaction models) even though all of these perspectives (data, process, and interaction modeling) are essential to specify a correct conceptual schema used in an MDD context [13].

In this article, we present an approach that allows the automatic verification of the conceptual models used in MDD environments with respect to defect types from the data, process, and interaction perspectives. We present a set of defect types related to data, process, and interaction models as well as a quality model that formalizes the elements involved in the identification of the different defect types proposed. This quality model, which is defined using current metamodeling standards, is the main contribution of this article. It is oriented to represent the abstract syntax of the constructs involved in the conceptual specification of software applications generated in MDD environments. From this quality model, defect detection can be automated by means of OCL [14] rules that verify the properties of the conceptual constructs according to the set of defects types defined.

The remainder of the paper is organized as follows. Section 2 presents the related work, including a list with the defect types found in the literature. Section 3 presents a set of conceptual constructs of the conceptual model of an MDD approach. Section 4 presents the quality model (metamodel) in detail. Section 5 presents our conclusions and suggestions for further work.

3.2 RELATED WORK

In the literature, there is no consensus for the definition of the quality of conceptual models. There are several proposals that use different terminologies to refer to the same concepts. There are also many proposals that do not even define what they mean by quality of conceptual models. In order to achieve consensus about the definition of quality and to improve the conceptual models, we have adopted the definition proposed by Moody [3]. This definition is based on the definition of quality of a product or service in the ISO 9000 standard [15]. Therefore, we define the quality of a conceptual model as "the total of features and characteristics of a conceptual model that bear on its ability to satisfy stated or implied needs".

In order to design a quality model, the types of defects that the conceptual models used in MDD environments must be known. Defect detection refers to identifying anomalies in software products in order to correct them to be able to obtain better software products. The IEEE 1044 [16] presents a standard classification for software anomalies, which defines an anomaly as any condition that deviates from expectations based on requirements specifications, design documents, user documents, standards, and so forth, or from someone's perceptions or experiences. This definition is so broad that different persons can identify different anomalies in the same software artifact, and anomalies that one person identifies may not be perceived as anomalies for another person. Therefore, many researchers have had to redefine the concepts of error, defect, failure, fault, and so forth, while other researchers have used these concepts indistinctly [17]. To avoid the proliferation of concepts related to the software anomalies, in this article, we analyze the proposals of defect detection in conceptual models by adopting the terminology defined by Meyer in [18].

1. Error. It is a wrong decision made during the development of a conceptual model.
2. Defect. It is a property of a conceptual model that may cause the model to depart from its intended behavior.
3. Fault. It is an event of a software system that departs from its intended behavior during one of its executions.

Taking into account that the cost of fault correction increases exponentially over the development life cycle [3], it is of paramount importance to discover faults as early as possible: this means detecting errors or defects before the implementation of the software system.

Travassos et al. [19] use reading techniques to perform software inspections in high-level, object-oriented designs. They use UML diagrams that are focused on data structure and behaviour. These authors advocate that the design artifacts (a set of well-related diagrams) should be read in order to determine whether they are consistent with each other and whether they adequately capture the requirements. Design defects occur when these conditions are not met. These authors use a defect taxonomy that is borrowed from requirements defects [20], which classifies the defects as Omission, Incorrect Fact, Inconsistency, Ambiguity, and Extraneous Information. However, they do not present the types of defects that were found in their study.

Laitenberger et al. [21] present a controlled experiment to compare the checklist-based reading (CBR) technique with the perspective-based reading (PBR) technique for defect detection in UML models. The authors define three inspection scenarios in the UML models in order to detect defects from different viewpoints (designers, testers, and programmers). These authors do not explicitly identify the types of defects found in UML models. However, they present a set of concepts that must be checked in the UML models from different viewpoints, and it is possible to infer the types of defects from these concepts.

Conradi et al. [22] present a controlled experiment that was designed to perform a comparison between an old reading technique used by the Ericsson company and an Object-Oriented Reading Technique (OORT) for detecting defects in UML models. The authors present a summary of the defects detected using both inspection techniques for the same project. The findings of the controlled experiment are that one group of subjects detected 25 defects using the old technique (without any overlaps of the defects detected) while the other group of subjects detected 39 defects using the OORT technique (with 8 overlaps in the defects detected). However, the authors did not present the types of defects found in the models inspected in the experiment.

Gomma and Wijesekera [23] present an approach for the identification and correction of inconsistency and incompleteness across UML views. It is applied in the COMET method [24], which uses the UML notation. The authors present 7 defect types related to the consistency between models: 1 defect type for the consistency between use-case diagrams and sequence diagrams, 4 defect types for the consistency between class diagrams and state transition diagrams, and 2 defect types for the consistency between sequence diagrams and state transition diagrams.

Kuzniarz [25] presents a set of inconsistencies found in student designs produced in a sample didactic development process. This proposal corresponds to a case study that was developed to explore the nature of inconsistency in UML designs. The authors present 8 defect types based on subjective but common-sense judgment.

Berenbach [26] presents a set of heuristics for analysis and design models that prevents the introduction of defects in the models. This allows semantically correct models to be developed. In addition, Berenbach presents the Design Advisor tool created by Siemens to facilitate the inspection of large models. This tool implements the heuristics proposed by Berenbach for evaluating the goodness of the analysis and design models. For the analysis models, Berenbach presents 10 heuristics for model organization, 5 heuristics for use case definition, 3 heuristics related to the use-case relationships, and 14 heuristics related to business object modeling. For the design models, he presents 2 heuristics for the class model.

Lange and Chaudron [27] identify the incompleteness of UML diagrams as a potential problem in the subsequent stages of a model-oriented software development. These authors refer to the completeness of a model by means of the aggregation of three characteristics: (1) the well-formedness of each diagram that comprises the model, (2) the consistency between the diagrams that comprise the model, and (3) the completeness among the diagrams that comprise the model. Note that the authors use the completeness concept to define the completeness of a model. Since this is equivalent to reusing the same concept (completeness) for its own definition, they do not really describe what is understood by completeness. These authors identify eleven types of defects of UML models: 5 types of defects related to the well-formedness of the diagrams, 3 types related to the consistency among the diagrams, and 3 other types related to the completeness among the diagrams.

Leung and Bolloju [28] present a study that aims to understand the defects frequently committed by novice analysts in the development of UML Class models. These authors use Lindland et al.'s quality framework [4] to evaluate the quality of the class diagrams. They distinguish five classifications that allow the evaluation of the syntactic quality, semantic quality, and pragmatic quality. These five classifications are syntactic (for the syntactic quality), validity and completeness (for the semantic quality), and the expected is missing and the unexpected is present (for the pragmatic quality). The authors obtain 103 different types of defects in 14 projects. However, the authors only detail 21 types of defects for one class diagram.

Bellur and Vallieswaran [12] perform an impact analysis of UML design models. This analysis evaluates the consistency of the design and the impact of a design change over the code. In order to evaluate the consistency of the design models, these authors propose evaluating the well-formedness of UML diagrams. The proposal of Bellur and Vallieswaran [12] extends the proposal of Lange and Chaudron [27] focusing on the quality of UML conceptual models as well as on the code. These authors identify 4 types of defects for use-case diagrams, 2 types of defects for sequence diagrams, 5 types of defects for the specification of the method sequences, 3 types of defects for the class diagram, 8 types of defects for the state transition diagrams, 2 types of defects for the component diagram, and 2 types of defects for the deployment diagram.

Summarizing, the above proposals present defect types that are related to the consistency (consistency is defined in the IEEE 610 standard as the degree of uniformity, standardization, and freedom from contradiction among the documents or parts of a system or component) [29] among diagrams and defect types that are related to the correctness (correctness is defined in the IEEE 610 standard as the degree to which a system or component is free from faults in its specification, design, and implementation) [29] of a particular diagram. Table 1 presents the defect types of the different proposals analyzed. The first column, "Quality Characteristic", divides the defect types into two groups, the consistency characteristic and the correctness characteristic. The second column, "Authors", presents the authors who have proposed these defect types and the corresponding year of the proposals. The third column, "Model", presents the conceptual models (or diagrams) where the defect types have been found. The last column, "Defect Types", presents the defect types.

In the systematic revision of the state of the art, we noticed that all the proposals for defect detection in conceptual models are focused on UML models. However, it is well known that UML diagrams [30] do not have enough semantic precision to allow the specification of a complete and unambiguous software application [31–33], which is clearly observed in the semantic extension points that are defined in the UML specification [30]. For this reason, many methodologies have selected a subset of UML diagrams and conceptual constructs and have aggregated the needed semantic expressiveness in order to completely specify the final applications in the conceptual model, making the implementation of MDD technology a reality.

Since MDD proposals select a set of conceptual constructs and aggregate others to specify the conceptual models, it is important to note that a great number of conceptual constructs increase the complexity of the specification of the models and may cause the introduction of more defects into the conceptual models. For this reason, the conceptual constructs of an MDD proposal must be carefully selected so that the number of constructs that allow the complete specification of software applications at the conceptual abstraction level is as low as possible. In the following section, we present a minimal set of the conceptual constructs for an MDD environment.

3.3 CONCEPTUAL CONSTRUCTS OF AN MDD PROPOSAL

Model-Driven Development environments generally use Domain-Specific Modeling Languages (DSMLs), which define the set of conceptual constructs in order to represent the semantics of a particular domain in a precise way [34]. For example, the DSMLs for the Management Information Systems (MIS) domain share a well-known set of conceptual constructs. In order to allow the complete specification of MIS applications, the DSMLs must add specific conceptual constructs to the conceptual models.

The MDD methods use models at different levels of abstraction to automate their transformations to generate software products. Model-Driven Architecture (MDA) is a standard proposed by OMG [35] that defends MDD principles and proposes a technological architecture to construct MDD methods. This architecture divides the models into the following categories: Computation-Independent Models (CIMs), Platform-Independent Models (PIMs), and Platform-Specific Models (PSMs). CIMs are requirement models (e.g., use-case diagrams, i* models, etc.), which by nature do not allow the complete specification of final software applications. In contrast, PIMs and PSMs allow the complete specification of final applications in an abstract way, but the PSMs use constructs that are specific to the technological platform in which the final applications will be generated (e.g., java, c#, etc.). Therefore, in this article, we focus on the PIM models (which we refer to as conceptual models of MDD proposals) since they can be used independently of the platform.

To provide details of the conceptual constructs of MDD proposals for the MIS domain, we have selected a specific MDD environment as reference: the OO-Method approach [36, 37]. This approach is an object-oriented method that puts MDD technology into practice [36] by separating the business logic from the platform technology to allow the automatic generation of final applications by means of well-defined model transformations [37]. The OO-Method approach provides the semantic formalization that is needed to define complete conceptual models, which allows the specification of all the functionality of the final application at the conceptual level. The OO-Method approach has been implemented in an industrial tool [26] that automatically generates fully working applications.

These applications can be either desktop or web MIS applications and can be generated in several technologies (java, C#, visual basic, etc.).

The conceptual model of an MDD proposal must be able to specify the structure, the behavior, and the interaction of the components of an MIS in an abstract way. Therefore, we distinguish three kinds of models that together provide the complete specification of software systems: a structural model, a behavior model, and an interaction model.

3.3.1 THE STRUCTURAL MODEL

The structural model describes the static part of the system and is generally represented by means of a class model. A class describes a set of objects that share the same specifications of characteristics, constraints, and semantics. A class can have attributes, integrity constraints, services, and relationships with other classes. The attributes of a class represent characteristics of this class. The attributes of a class can also be derived attributes, which obtain their value from the values of other attributes or constants. The integrity constraints are expressions of a semantic condition that must be preserved in every valid state of an object.

The services of a class are basic components that are associated with the specification of the behavior of a class. The services can be events, transactions, or operations. The events are indivisible atomic services that can assign a value to an attribute. The transactions are a sequence of events or other transactions that have two ways to end the execution: either all involved services are correctly executed or none of the services are executed. The operations are a sequence of events, transactions, or other operations, which are executed sequentially independently of whether or not the involved services have been executed correctly. The services can have preconditions that limit their execution because the preconditions are conditions that must be true for the execution of a service.

The relationships between classes in the structural model can be the following: agent, association, aggregation, composition, and specialization. Agents are relationships that indicate the classes that can access specific attributes or services of other classes of the model. Agents are specifically defined in the reference MDD approach.

3.3.2 THE BEHAVIOR MODEL

The behavior model describes the dynamic part of a system. These dynamics include the behavior of each class and the interaction among the objects of the system. For the specification of the behavior of a system, we select the functional model of the reference MDD approach, which defines the behavior of the services defined inside the classes of the structural model.

The functional model specifies a formula with the sequence of events, transactions, or operations that must be executed when a service is used. This formula must be specified by means of well-formed, first-order logic formulae that are defined using the OASIS language [38].

The functional model specifies the effects that the execution of an event has over the value of the attributes of the class that owns the event. To do this, the functional model uses valuations to assign values to the corresponding attributes. The effect of a valuation is also specified using formulae within the syntax of the OASIS language. The change that a valuation produces in the value of an attribute is classified into three different categories: state, cardinal, and situation. The state category implies that the change of the value of an attribute depends only on the effect specified in the valuation for the event, and it does not depend on the value in the previous state. The cardinal category increases, decreases, or initializes the numeric-type attributes. The situation category implies that the valuation effect is applied only if the value of the attribute is equal to a predefined value specified as the current value of the attribute.

Since services can have preconditions, the conditions and the error messages of the preconditions are also specified using OASIS formulae. The integrity constraints of a class are also specified using OASIS formulae.

3.3.3 THE INTERACTION MODEL

The interaction model describes the presentation (static aspects of a user interface like widgets, layout, contents, etc.) and the dialogs (dynamic aspects of a user interface like controls, dynamic page change, etc.) of the system [39]. In order to specify the interaction between the users of an application and the system, the OO-Method MDD approach specifies views. A view corresponds to a set of interfaces, which are the communication point between agents and classes of the structural model. When the views of a system have been defined, the interaction model of each view must be specified.

The interaction model allows the specification of the graphical user interface of an application in an abstract way [40]. To do this, the interaction model has a set of abstract presentation patterns that are organized hierarchically in three levels: access structure, interaction units, and auxiliary patterns. The first level allows the specification of the system access structure. In this level, the set of entry options that each user of the application will have available is specified by means of a Hierarchy Action Tree (HAT).

Based on the menu-like view provided by the first level, the second level allows the specification of the interaction units of the system. The interaction units are groups of functionality that allow the users of the application to interact with the system. Thus, the interaction units of the interaction model represent entry-points for the application. These units can be the following.

1. Service Interaction Unit (SIU). This interaction unit represents the interaction between a user of the application and the execution of a system service. In other words, the SIUs allow the users of the application to enter the values for the arguments of a service and to execute the service. They also provide the users with the feedback of the results of the execution of the service.

2. A Population Interaction Unit (PIU). This interaction unit represents the interaction with the system that deals with the presentation of a set of instances of a class. In a PIU, an instance can be selected, and the corresponding set of actions and/or navigations for the selected instance are offered to the user.

3. An Instance Interaction Unit (IIU). This interaction unit represents the interaction with an object of the system. In an IIU, the corresponding set of actions and/or navigations for the instance are offered to the user.

4. A Master Detail Interaction Unit (MDIU). This interaction unit represents the interaction with the system through a composite

interaction unit. An MDIU corresponds to the joining of a master interaction unit (which can be an IIU or a PIU) with a detail interaction unit (which can be a set of IIUs, PIUs, or SIUs).

The third level of the interaction model allows the specification of the auxiliary patterns that characterize lower level details about the behavior of the interaction units. These auxiliary patterns are the following.

1. The entry pattern is used to indicate that the user can enter values for the arguments of the SIUs.
2. The defined selection pattern is used to specify a list of specific values to be selected by the user.
3. The arguments dependency pattern is used to define dependencies among the values of the arguments of a service. To do this, Event-Condition-Action (ECA) rules are defined for each argument of the service. The ECA rules have the following semantics: when an interface event occurs in an argument of a service (i.e., the user enters a value), an action is performed if a given condition is satisfied.
4. The display set pattern is used to specify which attributes of a class or its related classes will be shown to the user in a PIU or an IIU.
5. The order criteria pattern allows the objects of a PIU to be ordered. This pattern consists of the ascendant/descendant order over the values of the attributes of the objects presented in the PIU.
6. The action pattern allows the execution of services by joining and activating the corresponding SIUs by means of actions.
7. The navigation pattern allows the navigation from an interaction unit to another interaction unit.
8. The filter pattern allows a restricted search of objects for a population interaction unit. A filter can have data-valued variables and object-valued variables. These variables can have a defined default value, an associated PIU to select the value of the object-valued variables, and precharge capabilities for the values of the object-valued arguments.

Each auxiliary pattern has its own scope that states the context in which it can be applied. With these conceptual constructs we can completely specify applications that correspond to the MIS domain in an abstract way. To formalize the concepts and the relationships among them, we present a generic metamodel for MDD proposals.

3.4 A QUALITY MODEL FOR MDD ENVIRONMENTS

The quality model proposed in this article is specified by means of the modeling facilities that current metamodeling standards provide, specifically, the EMOF specification [41]. The EMOF was selected for its metamodeling language, which is supported by open-source tools such as the Eclipse EMF [42] (for metamodeling purposes) or Eclipse GMF [43] (for the generation of model editors). EMOF is also used by technologies such as ATL [44, 45] or QVT [46] for the implementation of model-to-model transformations. In the following subsections, we present the metamodel, the procedure proposed for defect detection, and a list of defect types found in MDD-oriented conceptual models.

3.4.1 A METAMODEL FOR DEFECT DETECTION IN MDD-ORIENTED CONCEPTUAL MODELS

In general terms, a metamodel is the artifact used to specify the abstract syntax of a modeling language: the structural definition of the involved conceptual constructs with their properties, the definition of relationships among the different constructs, and the definition of a set of rules to control the interaction among the different constructs specified [47]. In EMOF, a metamodel is represented by means of a class diagram, where each class of the diagram corresponds to a construct of the modeling language involved. We use the OCL specification [14] for the definition of the controlling rules of the metamodel since it is part of the OMG standards and can work with EMOF metamodels. Also, OCL rules provide a computable language for rule specification, which allows the defined rules to be automatically evaluated by existent tools such as Eclipse OCL tools [48].

With EMOF, the quality metamodel can specify the constructs involved in the different types of defects as well as the properties that must be present in the different conceptual constructs for the detection of defects. The OCL language used for the metamodeling rules can be used to define specific rules to automate defect detection. The final quality model is comprised of two main elements: (1) a metamodel for the description of the conceptual constructs that are used in MDD environments (which includes all the properties involved in defect detection) and (2) a set of OCL rules that allows the automatic detection of defects according to the list of defects presented in this article.

Figure 1 presents our quality metamodel. As this figure shows, a generic ConceptualModel of an MDD approach is comprised of a structural model (class StructuralModel), a behaviour model (class BehaviourModel), and an interaction model (PresentationModel). The structural model has a set of classes (class Class). Each class has several features (class ClassFeature), which can be services (class Service) or properties (class Property). In turn, the properties can be typed properties (class TypedProperty) or association ends (class AssociationEnd). The typed properties correspond to the attributes of a class, which must have a data type (class DataType) specified (attribute Kind). The typed properties can be derived (class DerivedAttribute) or not derived (class Attribute). The services can be events (class Event), transactions (class Transaction), or operations (class Operation). The events have valuations (class Valuation) to change the value of the attributes of a class. Each service has a set of arguments (class Argument) with their corresponding types (class Type), and it can also have a set of preconditions (association precondition). There are relationships between the classes of the model (represented by the class RelationShip), which can be associations (class Association), generalizations (class Generalization), and agents (class Agent). The agent definition is oriented to state the visibility and execution permissions over the classes of the defined model (association agent). The associations can be aggregations, compositions, or normal associations (attribute aggregation of the class AssociationEnd). Each class has a set of integrity constraints (association integrityConstraint). The classes, class features, arguments, and relationships must have a name (class NamedElement).

The derived attributes, services, preconditions, and integrity constraints require the specification of the functionality that they perform.
This functionality is specified by means of the behaviour model. The behaviour model has elements (class BehaviourElement) that can be conditional elements (ConditionalBehaviourElement) or constraint elements
(Constraint). The conditional elements correspond to formulae (class Formula) with a condition (association condition) and an effect (association
effect). The constraint elements correspond to formulae (class Formula)
with an error message (attribute errorMsg). The formulae are defined (attribute value) by means of a particular language called OASIS, which is
similar to the OCL language. Thus, the valuations and the specification of
the derived attributes (class ValueSpecification) correspond to conditional
behaviour elements, and the transactions, and operations correspond to
behaviour elements. The preconditions and the integrity constraints correspond to constraint behaviour elements.

The interaction model has a set of interaction units (class Interactio-
nUnit) and a set of auxiliary patterns (class AuxPattern) that allow the
specification of the graphical user interface at an abstract level. The interaction units can be instances (InstanceIU), set of instances (Popula-
tionIU), services (ServiceIU), and composite units (MasterDetailIU).
The master-detail interaction units correspond to composite interaction
units (class DependentIU), which are comprised of a master part (class
IndependentIU) and a set of detail interaction units (class DependentIU).
In the master part, only instances or populations can be used. In the detail part, instances, populations and other master detail interaction units
can be used. Since, the instance interaction units and the population interaction units can be used independently of other interaction units; we
classify them in the class IndependentIU. However, these interaction
units can also be used inside the detail part of master detail interaction
units, so we classify them in the class DependentIU. The independent interaction units have display sets (class DiaplaySet) to present the data.
Each display pattern has a set of attributes (association relatedattribute)
that are specified in the structural model, from which the data will be recovered to show the users of the application. The independent interaction units can have actions (class ActionSet) to present the set of services
(throw a ServiceIU) that can be executed by the users over the instances

shown in the interaction units. In addition, the independent interaction units can have navigations (class NavigationSet) to present the interaction units that can be accessed. The population interaction units can also have filters (class Filter) to search for information in a set of instances, which must be specified with the corresponding formula (class Formula). The service interaction units have entry (class EntryPattern) and selection patterns (class SelectionPattern), which have associated formulae composed of a condition (association condition) and an effect (association effect).

Since the quality metamodel has been specified using the standards of metamodelling, this metamodel eliminates redundancy of the elements defined and can be implemented using open-source modeling tools.

3.4.2 THE OOMCFP PROCEDURE TO IDENTIFY DEFECTS

Before the specification of the OCL rules, the types of defects that the conceptual models used in MDD environments must be known. To do this, we use a Functional Size Measurement (FSM) procedure designed for the OO-Method MDD approach, which is called OOmCFP [49]. This FSM procedure was developed to measure the functional size of the applications generated in an MDD environment from the conceptual models. The OOm CFP measurement procedure was defined in accordance with the COSMIC measurement manual version 3.0 [50]. Thus, a mapping between the concepts used in COSMIC and the concepts used in the conceptual model of the MDD approach has been defined [51].

The OOmCFP procedure is structured using three phases: the strategy phase, the mapping phase, and the measurement phase. The strategy phase addresses the four key parameters of software functional size measurement that must be considered before actually starting to measure: purpose of the measurement, scope of the measurement, identification of functional users, and level of granularity that should be measured. The mapping phase presents the rules to identify the functional processes, data groups, and data attributes in the software specification (i.e., in the conceptual model) depending on the parameters defined in the strategy phase. The measurement phase presents the rules to identify and measure the data movements that occur between the functional users and the functional processes.

OOmCFP starts with the definition of the strategy to perform the measurement. The purpose of the measurement in OOmCFP is defined as measuring the accurate functional size of the OO-Method applications generated in an MDD environment from the involved conceptual models. The scope of the measurement defines a set of functional user requirements that will be included in a measurement exercise. For OOmCFP, the scope of the measurement in OOmCFP is the OO-Method conceptual model, which is comprised of four models (Object, Dynamic, Functional, and Presentation), which allow a fully working software application to be generated.

Once the scope of the measurement has been determined, it is important to identify the layers, the pieces of software, and the peer components that make up the applications. Since the OO-Method software applications are generated according to a three-tier software architecture, we distinguish three layers: a client layer, which contains the graphical user interface; a server layer, which contains the business logic of the application; and a database layer, which contains the persistence of the applications (see Figure 2). In each layer of an OO-Method application, there is a piece of software that can interchange data with the pieces of software of the other layers. Thus, we distinguish, respectively, three pieces of software in an OO-Method application: the client piece of software, the server piece of software, and the database piece of software (see Figure 2).

Since the functional users are the types of users that send (or receive) data to (from) the functional processes of a piece of software, the functional users of the OO-Method applications are the human users, the client component of the software, the server component of the software, and the legacy views (see Figure 2). We called these users as "human functional user", "client functional user", "server functional user", and "legacy functional user", respectively.

Once the strategy is defined, OOmCFP starts a mapping phase. A functional process corresponds to a set of Functional User Requirements comprising a unique, cohesive, and independently executable set of data movements. A functional process starts with an entry data movement carried out by a functional user given that an event (triggering event) has happened. A functional process ends when all the data movements needed to generate the answer to this event have been executed. In the context of OOmCFP, the "human functional user" carries out the triggering events that occur in the real world. This functional user starts the functional processes that occur in the client layer of the application. In this layer, the functional processes are represented by the interaction units of the conceptual model that can be directly accessed by the "human functional user". The "client functional user" activates triggering events that occur in the interaction units of the presentation model. The "client functional user" starts functional processes, which are the actions that carry out the server layer of the software in response to the triggering events that occur in the client layer of the software. The "server functional user" carries out the triggering events that occur in the server layer of the software. The "server functional user" starts functional processes, which are the actions that the database layer carries out in response to the triggering events of the server layer, and the actions that the client layer carries out in response to triggering events of the server layer of the software. The "legacy functional user" activates triggering events that occur in the legacy system. The "legacy functional user" starts functional processes, which are the actions that the server layer of the software carries out to interact with the legacy system. The data groups correspond to the classes of the structural model that participate in the functional processes. The data attributes correspond to the attributes of the classes identified as data groups.

In the measuring phase, the data movements correspond to the movements of data groups between the users and the functional processes. Each functional process has two or more data movements. Each data movement moves a single data group. A data movement can be an Entry (E), an Exit (X), a Read (R), or a Write (W) data movement. This proposal has 65 rules to identify the data movements that can occur in the OO-Method applications (see Figure 3). Each rule is structured with a concept of the COSMIC measurement method, a concept of the OO-Method approach, and the cardinalities that associate these concepts. These mapping rules detect the data movements (E, X, R, and W) of all the functionality needed for the correct operation of the generated application, which must be built by the developer of the application. This proposal has three measurement rules to obtain the functional size of each functional process of the application, each piece of software of the application, and the whole application. A complete description of OOm-CFP can be found in its measurement guide (http://oomethod.dsic.upv.es/labs/images/OOmCFP/guide.pdf).

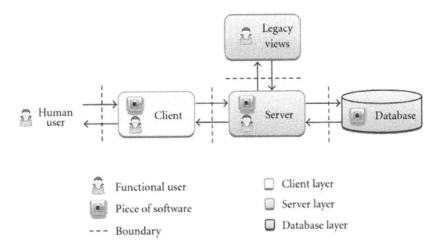

FIGURE 2: Layers, pieces of software, and functional users of the OO-Method applications.

Since the OOmCFP procedure has been designed to obtain accurate measures of the applications that are generated from the OO-Method conceptual model [52] and has been automated to provide measurement results in a few minutes using minimal resources [53], we use it to verify the quality of conceptual models in three case studies. The OOmCFP measurement procedure assumes that the conceptual model is of high quality; that is, the OOmCFP procedure assumes that the conceptual model is consistent, correct, and complete. This is obviously an unreal assumption because conceptual models often have defects. Since a measurement procedure analyzes all the conceptual constructs that are related to the functionality of a system, we consider that a measurement procedure is a valuable tool for finding defects in conceptual models.

3.4.3 DEFECT TYPES

In order to determine the defect types of MDD conceptual models, the proposed metamodel and procedure were applied to three case studies with

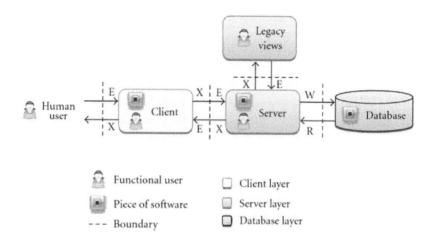

FIGURE 3: Data movements between the users and layers of an OO-Method application.

conceptual models of different functional sizes: a Publishing application (a small model), a Photography Agency application (a medium model), and an Expense Report application (a large model). We identified 39 defects and grouped them into 24 defect types (see [54]). For details, Table 2 shows the set of defect types that we identified using the OOmCFP procedure.

These defect types correspond to those related to structural models and those related to interaction models. This is one interesting contribution of our measurement procedure since, to our knowledge, there are no reported findings of defect types related to interaction models in the published literature. In order to formalize defect detection in the metamodel presented in Figure 1, we defined OCL rules to prevent the occurrence of the identified defects in the conceptual models. Table 3 shows the defect types and the OCL rules of our approach.

TABLE 2: Defect types of conceptual models found using OOmCFP.

Defect types found using OOmCFP
Defect: An object model without a specification of an agent class
Defect: An OO-Method Conceptual Model without a definition of the presentation model
Defect: A presentation model without the specification of one or more interaction units
Defect: An object model without the specifications of one or more classes
Defect: A class without a name
Defect: Classes with a repeated name
Defect: A class without the definition of one or more attributes
Defect: A class with attributes with repeated names
Defect: An instance interaction unit without a display pattern
Defect: A population interaction unit without a display pattern
Defect: A display pattern without attributes
Defect: Derived attributes without a derivation formula
Defect: A filer without a filter formula
Defect: An event of a class of the object diagram without valuations (excluding creation or destruction events)
Defect: A class without a creation event
Defect: Transactions without a specification of a sequence of services (service formula)
Defect: Operations without a specification of a sequence of services (service formula)
Defect: A service without arguments
Defect: A service with arguments with repeated names
Defect: A precondition without the specification of the precondition formula
Defect: A precondition without an error message
Defect: An integrity constraint without the specification of the integrity formula
Defect: An integrity constraint without an error message

In order to identify the maximum number of defects using the quality model, we aggregated the defect types already found in the literature (see Table 1) with the corresponding OCL rules (see Table 4). We selected the defect types related to the class model, which is a diagram commonly used by several MDD proposals. We ruled out the defect types of the literature that were also identified using the OOmCFP measurement procedure.

TABLE 3: 23 Defect types of conceptual models found using OOmCFP and OCL rules.

Defect types found using OOm-CFP	OCL rules
Defect: An object model without a specification of an agent class	context Agent inv: body self.allInstances-> size()>0
Defect: An OO-Method Conceptual Model without a definition of the presentation model	context ConceptualModel inv: body self.presentation->size()>0
Defect: A presentation model without the specification of one or more interaction units	context PresentationModel inv: body self.interactionUnit->size()>0
Defect: An object model without the specifications of one or more classes	context StructuralModel inv: body self.ownedClass->size()>0
Defect: A class without a name	context Class inv: body Class.allInstances()->select(c c.name.isEmpty())->isEmpty()
Defect: Classes with a repeated name	context Class inv: body self.allInstances()->forAll(c1, c2 | c1 <> c2 implies c1.name <> c2.name)
Defect: A class without the definition of one or more attributes	context Class inv: body self.features->select(t t.oclIsKindOf(TypedProperty))->collect(t | t.oclAsType (TypedProperty))->size()>0
Defect: A class with attributes with repeated names	context Class inv: body self.features->select(t |t.oclIsKindOf(TypedProperty))->collect(t | t.oclAsType (TypedProperty))->forAll(a1, a2 | a1 <> a2 implies a1.name a2.name)
Defect: An instance interaction unit without a display pattern	context InstanceIU inv: body self.displaySet->size()>0
Defect: A population interaction unit without a display pattern	context PopulationIU inv: body self.displaySet->size()>0
Defect: A display pattern without attributes	context DisplaySet inv: body self.relatedAttribute->size()>0
Defect: Derived attributes without a derivation formula	context DerivedAttribute inv: body self.derValue.effect->select(f f.value.isEmpty())->isEmpty()
Defect: A filter without a filter formula	context Filter inv: body self.filterFormula->select(f | f.value. isEmpty())->isEmpty()
Defect: An event of a class of the object diagram without valuations (excluding creation or destruction events)	context Event inv: body self.allInstances->select(e | (e.kind <> ServiceKind::creation and e.kind <> ServiceKind::destruction) implies e.valuation.size() >0)
Defect: A class without a creation event	context Class inv: body self.features->select(s |s.oclIsKindOf(Service))->collect(s | s.oclAsType (Service))- > select(s | s.kind = ServiceKind::creation)->notEmpty()

TABLE 3: *Cont.*

Defect types found using OOm-CFP	OCL rules
Defect: Transactions without a specification of a sequence of services (service formula)	context Transaction inv: body self.effect->select(f | f.value. isEmpty())->isEmpty()
Defect: Operations without a specification of a sequence of services (service formula)	context Operarion inv: body self.effect->elect(f | f.value. isEmpty())->isEmpty()
Defect: A service without arguments	context Service inv: body self.argument->size()>0
Defect: A service with arguments with repeated names	context Service inv: body self.argument->forAll(a1, a2 | a1 <> a2 implies a1.name <> a2.name)
Defect: A precondition without the specification of the precondition formula	context Service inv: body self.precondition.effect->select(f | f.value.isEmpty())->isEmpty()
Defect: A precondition without an error message	context Service inv: body self.precondition-> select (c | c.errorMsg.isEmpty())-> isEmpty()
Defect: An integrity constraint without the specification of the integrity formula	context Constraint inv: body self.effect-> select(f | f.value. isEmpty())-> isEmpty()
Defect: An integrity constraint without an error message	context Constraint inv: body self.allInstances-> select (c | c.errorMsg.isEmpty())->isEmpty()

In the three case studies mentioned above, the conceptual models did not achieve the characteristics of consistency and correctness due to the defect types presented in our approach. The OCL rules presented in Tables 3 and 4 can be implemented for the model compilers of MDD proposals in order to automatically verify the conceptual models with regard to these characteristics.

3.5 CONCLUSIONS

In this paper, we have presented a quality model to evaluate the conceptual models used in MDD environments to generate final applications through well-defined model transformations. The quality model is comprised of the following: (1) a metamodel that contains a minimal set of conceptual constructs, their properties, and their relationships, which allows the complete specification of applications in the conceptual model of an MDD environment; and (2) a set of rules for the detection of defects in the model, which have been specified using OCL constraints [14].

The design of the metamodel has been systematically performed using an MDD approach as reference. This approach, which is known as OO-Method, has been successfully applied in the software industry. However, it is important to note that even though some elements of the metamodel are specific to the OO-Method MDD approach, equivalent modeling constructs can be found in other object-oriented MDD methods. Thus, this metamodel can be used as a reference to improve existent MDD approaches or as a starting point for the specification of new MDD-oriented modeling languages. Moreover, the main modeling constructs that compose the metamodel are the same constructs present in the UML specification. For this reason, the quality model presented here can be applied to other MDD methods that use UML-like models.

TABLE 4: Five defect types of conceptual models found in the literature and OCL rules.

Defects types found in the literature	OCL rules
Defect: An attribute of a class without the specification of the type	context Class inv: body self.features->select(t | t.oclIsKindOf(TypedProperty))->collect(t | t.oclAsType (TypedProperty))->select(a | a.type.isEmpty())->isEmpty()
Defect: An argument of a service without the specification of the type	context Service inv: body self.features->select(s | s.oclIsKindOf(Service))->collect(s | s.oclAsType (Service)).argument.type-> size<1->isEmpty()
Defect: Associations replicated at sub-classes	Classifier::parents(): Set(Classifier); parents = generalization.generalClassifier::allParents(): Set(Classifier); allParents = self.parents()->union(self.parents()->collect(p | p.allParents())context AssociationEnd inv: body self.allInstances->forAll(r1, r2 | r1.name = r2.name and r1.owningClass.allParents()->select(c | c.name = r2.name)->isEmpty()
Defect: Associations with a repeated name	Context Relationship inv: body self.allInstances()->forAll(r1, r2 | r1 <> r2 implies r1.name <> r2.name)
Defect: An association without a source and target class	context Association inv: body self.role->select(e1,e2 | e1.role.kind = EndKind::source and e2.role.kind = EndKind::target)

We take advantage of modeling, metamodeling, and transformation techniques to avoid having to manually identify defects in the conceptual models, which is an error-prone activity. Thus, the quality model (metamodel + OCL rules) has been designed for easy application to other MDD proposals. This is feasible because the EMOF standard is used to define the metamodel, which is supported by existent open-source tools [41, 48] and is also used by other MDD proposals for the specification of their modeling languages. Therefore, we can firmly state that the quality model proposed here contributes substantially to improving the MDD processes and the quality of software products generated in this context.

For future works, we plan to apply the quality model into different MDD approaches by using an integration process that automatically generates metamodeling extensions [55–57]. By using the integration proposal, we plan to show how the proposed quality model allows the automatic verification of the list of defect types found in MDD proposals. We also plan to develop empirical studies to evaluate the quality of conceptual models for different MDD proposals. The findings from this evaluation will be used to build a knowledge base for further improvements in the evaluation of the quality of conceptual models related to MDD approaches.

REFERENCES

1. B. Selic, "The pragmatics of model-driven development," IEEE Software, vol. 20, no. 5, pp. 19–25, 2003.
2. S. J. Mellor, A. N. Clark, and T. Futagami, "Guest editors' introduction: model-driven development,," IEEE Software, vol. 20, no. 5, pp. 14–18, 2003.
3. D. L. Moody, "Theoretical and practical issues in evaluating the quality of conceptual models: current state and future directions," Data & Knowledge Engineering, vol. 55, no. 3, pp. 243–276, 2005.
4. O. I. Lindland, G. Sindre, and A. Solvberg, "Understanding quality in conceptual modeling," IEEE Software, vol. 11, no. 2, pp. 42–49, 1994.
5. T. H. Davenport and L. Prusak, Working Knowledge: How Organisations Manage What They Know, Business School Press, Boston, Mass, USA, 1998.
6. W. L. Neuman, Social Research Methods: Qualitative and Quantitative Approaches, Needham Heights, Mass, USA, Allyn & Bacon, 4th edition, 2000.
7. ISO/IEC, ISO/IEC 9126-1, Software Engineering—Product Quality—Part 1: Quality model,2001.
8. M. Genero, M. Piattini, and C. Calero, "A survey of metrics for UML class diagrams," Journal of Object Technology, vol. 4, no. 9, pp. 59–92, 2005.

9. S. S.-S. Cherfi, J. Akoka, and I. Comyn-Wattiau, "Conceptual modeling quality—from EER to UML schemas evaluation," in Proceedings of the 21st International Conference on Conceptual Modeling (ER '02), S. Spaccapietra, S. T. March, and Y. Kambayashi, Eds., vol. 2503 of Lecture Notes in Computer Science, Springer, Tampere, Finland, October 2002.

10. R. M. Wilson, W. B. Runciman, R. W. Gibberd, B. T. Harrison, J. D. Newby, and J. D. Hamilton, "The quality in Australian health care study," The Medical Journal of Australia, vol. 163, no. 9, pp. 458–471, 1995.

11. C. Lange and M. Chaudron, "Defects in industrial UML models—a multiple case study," in Proceedings of the 2nd Workshop on Quality in Modeling of MODELS (QiM '07), pp. 50–79, Nashville, Tenn, USA, 2007.

12. U. Bellur and V. Vallieswaran, "On OO design consistency in iterative development," in Proceedings of the 3rd International Conference on Information Technology: New Generations (ITNG '06), pp. 46–51, IEEE, April 2006.

13. J. Vanderdonckt, "Model-driven engineering of user interfaces: promises, successes, and failures," in Proceedings of the 5th Annual Romanian Conference on Human-Computer Interaction (ROCHI '08), S. Buraga and I. Juvina, Eds., pp. 1–10, Matrix ROM, Iasi, Romania, 2008.

14. OMG, Object Constraint Language 2.0 Specification, 2006.

15. ISO, ISO Standard 9000-2000: Quality Management Systems: Fundamentals and Vocabulary, 2000.

16. IEEE, IEEE 1044 Standard Classification for Software Anomalies, 1993.

17. N. E. Fenton and M. Neil, "A critique of software defect prediction models," IEEE Transactions on Software Engineering, vol. 25, no. 5, pp. 675–689, 1999.

18. B. Meyer, Object Oriented Software Construction, Prentice Hall, New York, NY, USA, 2nd edition, 2000.

19. G. H. Travassos, F. Shull, M. Fredericks, and V. R. Basili, "Detecting defects in object oriented designs: using reading techniques to increase software quality," in Proceedings of the Conference on Object-Oriented Programming Systems, Languages, & Applications (OOPSLA '99), pp. 47–56, Denver, Colo, USA, October 1999.

20. V. R. Basili, S. Green, O. Laitenberger et al., "The empirical investigation of perspective-based reading," Empirical Software Engineering Journal, vol. 1, no. 2, pp. 133–164, 1996.

21. O. Laitenberger, C. Atkinson, M. Schlich, and K. E. Emam, "Experimental comparison of reading techniques for defect detection in UML design documents," Journal of Systems & Software, vol. 53, no. 2, pp. 183–204, 2000.

22. R. Conradi, P. Mohagheghi, T. Arif, L. C. Hegde, G. A. Bunde, and A. Pedersen, "Object-oriented reading techniques for inspection of UML models—an industrial experiment," in Proceedings of the European Conference on Object-Oriented Programming (ECOOP '03), vol. 2749 of Lecture Notes in Computer Science, pp. 483–501, Springer, July 2003.

23. H. Gomaa and D. Wijesekera, "Consistency in multiple-view UML models: a case study," in Proceedings of the Workshop on Consistency Problems in UML-based Software Development II, pp. 1–8, IEEE, San Francisco, Calif, USA, 2003.

24. H. Gomaa, Designing Concurrent, Distributed, and Real-Time Applications with UML, Addison-Wesley, Reading, Mass, USA, 2000.

25. L. Kuzniarz, "Inconsistencies in student designs," in Proceedings of the Workshop on Consistency Problems in UML-Based Software Development II, pp. 9–17, IEEE, San Francisco,Calif, USA, 2003.
26. B. Berenbach, "The evaluation of large, complex UML analysis and design models," in Proceedings of the 26th International Conference on Software Engineering (ICSE '04), pp. 232–241, IEEE Computer Society, May 2004.
27. C. Lange and M. Chaudron, "An empirical assessment of completeness in UML designs," in Proceedings of the 8th Conference on Empirical Assessment in Software Engineering (EASE '04), pp. 111–121, IEEE, 2004.
28. F. Leung and N. Bolloju, "Analyzing the quality of domain models developed by novice systems analysts," in Proceedings of the 38th Annual Hawaii International Conference on System Sciences, pp. 1–7, January 2005.
29. IEEE, IEEE 610 Standard Computer Dictionary. A Compilation of IEEE Standard Computer Glossaries, 1990.
30. OMG, UML 2.1.2 Superstructure Specification, 2007.
31. K. Berkenkötter, "Reliable UML models and profiles," Electronic Notes in Theoretical Computer Science, vol. 217, pp. 203–220, 2008.
32. R. B. France, S. Ghosh, T. Dinh-Trong, and A. Solberg, "Model-driven development using UML 2.0: promises and pitfalls," IEEE Computer, vol. 39, no. 2, pp. 59–66, 2006.
33. A. L. Opdahl and B. Henderson-Sellers, "A unified modelling language without referential redundancy," Data & Knowledge Engineering, vol. 55, no. 3, pp. 277–300, 2005.
34. G. Giachetti, B. Marín, and O. Pastor, "Perfiles UML y desarrollo dirigido por modelos: desafíos y soluciones para utilizar UML como lenguaje de modelado específico de dominio," in Proceedings of the V Taller Sobre Desarrollo de Software Dirigido por Modelos (DSDM '09), Gijón, Spain, 2008.
35. OMG, MDA Guide Version 1.0.1, 2003.
36. O. Pastor, J. Gómez, E. Insfrán, and V. Pelechano, "The OO-Method approach for information systems modeling: from object-oriented conceptual modeling to automated programming," Information Systems, vol. 26, no. 7, pp. 507–534, 2001.
37. O. Pastor and J. C. Molina, Model-Driven Architecture in Practice: A Software Production Environment Based on Conceptual Modeling, Springer, New York, NY, USA, 2007.
38. O. Pastor, F. Hayes, and S. Bear, "OASIS: an object-oriented specification Language," in Proceedings of the 21st International Conference on Advanced Information Systems Engineering (CAiSE '92), pp. 348–363, Manchester, UK, 1992.
39. J. Vanderdonckt, "A MDA-compliant environment for developing user interfaces of information systems," in Proceedings of the 17th International Conference on Advanced Information Systems Engineering (CAISE '05), O. Pastor and J. Falcão e Cunha, Eds., vol. 3520, pp. 16–31, Springer, Porto, Portugal, 2005.
40. P. Molina, Especificación de Interfaz de Usuario: De los Requisitos a la Generación Automática, Universidad Politécnica de Valencia, Valencia, España, 2003.
41. Eclipse Modeling Project, February 2010, http://www.eclipse.org/modeling/.
42. Eclipse Modeling Framework Project, February 2010, http://www.eclipse.org/modeling/emf/.

43. Eclipse Graphical Modeling Framework Project, February 2010, http://www.eclipse. org/gmf/.
44. Eclipse ATL Project, February 2010, http://www.eclipse.org/m2m/atl/.
45. F. Jouault and I. Kurtev, "Transforming models with ATL," in Proceedings of the Satellite Events at the MoDELS 2005 Conference, vol. 3844 of Lecture Notes in Computer Science, pp. 128–138, Springer, 2006.
46. OMG, QVT 1.0 Specification, 2008.
47. B. Selic, "A systematic approach to domain-specific language design using UML," in Proceedings of the 10th IEEE International Symposium on Object and Component-Oriented Real-Time Distributed Computing (ISORC '07), pp. 2–9, May 2007.
48. Eclipse Model Development Tools, February 2010, http://www.eclipse.org/modeling/mdt/.
49. B. Marín, N. Condori-Fernández, O. Pastor, and A. Abran, "Measuring the functional size of conceptual models in an MDA environment," in Proceedings of the 20th International Conference on Advanced Information Systems Engineering (CAISE '08), Z. Bellahsene, C. Woo, E. Hunt, X. Franch, and R. Coletta, Eds., pp. 33–36, Montpellier, France, 2008.
50. A. Abran, J. Desharnais, A. Lesterhuis, et al., The COSMIC Functional Size Measurement Method—Version 3.0, 2007.
51. B. Marín, N. Condori-Fernández, and O. Pastor, "Design of a functional size measurement procedure for a model-driven software development method," in Proceedings of the 3rd Workshop on Quality in Modeling of MODELS (QiM '08), J.-L. Sourrouille, M. Staron, L. Kuzniarz, P. Mohagheghi, and L. Pareto, Eds., pp. 1–15, Touluse, France, 2008.
52. B. Marín, O. Pastor, and A. Abran, "Towards an accurate functional size measurement procedure for conceptual models in an MDA environment," Data & Knowledge Engineering, vol. 69, no. 5, pp. 472–490, 2010.
53. B. Marín, O. Pastor, and G. Giachetti, "Automating the measurement of functional size of conceptual models in an MDA environment," in Proceedings of the Product-Focused Software Process Improvement (PROFES '08), vol. 5089 of Lecture Notes in Computer Science, pp. 215–229, Springer, 2008.
54. B. Marín, G. Giachetti, and O. Pastor, "Applying a functional size measurement procedure for defect detection in MDD environments," in Proceedings of the 16th European Conference on Systems & Software Process Improvement and Innovation (EUROSPI '09), R.V. O' Connor, Ed., vol. 42 of Communications in Computer and Information Science, pp. 57–68, Springer, Madrid, Spain, 2009.
55. G. Giachetti, B. Marín, and O. Pastor, "Integration of domain-specific modelling languages and UML through UML profile extension mechanism," International Journal of Computer Science & Applications, vol. 6, no. 5, pp. 145–174, 2009.
56. G. Giachetti, B. Marín, and O. Pastor, "Using UML as a domain-specific modeling language: a proposal for automatic generation of UML profiles," in Proceedings of the 21st International Conference on Advanced Information Systems Engineering (CAiSE '09), P. van Eck, J. Gordijn, and R. Wieringa, Eds., vol. 5565 of Lecture Notes in Computer Science, pp. 110–124, Springer, Amsterdam, The Netherlands, 2009.

57. G. Giachetti, F. Valverde, and O. Pastor, "Improving automatic UML2 profile generation for MDA industrial development," in Proceedings of the 4th International Workshop on Foundations and Practices of UML (FP-UML '08), vol. 5232 of Lecture Notes in Computer Science, pp. 113–122, Springer, 2008.

There is one table and one figure that were too large to appear in this version of the article. To view this additional information, please use the citation on the first page of this chapter.

CHAPTER 4

FORMAL MODEL-DRIVEN ENGINEERING: GENERATING DATA AND BEHAVIORAL COMPONENTS

CHEN-WEI WANG AND JIM DAVIES

4.1 INTRODUCTION

Our society is increasingly dependent upon the behaviour of complex software systems. Errors in the design and implementation of these systems can have significant consequences. In August 2012, a 'fairly major bug' in the trading software used by Knight Capital Group lost that firm $461m in 45 minutes [15]. A software glitch in the anti-lock braking system caused Toyota to recall more than 400,000 vehicles in 2010 [25]; the total cost to the company of this and other software-related recalls in the same period is estimated at $3bn. In October 2008, 103 people were injured, 12 of them seriously, when a Qantas airliner [3] dived repeatedly as the fly-by-wire software responded inappropriately to data from inertial reference sensors. A modern car contains the product of over 100 million lines of source code [4], and in the aerospace industry, it has been claimed that "the current development process is reaching the limit of affordability of

Wang C-W and Davies J. Formal Model-Driven Engineering: Generating Data and Behavioural Components. Electronic Proceedings in Theoretical Computer Science 105 (2012); doi:10.4204/EPTCS.105.8. Copyright © C.-W. Wang and J. Davies. This chapter was originally published under the Creative Commons Attribution Licenses, http://creativecommons.org/licenses/by/3.0/

building safe aircraft" [10]. The solution to the problems of increasing software complexity lies in the automatic generation of correct, lower-level software from higher-level descriptions: precise models of structure and functionality.

The intention is that the same generation process should apply across a class of systems, or at least multiple versions of the same system. Once this process has been correctly implemented, we can be sure that the behaviour of the generated system will correspond to the descriptions given in the models. These models are strictly more abstract than the generated system, easier to understand and update, and more amenable to automatic analysis. This model-driven approach [11] makes it easier to achieve correct designs and correct implementations. Despite the obvious appeal of the approach, and that of related approaches such as domain-specific languages [8] and software product lines [18], much of the code that could be generated automatically is still written by hand; even where precise, abstract specifications exist, their implementation remains a time-consuming, error-prone, manual process.

The reason for the delay in uptake is simple: in any particular development project, the cost of producing a new language and matching generator, is likely to exceed that of producing the code by hand. As suitable languages and generators become available, this situation is changing, with significant implications for the development of complex, critical, software systems. In the past, developers would work to check the correctness of code written in a general-purpose programming language, such as C or Ada, against natural language descriptions of intended functionality, illuminated with diagrams and perhaps a precise, mathematical account of certain properties. In the future, they will check the correctness of more abstract models of structure and behaviour, written in a range of different, domain-specific languages; and rather than relying upon the correctness of a single, widely-used compiler, they will need to rely upon the correctness of many different code generators. The correctness of these generators, usually implemented as a sequence of model transformations, is thus a major, future concern.

In this paper, we present an approach to model-driven development that is based upon formal, mathematical languages and techniques. The objective is the correct design and implementation of components with complex state, perhaps comprising a large number of inter-related data objects. The approach is particularly applicable to the iterative design and deployment of systems in which data integrity is a primary concern. The modelling language employed has the familiar, structural features of object notations such as UML—classes, attributes, and associations—but uses logical predicates to characterise operations. An initial stage of transformation replaces these predicates with guarded commands that are guaranteed to satisfy the specified constraints: see, for example, [24]. The focus here is upon the subsequent generation of executable code, and the means by which we may prove that this generation process is correct.

The underlying thesis of the approach is that the increasing sophistication of software systems is often reflected more in the complexity of data models than in the algorithmic complexity of the operations themselves. The intended effect of a given event or action is often entirely straight-forward. However, the intention may be only part of the story: there may be combinations of inputs and before-states where the operation, as described, would leave the system in an inconsistent after-state; there may be other attributes to be updated; there may be constraints upon the values of other attributes that need to be taken into account. Furthermore, even if the after-state is perfectly consistent, the change in state may have made some other operation, or sequence of operations, inapplicable.

Fortunately, where the intended effect of an operation upon the state of a system is straightforward, it should be possible to express this effect as a predicate relating before and after values and generate a candidate implementation. Using formal techniques, we may then calculate the domain of applicability of this operation, given the representational and integrity constraints of the data model. If this is smaller than required, then a further iteration of design is called for; if not, then the generated implementation is guaranteed to work as intended. In either case, code may be generated to throw an exception, or otherwise block execution, should the operation be called outside its domain. Further, by comparing the possible outcomes with the calculated domains of other operations, we can determine whether or not one operation can affect the availability of others.

The application of formal techniques at a modelling level—to predicates, and to candidate implementations described as abstract programs—has clear advantages. The formal semantics of a modern programming language, considered in the context of a particular hardware or virtual machine platform, is rich enough to make retrospective formal analysis impractical. If we are able to establish correctness at the modelling level, and rely upon the correctness of our generation process, then we may achieve the level of formal assurance envisaged in new standards for certification: in particular, DO-178C [21]. We show here how the correctness of the process can be established: in Section 3, we present the underlying semantic framework; in Section 4, the translation of expressions; in Section 5, the implementation of operations; in Section 6, the approach to verification.

4.2 PRELIMINARIES

The BOOSTER language [6] is an object modelling notation in which model constraints and operations are described as first-order predicates upon attributes and input values. Operations may be composed using the logical combinators: conjunction, disjunction, implication, and both flavours of quantification. They may be composed also using relational composition, as sequential phases of a single operation or transaction. The constraints describing operations are translated automatically into programs written in an extended version of the Generalised Substitution Language (GSL), introduced as part of the B Method [1]. There may be circumstances under which a program would violate the model constraints, representing business rules, critical requirements, or semantic integrity properties. Accordingly, a guard is calculated for each operation, as the weakest precondition for the corresponding, generated program to maintain the model constraints. The result is an abstract program whose correctness is guaranteed, in a language defined by the following grammar:

$Substitution ::= skip$
$\qquad | <<PATH>> := <<Expression>>$
$\qquad | <<Predicate>> \rightarrow <<Substitution>>$
$\qquad | <<Substitution>> \, || \, <<Substitution>>$
$\qquad | <<Substitution>> \, ; \, <<Substitution>>$
$\qquad | <<Substitution>> \Box <<Substitution>>$
$\qquad | ! <<Variable>> : <<Expression>> \bullet <<Substitution>>$
$\qquad | @ <<Variable>> : <<Expression>> \bullet <<Substitution>>$

Here, the usual notation of assignable variables is replaced with paths, each being a sequence of attribute names, using the familiar object-oriented 'dot' notation as a separator. Predicate and Expression represent, respectively, first-order predicates and relational and arithmetic expressions. skip denotes termination, := denotes assignment, and → denotes a program guard: to be implemented as an assertion, a blocking condition, or as (the complement of) an exception. □ denotes alternation, and @ denotes selection: the program should be executed for exactly one of the possible values of the bound variable. Similarly, ‖ denotes parallel composition, with ! as its generalised form: all of the program instances should be performed, in parallel, as a single transaction. ; denotes relational or sequential composition. Inputs and outputs to operations need not be explicitly declared; instead, they are indicated using the decorations ? and ! at the end of the attribute name.

These abstract programs are interpreted as operations at a component applications programming interface (API), with the data model of the component given by a collection of class and association declarations in the usual object-oriented style. The integrity constraints and business rules for the data model can be given as predicates in the same notation, or using the object constraint language (OCL) of the Unified Modelling Language (UML) [11].

As a simple, running example, consider the following description of (a fragment of) the data model for a hotel reservations system:

class Hotel {   *class Reservation {*
  attributes   *attributes*
    reservations : seq(Reservation.host) [*] }   *host : Hotel.reservations }*

A single hotel may be the host for any number of reservations. It may also be the host of a number of rooms and allocations: see the class association graph [9] of Figure 1. The action of creating a new reservation may be specified using a simple operation predicate in the context of the Hotel class:

reserve {# allocations<limit & reservations' = reservations ^ <r!> & r!.room = m?}

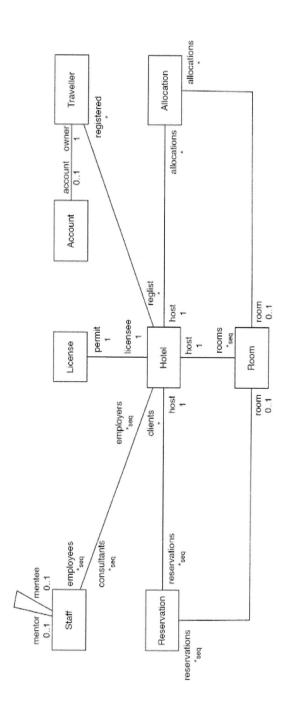

FIGURE 1: Hotel Reservation System (HRS)—Graph of Class Associations

This requires that a new reservation be created and appended to the existing list, modelled as an ordered association from Hotel to Room, and that the room involved is given by input m?. The operation should not be allowed if the number of reservations in the system has already reached a specified limit.

If the constructor operation predicate on Reservation mentions a set of dates dates?, then this will be added as a further input parameter. We might expect to find also a constraint insisting that any two different reservations associated with the same room should have disjoint sets of dates, and perhaps constraints upon the number of reservations that can held by a particular traveller for the same date. For the purposes of this paper, however, we will focus simply upon the required, consequential actions and the description of the operation as an abstract program.

reserve {
    r! : extent(Reservation) & dates? : set(Date) & m? : extent(Room)
    & card(allocations) < limit
==>
    r!.dates := r!.dates ∨ dates? || r!.status := "unconfirmed"
|| r!.host := this || reservations := ins(reservations, #reservations + 1, r!)
|| r!.room := m?||m?.reservations:= ins(m?.reservations, #m?.reservations+1, r!)}

In this abstract program, the two reservations attributes, in the hotel and room objects, are updated with a reference to the new reservation, the dates attribute of the new reservation is updated to include the supplied dates, and the status attribute is set to "unconfirmed", presumably as a consequence of the constructor predicate for the Reservation class.

4.3 A UNIFIED IMPLEMENTATION AND SEMANTIC FRAMEWORK

To illustrate our formal, model-driven approach, we will consider the case in which the target is a relational database platform. The above program would then be translated into a SQL query, acting on a relational equivalent of our original object model. The transformations can be described using the Haskell [2] functional programming language: in the diagram of

Figure 2, thin-lined, unshaded boxes represent to denote Haskell program data types, and thin arrows the executable transformations between them. These constitute an implementation framework. The thick-lined, shaded boxes denote the relational semantics of corresponding data types, thick lines with circles at one end the process of assigning a formal meaning, and arrows with circles at each end the relationship between formalised concepts. These constitute a corresponding semantic framework for establishing correctness.

Four kinds of models are involved in our transformation pipeline: 1) a BOOSTER model, in extended GSL notation, generated from the original predicates; 2) an OBJECT model representing an object-oriented relational semantics for that model; 3) an intermediate TABLE model reflecting our implementation strategy; 4) a SQL model expressed in terms of tables, queries, and key constraints. A final model-to-text transformation will be applied to generate a well-formed SQL database schema.

We use Haskell to define metamodels of model structures and operations as data types. Our transformations are then defined as Haskell functions: from BOOSTER to OBJECT, then to TABLE, and finally to SQL. Our relational semantics is most easily described using the Z notation [26]. Other formal languages with a transformational semantics would suffice for the characterisation of model and operation constraints, but Z has the distinct advantage that each operation, and each relation, may be described as a single predicate: rather than, for example, a combination of separate pre- and post-conditions; this facilitates operation composition, and hence a compositional approach to verification.

4.4 PATH & EXPRESSION TRANSFORMATION

The descriptions of operations in the BOOSTER, OBJECT, and TABLE models are all written in the GSL language; the difference between them lies in the representation of attribute and association references. Instead of creating three versions of a language type Substitution, one for each of the reference notations, we employ a type PATH as a generic solution: see Figure 3.

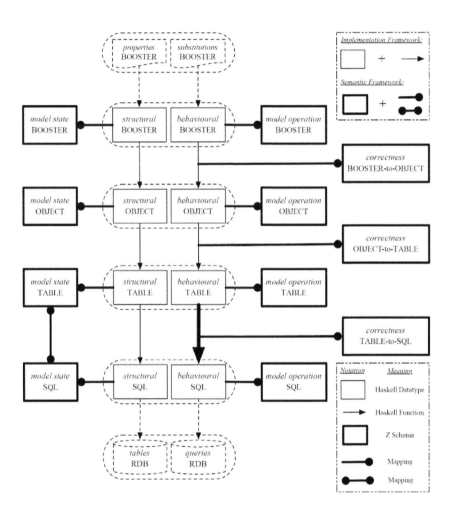

FIGURE 2: BOOSTER Model to SQL Database: Implementation & Semantic Framework

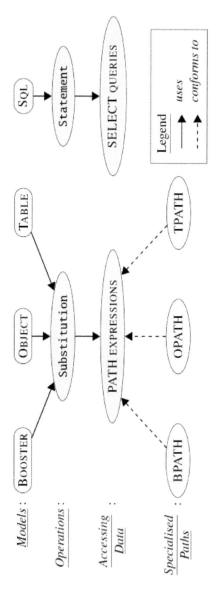

FIGURE 3: Datatypes of Behavioural Models

We define

*data PATH = **BPath** BPATH | **OPath** OPATH | **TPath** TPATH*

where BPath, OPath, and TPath are type constructors. A BOOSTER model path (of type BPATH) is represented as a sequence $<a_1, \ldots, a_n>$ of name references to attributes/properties. We will refer to this range 1 . . n of indices for explaining the corresponding OBJECT and TABLE model paths.

We consider structures of the types OPATH and TPATH in detail. Paths of type OPATH are used to indicate explicitly which properties/classes are accessed, along with its chain of navigation starting from the current class.

data OPATH	*= BaseOPath REF_START*	*|RecOPath OPATH TARGET*
data REF_START	*= ThisRef BASE*	*|SCRef IDEN_PROPERTY EXPRESSION BASE*
data TARGET	*= EntityTarget IDEN_PROPERTY*	*|SCTarget IDEN_PROPERTY EXPRESSION*
data BASE	*= ClassBase N_CLASS*	*|SetBase N_SET | IntBase | StrBase*
type IDEN_PROPERTY	*= (N_CLASS, N_ATTRIBUTE)*	

An object path is a left-heavy binary tree, where the left-most child refers to its starting reference and all right children represent target classes/properties that are accessed. The starting reference of an object path—which denotes access to, e.g the current object, an element of a sequence-valued property through indexing, etc.—provides explicit information about the base type of that reference. All intermediate and the ending targets of an object path contextualise the properties with their enclosing classes (i.e. IDEN_PROPERTY).

For each context path $<a_1, \ldots, a_i>$, where ($1 \leq i \leq n-1$), an OBJECT model path (of type OPATH) identifies a target class C; if the source BOOSTER path is valid, then attribute a_{i+1} must have been declared in C.

Example object path. As an example of how the transformation on paths works in practice, consider the Account class (Figure 1 shown on page 4). The path this.owner.reglist denotes a list of registered hotels and has its OPATH counterpart:

RecOPath (RecOPath (BaseOPath (ThisRef (ClassBase Account)))
(EntityTarget (Account, owner)))
(EntityTarget (Traveller reglist))

where RecOPath and BaseOPath are constructors for, respectively, recursive and base OBJECT paths. EntityTarget and ClassBase construct type information about the three context paths: (Account) for this, (Account, owner) for this.owner, and Traveller, reglist for this.owner.reglist.

On the other hand, we use a path of type TPATH to indicate, for each navigation to a property in the OBJECT model, the corresponding access to a table which stores that property.

data TPATH	*= BaseTPath*		*REF_START*	
	| RecTPath	*TPATH*	*T_ACCESS*	
data T_ACCESS	*=ClassTAccess*	*IDEN_PROPERTY*		
	|AssocTAccess	*IDEN_PROPERTY*		
	|SetTAccess	*IDEN_PROPERTY*		
	|SeqTAccess	*IDEN_PROPERTY*		*-- retrieve all indexed components*
	|SeqTCAccess	*IDEN_PROPERTY*	*EXPRESSION*	*-- retrieve an indexed component*

A table path is left-heavy (as is an OPATH), where the left-most child refers to its starting reference and all right children represent target tables that are accessed. The starting reference of a table path provides exactly the same information as its OPATH counterpart (i.e. REF START). All intermediate and the ending targets of a table path denote accesses to a variety of tables, predicated upon our implementation strategy. When the target property is sequence-valued, we distinguish between the two cases where one of its indexed components is to be accessed (SeqTCAccess) and where all indexed components are to be accessed (SeqTAccess).

For each attribute a_i, where $(1 \leq i \leq n)$, a TABLE model path (of type TPATH) recursively records which sort of table (e.g. class tables, association tables, or set tables) it is stored, based on the target class of its context path. Example table path. The above OBJECT path has its TPATH counterpart:

RecTPath (RecTPath (BaseTPath** *(ThisRef (*ClassBase*** *Account)))*
            *(****AssocTAccess*** *(Account, owner)))*
       *(****AssocTAccess*** *(Traveller reglist))*

where RecTPath and BaseTPath construct, respectively, recursive and base TABLE paths. Properties owner and reglist are accessed in the two corresponding association tables.

Path transformation. We now specify the above OPATH-to-TPATH transformation in Haskell:

objToTabPath :: OBJECT_MODEL -> PATH -> PATH
objToTabPath om (OPath opath) = ***TPath*** *(objToTabPath' om opath)*

where the first line declares a function objToTabPath, and the second line gives its definition: matching an input object model as om and an input path as (OPath opath), whereas the RHS constructs a new PATH via TPath. The transformation of object paths is given by

```
objToTabPath' om (RecOPath op tar) =
case tar of
  EntityTarget (c, p) | (c, p) `elem` biAssoc' om c -> RecTPath tp (AssocTAccess (c, p))
                      | (c, p) `elem` classTables tm c -> RecTPath tp (ClassTAccess (c, p))
                      | (c, p) `elem` setTables tm -> RecTPath tp (SetTAccess (c, p))
                      | (c, p) `elem` seqTables tm -> RecTPath tp (SeqTAccess (c, p))
  SCTarget (c, p) oe -> let te = objToTabExpr om oe in RecTPath tp (SeqTCAccess (c, p)
te)
where tm = objToTab om
      tp = objToTabPath' om op
```

where each condition specified between | and -> denotes a special case of the matched entity target, consisting of class c and property p. For example, the condition (c, p) `elem` classTables tm c denotes properties that are stored in the table for class c.

Each recursive object path is structured as (RecOPath op tar), where op is its prefix (i.e. context) of type OPATH, which we recursively transform into a table path equivalent tp; and tar is its target property. For each given tar, table access is determined by checking membership against various domains: a bidirectional association will be accessed by means of an association table. If the target property is sequence-valued (i.e. the case of SCTarget), it cannot be accessed for its entirety, but only one of its members through indexing. The function objToTabExpr transforms the index expression oe that contains paths of type OPATH to te that contains paths of type TPATH. The function objToTab transforms an object model om to an equivalent table model tm.

SQL database statements express paths via (nested) SELECT queries. For example, the above TABLE path has its SQL statement counterpart:

*SELECT (**VAR** `reglist`)*
        *(**TABLE** `Hotel_registered_Traveller_reglist`)*
        *(**VAR** `oid` = (**SELECT** (**VAR** `owner`)*
                                *(**TABLE** `Account_owner_Traveller_account`)*
                                *(**VAR** oid = **VAR** this)))*

where oid is the default column (declared as the primary key) for each table that implements an association. We can show [23] by structural induction that the transformation from BPATH to OPATH, from OPATH to TPATH, and from TPATH to SELECT statements are correct.

Expression transformation. We transform both predicates and expressions on TABLE model into SQL expressions:

toSqlExpr :: TABLE_MODEL -> Predicate -> SQL_EXPR
toSqlExpr' :: TABLE_MODEL -> Expression -> SQL_EXPR

Some transformations are direct

*toSqlExpr tm (**And** p q) = toSqlExpr tm p `**AND**` toSqlExpr tm q*

whereas others require an equivalent construction:

*toSqlExpr' tm (Card e) | isPathExpr e = **SELECT [COUNT (VAR oid)]***
*(toSqlExpr' tm e) **TRUE***

4.5 ASSIGNMENT TRANSFORMATION

The most important aspect of the model transformation is the handling of attribute assignments and collection updates. There are 36 distinct cases to consider, given the different combinations of attributes and bidirectional (opposite) associations. We present a single, representative case in Table 1, for an association between an optional attribute (multiplicity 0..1) and a sequence-valued attribute (ordered with multiplicity *) .

TABLE 1: Assignment Transformation Pattern for sequence-to-optional Bi-Association

Bi-Assoc. Decl.		#	GSL Substitution	SQL Queries
seq-to-opt		23	*bs* := ins (*bs; i; that*)	UPDATE t SET *index* = *index*+1
class A	class B		‖	WHERE ao = *this* AND *index* ≥ i;
bs: seq(B.ao)	ao: [A.bs]		*that:ao* := *this*	INSERT INTO t (*bs;ao; index*)
				VALUE (*that; this; i*);

From left to right, the columns of the table present declarations of properties, numerical identifiers of patterns, their abstract implementation in the substitution program, and their concrete implementation in database queries. The dummy variables this and that are used to denote instances of, respectively, the current class and the other end of the association. For each case (for each row of the completed table), we define a transformation function toSqlProc that turns a substitution into a list of SQL query statements.

toSqlProc tm _ s@(Assign _ _) = transAssign tm s
transAssign :: TABLE_MODEL -> Substitution -> [STATEMENT]

The function toSqlProc delegates the task of transforming base cases, i.e. assignments, to another auxiliary function transAssign that implements the 36 patterns. The recursive cases of toSqlProc are straightforward. For example, to implement a guarded substitution, we transform it into an If-ThenElse pattern that is directly supported in the SQL domain; and to implement iterators (ALL, ANY), we instantiate a loop pattern, declared with an explicit variant, that is guaranteed to terminate.

4.6 CORRECTNESS PROOFS

The correctness of both BOOSTER-to-OBJECT and OBJECT-to-TABLE transformations can be established by constructing a relational model mapping identifiers and paths to references and primitive values, and then showing that the different reference mechanisms identify the same values in each case. To prove the correctness of the TABLE-to-SQL transformation (shown as the vertical, thick arrow in Figure 2 on page 104), we need also to introduce linking invariants between model states. We first formalise states and operations for each model domain. In the Z notation, sets and relations may be described using a schema notation, with separate declaration and constraint components and an optional name:

name
declaration
constraint

Either component may include schema references, with the special reference Δ denoting two copies of another schema, typically denoting before- and after-versions, the attributes of the latter being decorated with a prime ('). The remainder of the mathematical notation is that of standard, typed, set theory. We map the state OBJECT model into a relational semantics S_{obj}, characterised by:

OBJECT MODEL
extent : N CLASS $\mapsto$ PObjectId
value : ObjectId $\mapsto$ N PROPERTY $\mapsto$ Value
domextent = domclass
$\forall c : N$ CLASS; o : ObjectId |
c $\in$ domextent $^\wedge$ o $\in$ extent (c) $\bullet$ dom(value (o)) = dom((classc):property)

The inclusion of OBJECT MODEL (whose details are omitted here) enables us to constrain the two mappings according to the type system of the object model in question. Value denotes a structured type that encompasses the possibilities of undefined value (for optional properties), primitive value, and set and sequence of values.

The state of a table model will be composed of: 1) the type system of the object model in context; and 2) functions for querying the state of such a context object model. More precisely,

---

TABLE MODEL
_____

OBJECT MODEL
nTableModel : N MODEL
assocTables; setTables : P(N CLASS N PROPERTY)
_____

where assocTables, setTables and seqTables are reflective queries: for example, assocTables returns the set of attributes/properties (and their context classes) that are stored in the association tables. We formalise the TABLE model state as:

S_{tab}
_____

S_{obj}
TABLE MODEL
_____

For each instance of S_{obj}, there should be a corresponding configuration of TABLE MODEL. A SQL database corresponds to a set of named tables, each containing a set of column-value mappings:

S_{sql}	*Tuple*
tuples : N TABLE!7 PTuple	*values : N COLUMN $\mapsto$ ScalarValue*

We use ScalarValue to denote the collection of basic types: strings, integers, and Booleans. We require mapping functions to retrieve values from TABLE and SQL:

$M : S_{tab}$ *(NClass NProperty) $\mapsto$ P(Value Value)*

These return reference–value pairs for each kind of property. For example, set-valued properties are returned by

$$\mathcal{M}_{set} == \lambda\, s : \mathcal{S}_{tab};\ p : NClass \times NProperty \bullet$$

$$\bigcup \left\{ \begin{array}{l} o : ObjectId;\ v : Value;\ vs : \mathbb{P}\, Primitive\ | \\ \quad o \in s.extent\,(fst\,p) \wedge v = s.value\,(o)\,(snd\,p) \wedge v = setValue\,(vs) \bullet \\ \quad \{v' : vs \bullet [\![o]\!]^{SV} \mapsto [\![v']\!]^{SV}\} \end{array} \right\}$$

The set of mappings for a particular table is given by

$\lambda\, s : S_{sql};\ n : NTable;\ c1;c2 : NColumn \bullet \{row : s{:}tuples\,(n) \bullet row{:}values\ (c1) \mapsto row{:}values\,(c2)\,\}$

and the necessary linking invariant is:

TABLE $\leftrightarrow$ SQL
S_{tab}
S_{sql}
C

where C comprises six conjuncts, one for each possible unordered combination of association end multiplicities.

Each operation is implemented as an atomic transaction. R_{obj} represents the formal context, with the effect upon the state being described as a binary relation ($\leftrightarrow$).

R_{obj}
input : PN VARIABLE
output : PN VARIABLE
effect : (S_{obj} IOobj) $\leftrightarrow$ ($S_{obj} \times IO_{obj}$)
effect $\in S_{obj}$ (input$\rightarrow$ Value) $\leftrightarrow S_{obj}$ (output $\rightarrow$ Value)

Each element of $IO_{obj} ==$ N VARIABLE $\mapsto$ Value represents a collection of inputs and outputs.

Using S_{obj} and R_{obj}, we may write System$_{obj}$ to denote the set of possible object system configurations, each characterised through its current state (of type S_{obj}) and its set of indexed operations (of type R_{obj}). More precisely,

---

System$_{obj}$
_____

state : S$_{obj}$

relation : N CLASS ↦ N OPERATION ↦ R$_{obj}$

We will describe the effect of a primitive assignment (:=), and use this as the basis for a recursive definition of effect, based on the grammar of the GSL notation. If AssignInput is the schema [path? : PATH; e? : Expression], then we may define

---

AssignEffect
_____

s; s0 : S$_{obj}$

AssignInput
_____

s:nObjModel = s':nObjModel

s:sets = s':sets

s:classes = s':classes

s:extent = s':extent

let *p == target [[path?]] ; o == context [[path?]] • s':value = s:value ⊕*
                                    {o ↦ s:value (o) ⊕ {p ↦ eval (e?)}}

The input path? can be either OPATH and TPATH: for the former, the other input expression e? involves paths, if any, of type OPATH; for the latter, it is TPATH. The (let es • p) expression, where es consists of a list of expression-to-variable bindings, denotes a predicate p on the variables of es.

We start by relating domains of the OBJECT model and TABLE model, where assignment paths are specified in, respectively, OPATH and TPATH (Fig 3). In the OBJECT model domain, an assignment is parameterised by a path of type BPATH and an expression that consists of paths, if any, of the consistent type. We formalise each OBJECT model assignment under the formal context of R_{obj}, by defining its effect mapping though the constraint of AssignEffect and by requiring that the sets of external inputs and outputs are empty.

Assign$_{obj}$

R_{obj}

op? : OPATH

oe? : Expression

$\forall s; s': S_{obj}; AssignInput \mid path? = OPath (op?) \wedge e? = oe? \bullet$
$\qquad\qquad AssignEffect \leftrightarrow (s, \{\}) \mapsto (s', \{\}) \in effect$

The characterisation Assign$_{tab}$ of an assignment in the TABLE model domain is similar to that of
Assign$_{obj}$, except that the target is now of type TPATH, and the source is now of type Expression. We may then map our extended GSL substitution into a relation:

$$[[-]]_{obj} : Substitution \rightarrow ((S_{obj} \times IO_{obj}) \leftrightarrow (S_{obj} \times IO_{obj}))$$

of the same type as the effect component of R_{obj}. Given a TABLE path tp? and an expression te?, we represent the assignment substitution tp? := te? by the effect relation of Assign$_{tab}$ that exists uniquely with respect to tp? and te?. More precisely,

$$[[tp? := te?]]_{obj} = (\mu\ Assign_{tab}):effect$$

where μ Assign$_{tab}$ denotes the unique instance of S_{tab} such that the constraint as specified in Assign$_{tab}$ holds, and :effect retrieves its relational effect on the model state. The definition of Assign$_{tab}$ is very similar to that of Assign$_{obj}$, except that the input path is constrained as path? = TPath (...).

We interpret a guarded substitution g $\rightarrow$ S as a relation that has the same effect as $[[S]]_{obj}$ within the domain of satisfying states of guard g (denoted as $[[g]]_{obj}^{states}$); otherwise, it just behaves like skip as it will be blocked and cannot achieve anything. More precisely, we have:

$$[[g \rightarrow S]]_{obj} = id\ (S_{obj} \times IO_{obj}) \oplus (\ [[g]]_{obj}^{states} \lhd C[[S]]_{obj}\ )$$

Similar rules may be defined for other combinators.

Each transaction is composed of SQL queries, and similar to R_{obj}, we collect and produce, respectively, its list of inputs and outputs upon its initiation and completion. We use R_{sql} to denote such formal context, under which the transformational effect on the state of database is defined accordingly as a function, reflecting the fact that the database implementation is deterministic in its effect.

R_{sql}

---
input; output : PN_VARIABLE

effect : $(S_{sql} \times IO_{sql}) \rightarrow (S_{sql} \times IO_{sql})$

---
this $\in$ input

The mechanism of referencing the current object (via this) is simulated through providing by default the value of this for each generated stored procedure or function. We model inputs and outputs in the same way as we do for IO_{obj}, except that the range of values is now of type ScalarValue.

For each SQL statement, we assign to it a relational semantics by mapping it to a relation on states (of type S_{sql}). This is a similar process to that for $[[-]]_{obj}$. More precisely, we define:

$$[[-]]_{sql} : Statement \rightarrow ((S_{sql} \times IO_{sql}) \leftrightarrow (S_{sql} \times IO_{sql}))$$

And since a SQL stored procedure is defined as a sequential composition, we also define

$$[[-]]_{seqsql} : seq\ Statement \rightarrow ((S_{sql} \times IO_{sql}) \leftrightarrow (S_{sql} \times IO_{sq}))$$

to derive its effect through combining those of its component statements via relational composition. For primitive query statements, we refer to their schema definitions. For example, we have:

$$[[UPDATE\ t\ SET\ sets\ WHERE\ cond\ ]]_{sql} = (\mu\ UPDATE):effect$$

where the state effect of query (UPDATE table? SET sets? WHERE cond?) is formally specified in a schema named UPDATE. The UPDATE query modifies in a table those tuples that satisfy a condition and takes as inputs table? a table name, sets? a mapping that specifies how relevant columns should be modified, and cond? a Boolean condition that chooses the range of tuples to be modified. The schema UPDATE is defined similarly as is $Assign_{tab}$, except that it imposes constraints on the model state S_{sql}. We formalise an IF...THEN...ELSE... statement as the union of the semantic interpretations of the two sequences of statements in its body, each suitably restricted on its domain.

$$[[IF\ b\ THEN\ stmts_1\ ELSE\ stmts_2]]_{sql} = ([[b]]_{sql}^{states} \lhd [[stmts_1]]_{seqsql}) \cup$$
$$([[NOTb]]_{sql}^{states} \lhd [[stmts_2]]_{seq\ sql})$$

where $[[b]]_{sql}^{states}$ denotes the set of satisfying state of a SQL expression b.

To define the semantics of a WHILE loop, we intend for the following equation to hold

$$[[WHILE\ b\ DO\ stmts\ END\ WHILE]]_{sql} = [[IF\ b\ THEN\ stmts \cap WHILE\ b$$
$$DO\ stmts\ END\ WHILEi\ ELSE\ <>]]_{sql}$$

where $\cap$ is the operator for sequence concatenation. By applying the definition of $[[-]]sql$ on IF...THEN...ELSE... and $[[-]]_{seq\ sql}$ on $<>$, we have

$$[[WHILE\ b\ DO\ stmts\ END\ WHILE]]_{sql} = [[b]]_{sql}^{states} \lhd ([[stmts]]_{seq\ sql\ o}^{9}$$
$$[[WHILE\ b\ DO\ stmts\ END\ WHILE]]_{sql})$$
$$\cup [[NOTb]]_{sql}^{states} \lhd id\ (S_{sql} \times IO_{sql})$$

Let us define a function

$$F(X) = ([[b]]_{sql}^{states} \lhd ([[stmts]]_{seqsql\ o}^{9} X)) \cup ([[NOTb]]_{sql}^{states} \lhd id\ (S_{sql} \times IO_{sql}))$$

When $X = [[WHILE\ b\ DO\ stmts\ END\ WHILE]]_{sql,}$ we obtain

$$[[WHILE\ b\ DO\ stmts\ END\ WHILE]]_{sql} = F([[WHILE\ b\ DO\ stmts\ END\ WHILE]]_{sql})$$

which means that $[[\text{WHILE b DO stmts END WHILE}]]_{sql}$ should be a fixed-point of function F. The least fixedpoint (LFP) of function F—i.e. $\bigcup_{n \in \mathbb{N}} F^n (\emptyset)$—exists by Kleene's fixed-point theorem, since F is easily provable to be continuous. We choose this LFP of F for the value of $[[\text{WHILE b DO stmts END WHILE}]]_{sql}$.

We are now able to establish the correctness of the transformation with respect to the linking invariant. The commuting diagram of Figure 4 shows how a substitution program prog and its context TABLE model (i.e. qTableModel), are mapped by the transformation toSqlProc(q TableModel) (prog) to produce an SQL implementation. The linking invariant holds for the before states TABLE $\leftrightarrow$ SQL and for the after states TABLE $\leftrightarrow$ SQL'. We then establish that for each state transformation, characterised by the relational effect of the generated SQL code from prog, there is at least a corresponding state transformation, characterised by the relational effect of the TABLE program, $[[\text{prog}]]_{obj}$. This is an example of simulation between abstract data types [19].

We use a universal quantification $(\forall x \mid R(x) \bullet P(x))$ to state our correctness criterion: the x part declares variables, the R(x) part constrains the range of state values, and the P(x) part states our concern. Schemas defined above (i.e. S_{obj}, S_{sql}, and TABLE $\leftrightarrow$ SQL) are used as both declarations and predicates. If we declare

TransInput
TableModel
prog : Substitution

to represent the inputs to the transformation, then

$\forall TransInput; \Delta S_{obj}; \Delta S_{sql} \mid$
  $TABLE \leftrightarrow SQL \wedge [[toSqlProc(\theta TableModel)(prog)]]_{seqsql} \bullet (\exists S'_{obj} \bullet$
  $(TABLE \leftrightarrow SQL)' \wedge [[prog]]_{obj})$

With the relational semantics outlined above, we may establish this result through a combination of case analysis and structural induction.

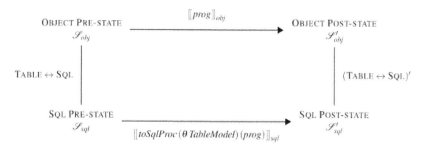

FIGURE 4: Correctness of Model Transformation

4.7 EXAMPLE IMPLEMENTATION

Consider the implementation, on a relational database platform, of the operation reserve introduced in Section 2. Having translated the object model into a collection of database tables, the generation process will produce a stored procedure for each operation. The guard for reserve requires that the current number of allocations—characterised through the cardinality of the set-valued attribute allocations—is below a specific bound. We might include such a condition, for example, to ensure that the memory or storage requirements of the system remain within particular bounds; this may not be an issue for a hotel reservation system, but is a realistic concern in critical systems development. In the implementation, a stored function is generated that will establish whether or not the guard constraint holds for the current state, together with any input values. The remainder of the generated code will achieve the effect specified in the original operation constraint, translated into the representation, or orientation, of the database platform.

Class Reservation has status as an attribute, and this is stored in the corresponding class table. In the function, AUTO INCREMENT allows the target SQL platform to generate a unique identifier for each inserted row. Set-valued properties, like attribute dates in class Reservation are stored in separate tables, with an oid column to identify the current object in a given method call. Associations such as host and reservations are stored in separate tables, with an oid column to identify the exact association instance. Since attribute reservations are also sequence-valued, an index column is required.

Schema of Tables Updated by 'reserve'

1 CREATE TABLE `Reservation`(`oid` INTEGER AUTO_INCREMENT, PRIMARY KEY (`oid`), `status` CHAR(30));
2 CREATE TABLE `Room_reservations_Reservation_room`(`oid` INTEGER AUTO_INCREMENT,
3 PRIMARY KEY (`oid`), `reservations` INTEGER, `room` INTEGER, `index` INTEGER);

We generate also integrity constraints for association tables: although the generated procedures are guaranteed to preserve semantic integrity, this affords some protection against errors in the design of additional, manually-written procedures.

The value of the model-driven approach should be apparent following a comparison of the original specification for reserve with the fragments of the following SQL implementation. Manual production of queries that need to be take account of a large number of complex model constraints—as well as, for examples, constraints arising from data caching strategies—is time-consuming and error-prone. Furthermore, we may expect the design of a system to evolve during use: the challenge of maintaining correctness in the face of changing specifications (and platforms) adds another dimension of complexity to systems development; some degree of automation, in production and in proof, is essential.

In the following, variable names have been preserved from the BOOSTER domain, e.g. the input and output parameters dates? and r! at line 2, as well as caching variables `r!.status`, `r!.host`, and `r!.room` at line 4. Meta-variables are used to implement the ALL iterator in method reserve: Line 5 declares, respectively, the bound variable `x` and `x variant` the variant of the loop, and Line 6 declares a cursor over the set-valued input dates?.

Queries Implementing 'reserve': Declarations

1 CREATE PROCEDURE `Hotel_reserve` (IN `this?` INTEGER,
2 IN `dates?` CHAR(30), IN `m?` INTEGER, OUT `r!` INTEGER)
3 BEGIN
4 DECLARE `r!.status` CHAR(30); DECLARE `r!.host` INTEGER; DECLARE `r!.room` INTEGER;
5 DECLARE `x` Date; DECLARE `x_variant` INTEGER;
*6 DECLARE `x_cursor` CURSOR FOR (SELECT * FROM `dates?` WHERE TRUE);*

Line 7 first creates a new instance of Reservation by inserting, for output r!, a row formatted as <oid...> into the appropriate class table, where oid is a unique value generated by the built-in function last insert id(), with the guarantee that each subsequent call to this functions returns a new value. It then assigns this unique identifier to r! for queries in later fragments to refer to.

Queries Implementing 'reserve': Creating an Empty Output

7 INSERT INTO `Reservation` () VALUE (); SET `r!` = last_insert_id ();

In Lines 8 to 10 the pair of DROP TEMPORARY TABLE and CRE-ATE TEMPORARY TABLE queries update the value of a cache variable `m?.reservations` that denotes a multi-valued property: this kind of caching is useful in large database implementations. In Line 11 we update the caching variable `r!.host` of single-valued types of properties through a SELECT INTO query. We cache the value of attribute host possessed by the reservation r!. Any later paths with `r!.host` or `m?.reservations` as its prefix will be able to use its value directly without re-evaluation.

Queries Implementing 'reserve': Updating Caching Vars

8 DROP TEMPORARY TABLE IF EXISTS `m?.reservations`;
9 CREATE TEMPORARY TABLE `m?.reservations` AS
10 SELECT `reservations` FROM `Room_reservations_Reservation_room` WHERE `room` = `m?`;
11 SELECT `status` INTO `r!.status` FROM `Reservation` WHERE `oid` = `r!`;

Lines 12 to 20 instantiate a finite loop pattern. In Line 12 we activate the declared cursor and and fetch its first available value. In Line 13 we also calculate the size of the data set that the cursor will iterate over and use it as the variant of the loop defined in Lines 14 to 20. The exit condition (Line 14) is characterised through decreasing—via the 2nd statement in Line 19—the value of x cursor; the bound variable x is updated to the next data item at the end of each iteration (via the 1st statement in Line 19). In each iteration of the loop, from Lines 15 to 17 we re-cache the value of the set-valued path r!.dates, in case there are other paths which contain it as a prefix and are used later in the loop. In Line 18 we perform the first substitution in the specification of method reserve: we implement the substitution r!.dates := r!.dates $\lor$ dates? via iterating through the input dates? with a bound variable `x`.

Queries Implementing 'reserve': Terminating Loop

```
12 OPEN `x_cursor`; FETCH `x_cursor` INTO `x`;
13 SELECT COUNT(*) INTO `x_variant` FROM `dates?` WHERE
TRUE;
14 WHILE (`x_variant`) > (0) DO
15 DROP TEMPORARY TABLE IF EXISTS `r!.dates`;
16 CREATE TEMPORARY TABLE `r!.dates` AS
17 SELECT `dates` FROM `Reservation_dates` WHERE `oid` = `r!`;
18 INSERT INTO `Reservation_dates` (`oid`, `dates`) VALUE (`r!`, `x`);
19 FETCH `x_cursor` INTO `x`; SET `x_variant` = `x_variant` - 1;
20 END WHILE; CLOSE `x_cursor`;
```

Line 21 implements the update r!.status := unconfirmed. The two generated query statements— that are located in Lines 22 to 27 and Lines 28 to 31—implement the last two parallel assignments in reserve that update the optional-to-sequence association. They correspond exactly to the rules specified for pattern 23 in Section 5. The queries for the middle two parallel assignments in reserve, updating the one-to-sequence association, are entirely similar.

Queries Implementing 'reserve': Performing Updates

21 UPDATE `Reservation` SET `status` = 'unconfirmed' WHERE (`oid`)   *= (`r!`);*
22 UPDATE `Room_reservations_Reservation_room`
23 SET `index` = (`index`) + (1)
24 WHERE `room` = `m?` AND
25 `index` >=(SELECT COUNT(`oid`)
26 FROM (SELECT `reservations` FROM `m?.reservations` WHERE   *TRUE) AS reservations*
27 WHERE TRUE) + 1;
28 INSERT INTO `Room_reservations_Reservation_room` (`reserva-*   *tions`, `room`, `index`) VALUE
29 (`r!`, `m?`, (SELECT COUNT(`oid`)
30 FROM (SELECT `reservations` FROM `m?.reservations` WHERE   *TRUE) AS reservations*
31 WHERE TRUE) + 1);

4.8 DISCUSSION

The principal contribution of this paper is the presentation of a practical, formal, model-driven approach to the development of critical systems. Both the modelling notation and the target programming language are given a formal, relational semantics: the latter only for a specific subset of the language, sufficient for the patterns of implementation produced by the code generation process. The generation process is formalised as a functional program, easily related to the corresponding transformation on the relational semantics. It is perfectly possible to prove the generator correct; indeed, a degree of automatic proof could be applied here. The task of system verification is then reduced to the strictly simpler task of model verification or validation.

The implementation platform chosen to demonstrate the approach is a standard means of storing data, whether that data was originally described in a hierarchical, a relational, or an object-oriented schema. In particular, there are many products that offer a means of mapping [20] from object models (as used here) to a relational database implementation: Hibernate [5] is perhaps the best-known example. However, translating the data model to a data schema is relatively straightforward; the focus here is the generation of correct implementations for operations.

At the same time, much of the work on program transformation is focussed, unsurprisingly, upon code rewriting rather than the generation of complete software components with persistent data. The work on Vu-X [16], where modifications to a web interface are reflected back into the data model is an interesting exception, but has yet to be extended to a formal treatment of data integrity. The work on UnQL [12] supports the systematic development of model transformation through the composition of graph-based transformations: this is a powerful approach, but again no similar framework has been proposed.

Some work has been done in precise data modelling in UML, for example [7], but no formal account has been given for the proposed translation of operations. The Query/View/Transformation approach [17] focuses on design models, but the transformations [13] are described in an imperative, stateful, style, making proofs of correctness rather more difficult. Recent work on generating provably correct code, for example [22], is restricted to producing primitive getter and setter methods, as opposed to complex procedures. Mammar [14] adopts a formal approach to generating relational databases from UML models. However, this requires the manual definition of appropriate guards for predefined update methods: the automatic derivation of guards, and the automatic generation of methods from arbitrary constraint specifications, as demonstrated here, is not supported.

The unified implementation and semantic framework for transformation (Figure 2) presented here can be applied to any modelling and programming notation that admits such a relational semantics for the behaviour of components. It is important to note that the style of this semantics effectively limits the approach to the development of sequential data components: that is, components in which interactions with important data are managed as exclusive transactions; our semantic treatment does not allow us to consider the effects of two or more complex update operations executing concurrently.

In practice, this is not a significant limitation. Where data is encapsulated within a component, and is subject to complex business rules and integrity constraints, we may expect to find locking or caching protocols to enforce data consistency in the face of concurrent requests, by means of an appropriate sequentialisation. Where concurrency properties are important, they can be addressed using process semantics and model-checking techniques; a degree of automatic generation may even be possible, although this is likely to be at the level of workflows, rather than data-intensive programs.

Work is continuing on the development of the transformation and generation tools discussed here, with a particular emphasis upon the incremental development of operation specifications and models. It is most often the case that a precise model will prove too restrictive: when a property is written linking two or more attributes, it constrains their interpretation; if one of these attributes is used also elsewhere in the model, or within an operation, then that usage may not always be consistent with the now formalised interpretation. In our approach, such a problem manifests itself in the unavailability of one or more operations, in particularly circumstances.

As a guard is generated for each operation, sufficient to protect any data already acquired, each incremental version of the system can be deployed without risk of data loss. It can then be used in practice and in earnest, allowing users to determine whether or not the availability—or the overall design—of each operation and data view matches their requirements and expectations. Where an operation has a non-trivial guard, additional analysis may be required to demonstrate that the resulting availability matches requirements: in many cases, the necessary check or test can be automated. The work described here provides a sound foundation for this development process.

REFERENCES

1.   J.-R. Abrial (1996): The B-book: assigning programs to meanings. Cambridge University Press.
2.   R. Bird (1998): Introduction to Functional Programming using Haskell. Prentice Hall.
3.   Australian Transport Safety Bureau (2011): In-flight upset 154km West of Learmouth, WA, VH-QPA, Airbus

4. A330-303. Aviation Safety Investigations and Reports AO-2008-070.
5. R. N. Charette (2009): This car runs on code. IEEE Spectrum. Available at
6. http://www.spectrum.ieee.org/feb09/7649.
7. JBoss Community: Hibernate: Relational Persistence for Java and .NET. www.hibernate.org.
8. J. Davies, C. Crichton, E. Crichton, D. Neilson & I. H. Sørensen (2005): Formality, evolution, and
9. model-driven software engineering. ENTCS 130, pp. 39–55, doi:10.1016/j.entcs.2005.03.004.
10. B. Demuth & H. Hussmann (1999): Using UML/OCL Constraints for Relational Database Design. In:
11. UML, LNCS 1723, pp. 598–613, doi:10.1007/3-540-46852-8 42.
12. A. van Deursen, P. Klint & J. Visser (2000): Domain-Specific Languages: An Annotated Bibliography.
13. SIGPLAN Notices 35(6), pp. 26–36, doi:10.1145/352029.352035.
14. H.-E. Eriksson, M. Penker & D. Fado (2003): UML 2 Toolkit. Wiley.
15. P.H. Feiler (2010): Model-based validation of safety-critical embedded systems. In: Aerospace Conference,
16. IEEE, pp. 1 – 10, doi:10.1109/AERO.2010.5446809.
17. D. S. Frankel (2003): Model Driven Architecture: Applying MDA to Enterprise Computing. Wiley.
18. S. Hidaka, Z. Hu, H. Kato & K. Nakano (2009): Towards a compositional approach to model
19. transformation for software development. In: SAC, ACM, pp. 468–475, doi:10.1145/1529282.1529383.
20. F. Jouault, F. Allilaire, J. Bézivin & I. Kurtev (2008): ATL: A model transformation tool. Science of
21. Computer Programming 72(1–2), pp. 31–39, doi:10.1016/j.scico.2007.08.002.
22. A. Mammar (2009): A systematic approach to generate B preconditions: application to the database
23. domain. Software and Systems Modeling 8(3), pp. 385–401, doi:10.1007/s10270-008-0098-8.
24. A. Massoudi (2012): Knight Capital glitch loss hits $461m. Financial Times.
25. K. Nakano, Z. Hu & M. Takeichi (2009): Consistent Web site updating based on bidirectional
26. transformation. Int. J. Softw. Tools Technol. Transf. 11(6), pp. 453–468, doi:10.1007/s10009-009-0124-3.
27. OMG (2009): Meta Object Facility (MOF) 2.0 Query/View/Transformation Specification. OMG Document
28. ptc/09-12-05, Object Management Group. http://www.omg.org/spec/QVT/1.1/Beta2/PDF/.
29. K. Pohl, G. Böckle & F. J. van der Linden (2005): Software Product Line Engineering: Foundations,
30. Principles, and Techniques. Springer, doi:10.1007/3-540-28901-1.
31. W. P. de Roever & K. Engelhardt (1999): Data Refinement: Model-Oriented Proof Methods and Their

32. Comparison. Cambridge University Press.
33. C. Russell (2008): Bridging the Object-Relational Divide. ACM Queue 6(3), pp. 18–28,
34. doi:10.1145/1394127.1394139.
35. RTCA SC-205 (2011): DO-178C, Software Considerations in Airborne Systems and Equipment
36. Certification. Approved by Special Committee 205 of Radio Technical Commission for Aeronautic.
37. K. Stenzel, N. Moebius & W. Reif (2011): Formal Verification of QVT Transformations for Code
38. Generation. In: MoDELS, pp. 533–547, doi:10.1007/978-3-642-24485-8 39.
39. C.-W. Wang (2012): Model-Driven Development of Information Systems. Ph.D. thesis, University of
40. Oxford, Oxford University Research Archive.
41. J. Welch, D. Faitelson & J. Davies (2008): Automatic Maintenance of Association Invariants. Software and
42. Systems Modeling 7(3), pp. 287–301, doi:10.1007/s10270-008-0085-0.
43. M. Williams (2010): Toyota to recall Prius hybrids over ABS software. Computerworld.
44. J. Woodcock & J. Davies (1996): Using Z. Prentice Hall.

CHAPTER 5

CATEGORY THEORY AND MODEL-DRIVEN ENGINEERING: FROM FORMAL SEMANTICS TO DESIGN PATTERNS AND BEYOND

ZINOVY DISKIN AND TOM MAIBAUM

5.1 INTRODUCTION

There are several well established applications of category theory (CT) in theoretical computer science; typical examples are programming language semantics and concurrency. Modern software engineering (SE) seems to be an essentially different domain, not obviously suitable for theoretical foundations based on abstract algebra. Too much in this domain appears to be ad hoc and empirical, and the rapid progress of open source and collaborative software development, service-oriented programming, and cloud computing far outpaces their theoretical support. Model driven (software) engineering (MDE) conforms to this description as well: the diversity of modeling languages and techniques successfully resists all attempts to classify them in a precise mathematical way, and model transformations and operations — MDE's heart and soul — are an area of a diverse experimental activity based on surprisingly weak (if any) semantic foundations.

In this paper we claim that theoretical underpinning of modern SE could (and actually quite naturally) be based on CT. The chasm between SE and CT can be bridged, and MDE appears as a "golden cut", in which an abstract view of SE realities and concrete interpretations of categorical abstractions merge together: SE → MDE ← CT. The left leg of the cospan is extensively discussed in the MDE literature (see [47] and references therein); prerequisites and challenges for building the right leg are discussed in the present paper. Moreover, we aim to elucidate a claim that relationships between CT and MDE are more complex and richer than is normally assumed for "applied mathematics". CT provides a toolbox of design patterns and principles, whose added value goes beyond such typical applications of mathematics to SE as formal semantics for a language, or formal analysis and model checking.

Two aspects of the CT-MDE "marriage" are discussed in the paper. The first one is a standard argument about the applicability of a particular mathematical theory to a particular engineering discipline. To wit, there is a mathematical framework called CT, there is an engineering domain called MDE, and we will try to justify the claim that they make a good match, in the sense that concepts developed in the former are applicable for mathematical modeling of constructs developed in the latter. What makes this standard argument exciting is that the mathematical framework in question is known to be notoriously abstract, while the engineering domain is very agile and seemingly not suitable for abstract treatment. Nevertheless, the argument lies within the boundaries of yet another instance of the evergreen story of applying mathematics to engineering problems. Below we will refer to this perspective on the issue as Aspect A.

The second perspective (Aspect B) is less standard and even more interesting. It is essentially based on specific properties of categorical mathematics and on the observation that software engineering is a special kind of engineering. To wit, CT is much more than a collection of mathematical notions and techniques: CT has changed the very way we build mathematical models and reason about them; it can be seen as a toolbox of structural design patterns and the guiding principles of their application.

This view on CT is sometimes called arrow thinking. On the other hand, SE, in general, and MDE, in particular, essentially depend on proper structuring of the universe of discourse into subuniverses, which in their turn are further structured and so on, which finally results in tool architectures and code modularization. Our experience and attempts to understand complex structures used in MDE have convinced us that general ideas of arrow thinking, and general patterns and intuitions of what a healthy structure should be, turn out to be useful and beneficial for such practical concerns as tool architecture and software design.

The paper is structured as follows. In Section 2 we present two very general A-type arguments that CT provides a "right" mathematical framework for SE. The second argument also gives strong prerequisites for the B-side of our story. Section 3.1 gives a brief outline of MDE, and Section 3.2 reveals a truly categorical nature of the cornerstone notions of multimodeling and intermodeling (another A-argument). In Section 4 we present two examples of categorical arrangement of model management scenarios: model merge and bidirectional update propagation. This choice is motivated by our research interests and the possibility to demonstrate the B-side of our story. In Section 5 we discuss and exemplify three ways of applying CT for MDE: understanding, design patterns for specific problems, and general design guidance on the level of tool architecture.

5.2 TWO VERY GENERAL PERSPECTIVES ON SE AND MATHEMATICS

5.2.1 THE PLANE OF SOFTWARE x MATHEMATICS

The upper half of Fig. 1 presents the evolution of software engineering in a schematic way, following Mary Shaw [48] and José Fiadeiro [25]. Programming-in-the-head refers to the period when a software product could be completely designed, at least in principle, "inside the head" of one (super intelligent) programmer, who worked like a researcher rather than as an engineer. The increasing complexities of problems addressed by software solutions (larger programs, more complex algorithms and data structures) engendered more industrially oriented/engineering views and methods (e.g., structured programming). Nevertheless, for Programming-in-the-small, the software module remained the primary goal and challenge of software development, with module interactions being simple and straightforward (e.g., procedure calls). In contrast, Programming-in-the-large marks a shift to the stage when module composition becomes the main issue, with the numbers of modules and the complexity of module interaction enormously increased. This tendency continued to grow and widened in scope as time went on, and today manifests itself as Programming-in-the-world. The latter is characterized by a large, and growing, heterogeneity of modules to be composed and methods for their composition, and such essentially zdmodiffyin-the-largelarge modern technologies as service orientation, open source and collaborative software development, and cloud computing.

The lower part of Fig. 1 presents this picture in a very schematic way as a path from 1 to M to M_n with M referring to multiplicity in different forms, and degree n indicating the modern tendencies of growth in heterogeneity and complexity.

MDE could be seen as a reaction to this development, a way of taming the growth of n in a systematic way. Indeed, until recently, software engineers may feel that they could live without mathematical models: just build the software by whatever means available, check and debug it, and keep doing this throughout the software's life. (Note that the situation in classical (mechanical and electrical) engineering is essentially different:

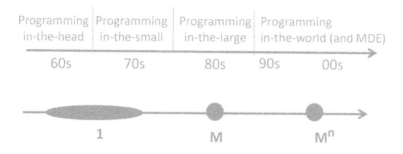

FIGURE 1: Evolution of software (M refers to Many/Multitude)

debugging, say, a bridge, would be a costly procedure, and classical engineers abandoned this approach long time ago.) But this gift of easily built systems afforded to SEs is rapidly degrading as the costs of this process and the liability from getting it wrong are both growing at an enormous rate. By slightly rephrasing Dijkstra, we may say that precise modeling and specification become a matter of death and life rather than luxury.

These considerations give us the vertical axis in Fig. 2, skipping the intermediate point. The horizontal axis represents the evolution of mathematics in a similar simplified way. Point 1 corresponds to the modern mathematics of mathematical structures in the sense of Bourbaki: what matters is operations and relations over mathematical objects rather than their internal structure. Skipped point M corresponds to basic category theory: the internal structure of the entire mathematical structure is encapsulated, and mathematical studies focus on operations and relations over structures considered as holistic entities. The multitude of higher degree, M^∞, refers to categorical facilities for reflection: enrichment, internalization, higher dimensions, which can be applied ad infinitum, hence, ∞-degree.

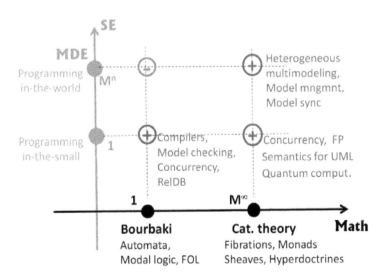

FIGURE 2: Software engineering and mathematics

This (over-simplified) schema gives us four points of Math **4** SE interaction. Interaction (1,1) turned out to be quite successful, as evidenced by such theory-based practical achievements as compilers, model checking, and relational DB theory. As for the point $(1;M^n)$, examining the literature shows that attempts at building theoretical foundations for MDE based on classical 1-mathematics were not successful. A major reason seems to be clear: 1-mathematics does not provide an adequate machinery for specifying and reasoning about inter-structural relationships and operations, which are at the very heart of modern software development. This point may also explain the general skepticism that a modern software engineer, and an academic teaching software engineering, feel about the practicality of using mathematics for modern software design: unfortunately, the only mathematics they know is the classical mathematics of Bourbaki and Tarski.

On the other hand, we view several recent applications of categorical methods to MDE problems [2, 5, 17, 37, 21, 45, 44, 22, 19, 43, 46] as promising theoretical attempts, with great potential for practical application. It provides a firm plus for the $(M^\infty;M^n)$-point in the plane.

Moreover, as emphasized by Lawvere, the strength of CT based modeling goes beyond modeling multi-structural aspects of the mathematical universe, and a categorical view of a single mathematical structure can be quite beneficial too. This makes point $(M^\infty;1)$ in the plane potentially interesting, and indeed, several successful applications at this point are listed in the figure.

5.2.2 MATHEMATICAL MODELING OF ENGINEERING ARTIFACTS: ROUND-TRIPPING ABSTRACTION VS. WATERFALL

Figure Fig. 3(a) shows a typical way of building mathematical models for mechanical and electrical engineering domains. Meta-mathematics (the discipline of modeling mathematical models) is not practically needed for engineering as such. The situation dramatically changes for software engineering. Indeed, category theory (CT) could be defined as a discipline for studying mathematical structures: how to specify, relate and manipulate

(a) Normal (waterfall) modeling chain

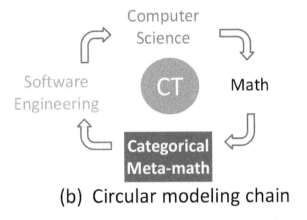

(b) Circular modeling chain

FIGURE 3: Modeling chains

them, and how to reason about them. In this definition, one can safely remove the adjective "mathematical" and consider CT as a mathematical theory of structures in a very broad sense. Then CT becomes directly applicable to SE as shown in Fig. 3(b). Moreover, CT has actually changed the way of building mathematical structures and thinking about them, and found extensive and deep applications in theoretical computer science. Hence, CT can be considered as a common theoretical framework for all modeling stages in the chain (and be placed at the center). In this way, CT provides a remarkable unification for modeling activities in SE.

The circular, non linear nature of the figure also illustrates an important point about the role of CT in SE. Because software artifacts are conceptual rather than physical entities, there is potential for feedback between SE and Mathematics in a way that is not possible in traditional scientific and engineering disciplines. Design patterns employed in SE can be, and have been, influenced by mathematical model of software and the way we develop them.

5.3 MDE AND CT: AN OVERALL SKETCH

We will begin with a rough general schema of the MDE approach to building software (Section 3.1), and then will arrange this schema in categorical terms (Section 3.2).

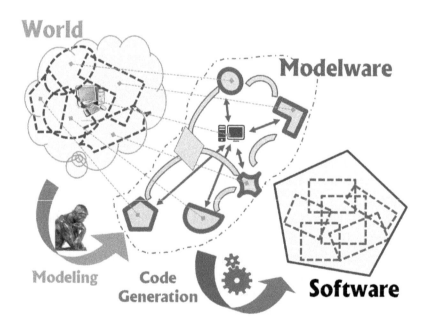

FIGURE 4: MDE, schematically

5.3.1 MDE IN A NUTSHELL

The upper-left corner of Fig. 4 shows a general goal of software design: building software that correctly interacts with different subsystems of the world (shown by figures of different shapes). For example, software embedded in a car interacts with its mechanical, electrical and electronic subsystems, with the driver and passengers, and with other cars on the road in future car designs. These components interact between themselves, which is schematically shown by overlaps of the respective shapes. The lower-right corner of Fig. 4 shows software modularized in parallel to the physical world it should interact with. The passage from the left to the right is highly non-trivial, and this is what makes SE larger and more challenging than mere programming. An effective means to facilitate the transition is to use models — a system of syntactical objects (as a rule, diagrammatic) that serve as abstractions of the "world entities" as shown in the figure (note the links from pieces of World to the respective parts of Modelware). These abstractions are gradually developed and refined until finally transformed into code. The modelware universe actually consists of a series of "modelwares"—systems of requirement, analysis, and design models, with each consecutive member in the list refining the previous one, and in its own turn encompassing several internal refinement chains. Modelware development consumes intelligence and time, but still easier and more natural for a human than writing code; the latter is generated automatically. The main idea of MDE is that human intelligence should be used for building models rather than code.

Of course, models have been used for building software long before the MDE vision appeared in the market. That time, however, after the first version of a software product had been released, its maintenance and further evolution had been conducted mainly through code, so that models had quickly become outdated, degraded and finally became useless. In contrast, MDE assumes that maintenance and evolution should also go through models. No doubts that some changes in the real world are much easier to incorporate immediately in the code rather than via models, but then MDE prescribes to update the models to keep them in sync with code. In fact, code becomes just a specific model, whose only essential distinction from other models in the modelware universe is its final position in the refinement chain. Thus, the Modelware boundary in Fig. 4 should be extended to encompass the Software region too.

5.3.2 MODELWARE CATEGORICALLY

Consider a modelware snapshot in Fig. 4. Notice that models as such are separated whereas their referents are overlapped, that is, interact between themselves. This interaction is a fundamental feature of the real world, and to make the model universe adequate to the world, intermodel correspondences/relations must be precisely specified. (For example, the figure shows three binary relations, and one ternary relation visualized as a ternary span with a diamond head.) With reasonable modeling techniques, intermodel relations should be compatible with model structures. The modelware universe then appears as a collection of structured objects and structure-compatible mappings between them, that is, as a categorical phenomenon. In more detail, a rough categorical arrangement could be as follows.

The base universe

Models are multi-sorted structures whose theories are called metamodels. The latter can be seen as generalized sketches [39, 20], that is, pairs $M = (G_M; C_M)$ with G_M a graph (or, more generally, an object of an apiori fixed presheaf topos G), and C_M a set of constraints (i.e., diagram predicates) declared over G_M. An instance of metamodel M is a pair $A = (G_A; t_A)$ with G_A another graph (an object in G) and $t_A : G_A \rightarrow G_M$ a mapping (arrow in G) to be thought of as typing, which satisfy the constraints, $A \models C_M$ (see [20] for details). An instance mapping $A \rightarrow B$ is a graph mapping $f : G_A \rightarrow G_B$ commuting with typing: $f ; t_B = t_A$. This defines a category **Mod(M)** $\subset$ **G**=G_M of M-instances.

To deal with the heterogeneous situation of models over different metamodels, we first introduce metamodel morphisms m: $M \rightarrow N$ as sketch morphisms, i.e., graph mappings m: $G_M \rightarrow G_N$ compatible with constraints. This gives us a category of metamodels **MMod**. Now we can merge all categories **Mod(M)** into one category **Mod**, whose objects are instances (= G-arrows) $t_A : G_A \to G_{M(A)}$, $t_B : G_B \to G_{M(B)}$ etc, each having its metamodel, and morphisms $f : A \to B$ are pairs $f_{data} : G_A \to G_B$, $f_{meta} : M(A) \to M(B)$ such that $f_{data};t_B = t_A$; f_{meta}, i.e., commutative squares in G. Thus, Mod is a subcategory of the arrow category $G^{\to}$.

It can be shown that pulling back a legal instance $t_B : G_B \to G_N$ of metamodel N along a sketch morphism m: $M \to N$ results in a legal instance of M [20]. We thus have a fibration **p: Mod** $\to$ **MMod**, whose Cartesian lifting is given by pullbacks.

Intermodel relations and queries

A typical intermodeling situation is when an element of one model corresponds to an element that is not immediately present in another model, but can be derived from other elements of that model by a suitable operation (a query, in the database jargon) [19]. Query facilities can be modeled by a pair of monads $(Q_{def};Q)$ over categories **MMod** and **Mod**, resp. The first monad describes the syntax (query definitions), and the second one provides the semantics (query execution).

A fundamental property of queries is that the original data are not affected: queries compute new data but do not change the original. Mathematical modeling of this property results in a number of equations, which can be summarized by saying that monad Q is **p**-Cartesian, i.e., the Cartesian and the monad structure work in sync. If can be shown [19] that a query language $(Q;Q_{def})$ gives rise to a fibration $\mathbf{p}_Q : \mathbf{Mod}_Q \to \mathbf{MMod}_{Qdef}$ between the corresponding Kleisli categories. These Kleisli categories have immediate practical interpretations. Morphisms in $\mathbf{MMod}_{Qdef}$ are nothing but view definitions: they map elements of the source metamodel to queries against the target one. Correspondingly, morphisms in $\mathbf{Mod}_Q$ are view executions composed from query execution followed by retyping. The fact that projection $\mathbf{p}_Q$ is fibration implies that the view execution mechanism is compositional: execution of a composed view equals the composition of executions.

Now a correspondence between models A;B over metamodels M;N can be specified by data shown in Fig. 5; these data consist of three components.. (1) span (m: $N \Leftarrow MN$; n: $MN \Rightarrow N$) (whose legs are Kleisli mappings) specifies a common view MN between the two metamodels.

(2) trapezoids (arrows in $\mathbf{Mod}_Q$) are produced by $\mathbf{p}_Q$-Cartesian "lifting", i.e., by executing views m and n for models A and B resp., which results in models $A\restriction_m$ and $B\restriction_n$ (here and below we use the following notation: computed nodes are not framed, and computed arrows are dashed). (3) span (p: $A\restriction_m \leftarrow AB$; q: $AB \rightarrow B\restriction n$) specifies a correspondence between the views. Note that this span is an independent modelware component and cannot be derived from models A;B.

Spans like in Fig. 5 integrate a collection of models into a holistic system, which we will refer to as a multimodel. Examples, details, and a precise definition of a multimodel's consistency can be found in [21].

It is tempting to encapsulate spans in Fig. 5 as composable arrows and work with the corresponding (bi)categories of metamodels and models. Unfortunately, it would not work out because, in general, Kleisli categories are not closed under pullbacks, and it is not clear how to compose Kleisli spans. It is an important problem to overcome this obstacle and find a workable approach to Kleisli spans,

Until the problem above is solved, our working universe is the Kleisli category of heterogeneous models fibred over the Kleisli category of metamodels. This universe is a carrier of different operations and predicates over models, and a stage on which different modeling scenarios are played. Classification and specification of these operations and predicates, and their understanding in conventional mathematical terms, is a major task of building mathematical foundations for MDE. Algebraic patterns appear here quite naturally, and then model management scenarios can be seen as algebraic terms composed from diagram-algebra operations over models and model mappings. The next section provides examples of such algebraic arrangements.

5.4 MODEL MANAGEMENT (MMT) AND ALGEBRA: TWO EXAMPLES

We will consider two examples of algebraic modeling of MMt scenarios. A simple one — model merging, and a more complex and challenging— bidirectional update propagation (BX).

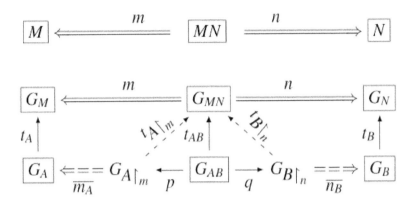

FIGURE 5: Correspondences between heterogeneous models

5.4.1 MODEL MERGE VIA COLIMIT

Merging several interrelated models without data redundancy and loss is an important MDE scenario. Models are merged (virtually rather than physically) to check their consistency, or to extract an integrated information about the system. A general schema is shown in Fig. 6. Consider first the case of several homogeneous models AB, C... to be merged. The first step is to specify correspondences/relations between models via Kleisli spans R1, R2,..., or perhaps direct mappings like r3. The intuition of merging without data loss and redundancy (duplication of correspondent data) is precisely captured by the universal property of colimits, that is, it is reasonable to define merge as the colimit of a diagram of models and model mappings specifying intermodel correspondences.

If models are heterogeneous, their relations are specified as in Fig. 5. To merge, we first merge metamodels modulo metamodel spans. Then we can consider all models and heads of the correspondence spans as instances of the merged metamodel, and merge models by taking the colimit of the entire diagram in the category of instances of the merged metamodel.

An important feature of viewing model merge as described above is a clear separation of two stages of the merge process: (i) discovery and specifying intermodel correspondences (often called model matching), and (ii) merging models modulo these correspondences. The first stage is inherently heuristic and context dependent. It can be assisted by tools based on AI-technologies, but in general a user input is required for final adjustment of the match (and of course to define the heuristics used by the tool). The second stage is pure algebra (colimit) and can be performed automatically. The first step may heavily depend on the domain and the application, while the second one is domain and application independent. However, a majority of model merge tools combine the two stages into a holistic merge algorithm, which first somehow relates models based on a specification of conflicts between them, and then proceeds accordingly to merging. Such an approach complicates merge algorithms, and makes a taxonomy of conflicts their crucial component; typical examples are [49, 42].

The cause of this deficiency is that tool builders rely on a very simple notion of model matching, which amounts to linking the-same-semantics elements in the models to be matched. However, as discussed above in Section 3.2, for an element e in model A, the-same-semantics B-element

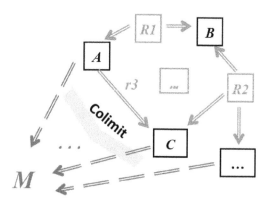

FIGURE 6: Model merge

e' can only be indirectly present in B, i.e., e' can be derived from other elements of B with a suitable operation (query) over B rather than being an immediate element of B. With complex (Kleisli) matching that allows one to link basic elements in one model with derived elements in another model, the algebraic nature of merge as such (via the colimit operation) can be restored. Indeed, it is shown in [9] that all conflicts considered in [42] can be managed via complex matching, that is, described via Kleisli spans with a suitable choice of queries, afterwards merge is computed via colimit.

5.4.2 BIDIRECTIONAL UPDATE PROPAGATION (BX)

Keeping a system of models mutually consistent (model synchronization) is vital for model-driven engineering. In a typical scenario, given a pair of inter-related models, changes in either of them are to be propagated to the other to restore consistency. This setting is often referred to as bidirectional model transformation (BX) [6].

5.4.2.1 BX VIA TILE ALGEBRA

A simple BX-scenario is presented in Fig. 7(a). Two models, A and B, are interrelated by some correspondence specification r (think of a span in a suitable category, or an object in a suitable comma category, see [21] for examples). We will often refer to them as horizontal deltas between models. In addition, there is a notion of delta consistency (extensionally, a class of consistent deltas), and if r is consistent, we call models A and B synchronized.

Now suppose that (the state of) model B has changed: the updated (state of the) model is B', and arrow b denotes the correspondence between B and B' (a vertical delta). The reader may think of a span, whose head consists of unchanged elements and the legs are injections so that B's elements beyond the range of the upper leg are deleted, and B''s elements beyond the range of the lower leg are inserted. Although update spans are denoted by bidirectional arrows, the upper node is always the source, and the lower is the target.

Suppose that we can re-align models A and B' and compute new horizontal delta r ∗ b (think of a span composition). If this new delta is not consistent, we need to update model A so that the updated model A' would be in sync with B'. More accurately, we are looking for an update a: A ↔ A' such that the triple (A'; r';B') is consistent. Of course, we want to find a minimal update a (with the biggest head) that does the job.

Unfortunately, in a majority of practically interesting situations, the minimality condition is not strong enough to provide uniqueness of a. To achieve uniqueness, some update propagation policy is to be chosen, and then we have an algebraic operation bPpg ('b' stands for 'backward'), which, from a given a pair of arrows (b; r) connected as shown in the figure, computes another pair (a; r') connected with (b; r) as shown in the figure. Thus, a propagation policy is algebraically modeled by a diagram operation of arity specified by the upper square in Fig. 7(a): shaded elements denote the input data, whereas blank ones are the output. Analogously, choosing a forward update propagation policy (from the A-side to the B-side) provides a forward operation fPpg as shown by the lower square.

The entire scenario is a composition of two operations: a part of the input for operation application 2:fPpg is provided by the output of 1:bPpg. In general, composition of diagram operations, i.e., operations acting upon configurations of arrows (diagrams), amounts to their tiling, as shown in the figure; then complex synchronization scenarios become tiled structures. Details, precise definitions and examples can be found in [15].

Different diagram operations involved in model synchronization are not independent and their interaction must satisfy certain conditions. These conditions capture the semantics of synchronization procedures, and their understanding is important for the user of synchronization tools: it helps to avoid surprises when automatic synchronization steps in. Fortunately, principal conditions (synchronization laws) can be formulated as universally valid equations between diagrammatic terms — a tile algebra counterpart of universal algebraic identities. In this way BX becomes based on an algebraic theory: a signature of diagram operations and a number of equational laws they must satisfy. The appendix presents one such theory—the notion of a symmetric delta lens, which is currently an area of active research from both a practical and a theoretical perspective.

5.4.2.2 BX: DELTA-BASED VS. STATE-BASED

As mentioned above, understanding the semantics of model synchronization procedures is important, both theoretically and practically. Synchronization tools are normally built on some underlying algebraic theory [28, 53, 40, 4, 1, 41, 30], and many such tools (the first five amongst those cited above) use algebraic theories based on state-based rather than delta-based operations. The state-based version of the propagation scenario in Fig. 7(a) is described in Fig. 7(b). The backward propagation operation takes models A;B;B', computes necessary relations between them (r and b on the adjacent diagram), and then computes an updated model A'. The two-chevron symbol reminds us that the operation actually consists of two stages: model alignment (computing r and b) and update propagation as such.

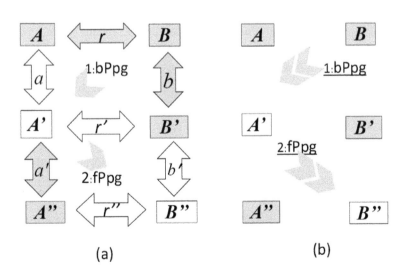

FIGURE 7: BX scenario specified in (a) delta-based and (b) state-based way

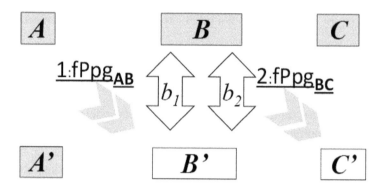

FIGURE 8: State-based BX: erroneous horizontal composition

The state-based frameworks, although they may look simpler, actually hides several serious deficiencies. Model alignment is a difficult task that requires contextual information about models. It can be facilitated by intelligent AI-based tools, or even be automated, but the user should have an option to step in and administer corrections. In this sense, model alignment is similar to model matching preceding model merge. Weaving alignment (delta discovery) into update (delta) propagation essentially complicates the semantics of the latter, and correspondingly complicates the algebraic theory. In addition, the user does not have an access to alignment results and cannot correct them.

Two other serious problems of the state-based frameworks and architectures are related to operation composition. The scenario described in Fig. 7(a) assumes that the model correspondence (delta) used for update propagation 2:fPpg is the delta computed by operation 1:bPpg; this is explicitly specified in the tile algebra specification of the scenario. In contrast, the state-based framework cannot capture this requirement. A similar problem appears when we sequentially compose a BX program synchronizing models A and B and another program synchronizing models B and C: composition amounts to horizontal composition of propagation opera-

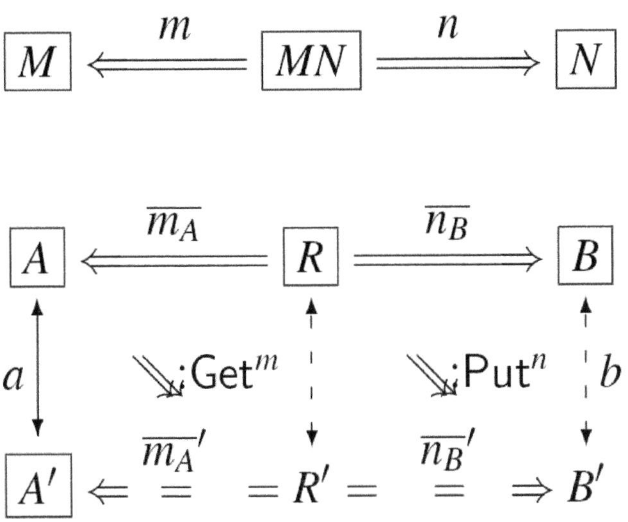

$$M \Longleftarrow \overset{m}{\rule{3cm}{0pt}} MN \overset{n}{\Longrightarrow} N$$

$$A \Longleftarrow \overset{\overline{m_A}}{\rule{2cm}{0pt}} R \overset{\overline{n_B}}{\Longrightarrow} B$$

$$a \downarrow \qquad \searrow_i \mathrm{Get}^m \quad \vert \qquad \searrow_i \mathrm{Put}^n \quad \vert\; b$$

$$A' \Longleftarrow \overset{\overline{m_A}'}{\rule{1.5cm}{0pt}} = R' = \overset{\overline{n_B}'}{\rule{1.5cm}{0pt}} \Rightarrow B'$$

FIGURE 9: Model transformation via GetPut-decomposition

tions as shown in Fig. 8, and again continuity, $b_1 = b_2$, cannot be specified in the state-based framework. A detailed discussion of delta- vs. state-based synchronization can be found in [22, 10].

5.4.2.3 ASSEMBLING MODEL TRANSFORMATIONS

Suppose M,N are two metamodels, and we need to transform M-instances (models) into N-ones. Such a transformation makes sense if metamodels are somehow related, and we suppose that their relationship is specified by a span (m: $M \Leftarrow M_N$; n: $M_N \Rightarrow N$) (Fig. 9), whose legs are Kleisli mappings of the respective query monad.

Now N-translation of an M-model A can be done in two steps. First, view m is executed (via its Cartesian lifting actually going down in the figure), and we obtain Kleisli arrow $m_A : A \Leftarrow R$ (with $R = A\restriction_m$). Next we need to find an N-model B such that its view along n, $B\restriction_n$, is equal to R.

In other words, given a view, we are looking for a source providing this view. There are many such sources, and to achieve uniqueness, we need to choose some policy. Afterwards, we compute model B related to A by span (m_A, n_B).

If model A is updated to A', it is reasonable to compute a correspond-ing update b: B ↔ B' rather than recompute B' from scratch (recall that models can contain thousands elements). Computing b again consists of two steps shown in the figure. Operations Get^m and Put^n are similar to fPpg and bPpg considered above, but work in the asymmetric situation when mappings m and n are total (Kleisli) functions and hence view R contains nothing new wrt. M and N. Because of asymmetry, operations Get ('get' the view update) and Put ('put' it back to the source) are different. Get^m is uniquely determined by the view definition m. Put^n needs, in addition to n, some update propagation policy. After the latter is chosen, we can realize transformation from M to N incrementally by composition fPpg = $Get^m;Put^n$ — this is an imprecise linear notation for tiling (composition of diagram operations) specified in Fig. 9.

Note that the initial transformation from M to N sending, first, an M-instance A to its view $R = A\restriction_m$, and then finding an N-instance $B \in N$ such that $B\restriction_n = R$, can be also captured by Get and Put. For this, we need to postulate initial objects Ω_M and Ω_N in categories of M- and N-instances, so that for any A over M and B over N there are unique updates $0_A : \Omega_M \to$ A and $0_B : \Omega_N \to B$. Moreover, there is a unique span $(m_\Omega : \Omega_M \Leftarrow \Omega_{MN}, n_\Omega : \Omega_{MN} \Rightarrow \Omega_N)$ relating these initial objects. Now, given a model A, model B can be computed as B' in Fig. 9 with the upper span being (m_Ω, n_Ω), and the update a being $0_A : \Omega_M \to A$.

The backward transformation is defined similarly by swapping the roles of m and n:

bPpg = $Get^n;Put^m$

The schema described above can be seen as a general pattern for defin-ing model transformation declaratively with all benefits (and all pains) of having a precise specification before the implementation is approached (and must obey). Moreover, this schema can provide some semantic guar-antees in the following way. Within the tile algebra framework, laws for operations Get and Put, and their interaction (invertibility), can be precisely specified [22] (see also the discussion in Section 5.1); algebras of this theory are called delta lenses. Then we can deduce the laws for the composed operations fPpg and bPpg from the delta lens laws. Also, operations Get^m, Put^m can themselves be composed from smaller blocks, if the view m is composed: $m = m_1, m_2:...:m_k$, via sequential lens composition. In this way, a complex model transformation is assembled from elementary transformation blocks, and its important semantic properties are guaranteed. More examples and details can be found in [15].

5.5 APPLYING CT TO MDE: EXAMPLES AND DISCUSSION.

We will try to exemplify and discuss three ways in which CT can be applied in MDE. The first one — gaining a deeper understanding of an engineering problem — is standard, and appears as a particular instantiation of the general case of CT's employment in applied domains. The other two are specific to SE: structural patterns provided by categorical models of the software system to be built can directly influence the design. We will use models of BX as our main benchmark; other examples will be also used when appropriate.

5.5.1 DEEPER UNDERSTANDING

As mentioned in Sect. 4.2, stating algebraic laws that BX procedures must obey is practically important as it provides semantic guaranties for synchronization procedures. Moreover, formulation of these laws should be semantically transparent and concise as the user of synchronization tools needs a clear understanding of propagation semantics. The original state-based theory of asymmetric BX [28] considered two groups of laws: invertibility (or round-tripping) laws, GetPut and PutGet, and history ignorance, PutPut. Two former laws say that two propagation operations, Get and Put, are mutually inverse. The PutPut law says that if a complex update is decomposed into consecutive pieces, it can be propagated incrementally, one piece after the other. A two-sorted algebra comprising two operations, Get and Put, satisfying the laws, is called a well-behaved lens.

Even an immediate arrow-based generalization of lenses to delta lenses (treated in elementary terms via tile algebra [15, 22]) revealed that the GetPut law is a simple law of identity propagation, IdPut, rather than of round-tripping. The benefits of renaming GetPut as IdPut are not exhausted by clarification of semantics: as soon as we understand that the original GetPut is about identity propagation, we at once ask what the real round-tripping law GetPut should be, and at once see that operation Put is not the inverse of Get. We only have the weaker 1.5-round-tripping GetPutGet law (or weak invertibility; see the Appendix, where the laws in question are named IdPpg and fbfPpg and bfbPpg). It is interesting (and remarkable) that papers [14, 31], in which symmetric lenses are studied in the state-based setting, mistakenly consider identity propagation laws as round-tripping laws, and correspondingly analyze a rather poor BX-structure without real round-tripping laws at all.

The tile algebra formulation of the PutPut law clarified its meaning as a composition preservation law [15, 22], but did not solve the enigmatic PutPut problem. The point is that PutPut does not hold in numerous practically interesting situations, but its entire removal from the list of BX laws is also not satisfactory, as it leaves propagation procedures without any constraints on their compositionality. The problem was solved, or at least essentially advanced, by a truly categorical analysis performed by Michael Johnson et al [35, 34]. They have shown that an asymmetric well-behaved lens is an algebra for some KZ monad, and PutPut is nothing but the basic associativity condition for this algebra. Hence, as Johnson and Rosebrugh write in [34], the status of the PutPut changes from being (a) "some law that may have arisen from some special applications and should be discarded immediately if it seems not to apply in a new application" to (b) a basic requirement of an otherwise adequate and general mathematical model. And indeed, Johnson and Rosebrugh have found a weaker—monotonic—version of PutPut (see Fig. 13 in the Appendix), which holds in a majority of practical applications, including those where the original (non-monotonic or mixed) PutPut fails. Hopefully, this categorical analysis can be generalized for the symmetric lens case, thus stating solid mathematical foundations for BX.

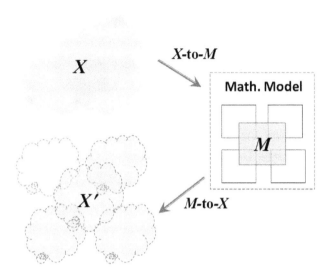

FIGURE 10: From mathematical models to design patterns

5.5.2 DESIGN PATTERNS FOR SPECIFIC PROBLEMS

Recalling Figure 3, Figure 10 presents a rough illustration of how mathematical models can reshape our view of a domain or construct X. Building a well-structured mathematical model M of X, and then reinterpreting it back to X, can change our view of the latter as schematically shown in the figure with the reshaped construct X'. Note the discrepancy between the reshaped X' and model M: the upper-left block is missing from X'. If X is a piece of reality (think of mathematical modeling of physical phenomena), this discrepancy means, most probably, that the model is not adequate (or, perhaps, some piece of X is not observable). If X is a piece of software, the discrepancy may point to a deficiency of the design, which can be fixed by redesigning the software. Even better to base software design on a wellstructured model from the very beginning. Then we say that model M provides a design pattern for X.

We have found several such cases in our work with categorical modeling of MDE-constructs. For example, the notion of a jointly-monic n-ary arrow span turns out to be crucial for modeling associations between object classes, and their correct implementation as well [17]. It is interesting to observe how a simple arrow arrangement allows one to clean the UML metamodel and essentially simplify notation [12, 8]. Another example is modeling intermodel mappings by Kleisli morphisms, which provide a universal pattern for model matching (a.k.a alignment) and greatly simplify model merge as discussed in Sect. 4.1. In addition, the Kleisli view of model mappings provides a design pattern for mapping composition — a problem considered to be difficult in the model management literature [3]. Sequential composition of symmetric delta lenses is also not evident; considering such lenses as algebras whose carriers are profunctors (see Appendix) suggests a precise pattern to be checked (this work is now in progress). Decomposition of a model transformation into Cartesian lifting (view execution) followed by the inverse operation of Cartesian lifting completion (view updating) as described in Section 4.2.3 provides a useful guidance for model transformation design, known to be laborious and error-prone. In particular, it immediately provides bidirectionality.

The graph transformation community also developed several general patterns applicable to MDE (with models considered as typed attributed graphs, see [23] for details). In particular, an industrial standard for model transformation, QVT [41], was essentially influenced by triple-graph grammars (TGGs). Some applications of TGGs to model synchronization (and further references) can be found in [30].

5.5.3 DIAGRAMMATIC MODELING CULTURE AND TOOL ARCHITECTURE.

The design patterns mentioned above are based on the respective categorical machinery (monads, fibrations, profunctors). A software engineer not familiar with these patterns would hardly recognize them in the arrays of implementation details. Even less probable is that he will abstract away his implementation concerns and reinvent such patterns from scratch; distillation of these structures by the CT community took a good amount of time. In contrast, simple arrow diagrams, like in Fig. 7(a) (see also the Appendix), do not actually need any knowledge of CT: all that is required is making intermodel relations explicit, and denoting them by arcs (directed or undirected) connecting the respective objects. To a lesser extent, this also holds for the model transformation decomposition in Fig. 9 and the model merge pattern in Fig. 6. We refer to a lesser extent because the former pattern still needs familiarity with the relations-are-spans idea, and the latter needs an understanding of what colimit is (but, seemingly, it should be enough to understand it roughly as some algebraic procedure of "merging things").

The importance of mappings between models/software artifacts is now well recognized in many communities within SE, and graphical notations have been employed in SE for a long time. Nevertheless, a majority of model management tools neglect the primary status of model mappings: in their architecture, model matching and alignment are hidden inside (implementations of) algebraic routines, thus complicating both semantics and implementation of the latter; concerns are intricately mixed rather than separated. As all SE textbooks and authorities claim separation of concerns to be a fundamental principle of software design, an evident violation of the principle in the cases mentioned above is an empirical fact that puzzles us. It is not clear why a BX-tool designer working on tool architecture does not consider simple arrow diagrams like in Fig. 7(a), and prefers discrete diagrams (b). The latter are, of course, simpler but their simplicity is deceiving in an almost evident way.

The only explanation we have found is that understanding the deceiving simplicity of discrete diagrams (b), and, simultaneously, manageability of arrow diagrams (a), needs a special diagrammatic modeling culture that a software engineer normally does not possess. This is the culture of elementary arrow thinking, which covers the most basic aspects of manipulating and using arrow diagrams. It appears that even elementary arrow thinking habits are not cultivated in the current SE curriculum, the corresponding high-level specification patterns are missing from the software designer toolkit, and software is often structured and modularized according to the implementation rather than specification concerns.

5.6 RELATED WORK

First applications of CT in computer science, and the general claim of CT's extreme usefulness for computer applications should be, of course, attributed to Joseph Goguen [29]. The shift from modeling semantics of computation (behavior) to modeling structures of software programs is emphasized by Jos´e Fiadeiro in the introduction to his book [36], where he refers to a common "social" nature of both domains. The ideas put forward by Fiadeiro were directly derived from joint work with Tom Maibaum on what has become known as component based design and software architecture [26, 27, 24]. A clear visualization of these ideas by Fig. 2 (with M standing for Fiadeiro's "social") seems to be new. The idea of round-tripping modeling chain Fig. 3 appears to be novel, its origin can be traced to [11].

Don Batory makes an explicit call to using CT in MDE in his invited lecture for MoDELS'2008 [2], but he employs the very basic categorical means, in fact, arrow composition only. In our paper we refer to much more advanced categorical means: sketches, fibrations, Cartesian monads, Kleisli categories.

Generalized sketches (graphs with diagram predicates) as a universal syntactical machinery for formalizing different kinds of models were proposed by Diskin et al, [18]. Their application to special MDE problems can be found in [17, 38] and in the work of Rutle et al, see [46], [43] and references therein. A specific kind of sketches, ER-sketches, is employed for a number of problems in the database context by Johnson et al [32]. Considering models as typed attributed graphs with applications to MDE has been extensively put forward by the graph transformation (GT) community [23]; their work is much more operationally oriented than our concerns in the present paper. On the other hand, in contrast to the generalized sketches framework, constraints seem to be not the first-class citizens in the GT world.

The shift from functorial to fibrational semantics for sketches to capture the metamodeling foundations of MDE was proposed in [13] and formalized in [20]. This semantics is heavily used in [15], and in the work of Rutle et al mentioned above. Comparison of the two semantic approaches, functorial and fibrational, and the challenges of proving their equivalence, are discussed in [52].

The idea of modeling query languages by monads, and metamodel (or data schema) mappings by Kleisli mappings, within the functorial semantics approach, was proposed in [16], and independently by Johnson and Rosebrugh in their work on ER-sketches [32]. Reformulation of the idea for fibrational semantics was developed and used for specifying important MDE constructs in [15, 21]. An accurate formalization via Cartesian monads can be found in [19].

Algebraic foundations for BX is now an area of active research. Basics of the state-based algebraic framework (lenses) were developed by Pierce with coauthors [28]; their application to MDE is due to Stevens [50]. Delta-lenses [22, 10] is a step towards categorical foundations, but they have been described in elementary terms using tile algebra [15]. A categorical approach to the view update problem has been developed by Johnson and Rosebrugh et al[33]; and extended to categorical foundations for lenses based on KZ-monads in [35, 34]. The notion of symmetric delta lens in Appendix is new; it results from incorporating the monotonic PutPut-law idea of Johnson and Rosebrugh into the earlier notion of symmetric delta lens [10]. Assembling synchronization procedures from elementary blocks is discussed in [15].

5.7 CONCLUSION

The paper claims that category theory is a good choice for building mathematical foundations for MDE. We first discuss two very general prerequisites that concepts and structures developed in category theory have to be well applicable for mathematical modeling of MDE-constructs. We then exemplify the arguments by sketching several categorical models, which range from general definitions of multimodeling and intermodeling to important model management scenarios of model merge and bidirectional update propagation. We briefly explain (and refer to other work for relevant details) that these categorical models provide useful design patterns and guidance for several problems considered to be difficult.

Moreover, even an elementary arrow arrangement of model merge and BX scenarios makes explicit a deficiency of the modern tools automating these scenarios. To wit: these tools' architecture weaves rather than separates such different concerns as (i) model matching and alignment based on heuristics and contextual information, and (ii) relatively simple algebraic routines of merging and update propagation. This weaving complicates both semantics and implementation of the algebraic procedures, does not allow the user to correct alignment if necessary, and makes tools much less flexible. It appears that even simple arrow patterns, and the corresponding structural decisions, may not be evident for a modern software engineer.

Introduction of CT courses into the SE curriculum, especially in the MDE context, would be the most natural approach to the problem: even elementary CT studies should cultivate arrow thinking, develop habits of diagrammatic reasoning and build a specific intuition of what is a healthy vs. illformed structure. We believe that such intuition, and the structural lessons one can learn from CT, are of direct relevance for many practical problems in MDE.

REFERENCES

1. Michal Antkiewicz, Krzysztof Czarnecki & Matthew Stephan (2009): Engineering of Framework-Specific Modeling Languages. IEEE Trans. Software Eng. 35(6), pp. 795–824. Available at http://doi. ieeecomputersociety.org/10.1109/TSE.2009.30.
2. Don S. Batory, Maider Azanza & Joao Saraiva (2008): The Objects and Arrows of Computational Design. In Czarnecki et al. [7], pp. 1–20. Available at http://dx.doi.org/10.1007/978-3-540-87875-9_1.
3. Philip A. Bernstein (2003): Applying Model Management to Classical Meta Data Problems. In: CIDR. Available at http://www-db.cs.wisc.edu/cidr/cidr2003/program/p19.pdf.
4. Aaron Bohannon, J. Nathan Foster, Benjamin C. Pierce, Alexandre Pilkiewicz & Alan Schmitt (2008): Boomerang: resourceful lenses for string data. In: Proceedings of the 35th annual ACM SIGPLAN-SIGACT symposium on Principles of programming languages, POPL '08, ACM, New York, NY, USA, pp. 407–419. Available at http://dx.doi.org/10.1145/1328438.1328487.
5. Artur Boronat, Alexander Knapp, Jos´e Meseguer & Martin Wirsing (2008): What Is a Multi-modeling Language? In Andrea Corradini & Ugo Montanari, editors: WADT, Lecture Notes in Computer Science 5486, Springer, pp. 71–87. Available at http://dx.doi.org/10.1007/978-3-642-03429-9_6.

6. Krzysztof Czarnecki, J. Nathan Foster, Zhenjiang Hu, Ralf L¨ammel, Andy Sch¨urr & James F. Terwilliger (2009): Bidirectional Transformations: A Cross-Discipline Perspective. In Richard F. Paige, editor: ICMT, Lecture Notes in Computer Science 5563, Springer, pp. 260–283. Available at http://dx.doi.org/10. 1007/978-3-642-02408-5_19.

7. Krzysztof Czarnecki, Ileana Ober, Jean-Michel Bruel, Axel Uhl & Markus V¨olter, editors (2008): Model Driven Engineering Languages and Systems, 11th International Conference, MoDELS 2008, Toulouse, France, September 28 - October 3, 2008. Proceedings. Lecture Notes in Computer Science 5301, Springer. Available at http://dx.doi.org/10.1007/978-3-540-87875-9.

8. Z. Diskin (2007): Mappings, maps, atlases and tables: A formal semantics for associations in UML2. Technical Report CSRG-566, University of Toronto. http://ftp. cs.toronto.edu/pub/reports/csrg/566/TR-566-umlAssons.pdf.

9. Z. Diskin, S. Easterbrook & R. Miller (2008): Integrating schema integration frameworks, algebraically. Technical Report CSRG-583, University of Toronto. http://ftp. cs.toronto.edu/pub/reports/csrg/583/TR-583-schemaIntegr.pdf.

10. Z. Diskin, Y. Xiong, K. Czarnecki, H. Ehrig, F. Hermann & F. Orejas (2011): From State- to Delta-Based Bidirectional Model Transformations: The Symmetric Case. In Whittle et al. [51], pp. 304–318. Available at http://dx.doi.org/10.1007/978-3-642-24485-8_22.

11. Zinovy Diskin (2001): On Modeling, Mathematics, Category Theory and RM-ODP. In Jose A. Moinhos Cordeiro & Haim Kilov, editors: WOODPECKER, ICEIS Press, pp. 38–54.

12. Zinovy Diskin (2002): Visualization vs. Specification in Diagrammatic Notations: A Case Study with the UML. In Mary Hegarty, Bernd Meyer & N. Hari Narayanan, editors: Diagrams, Lecture Notes in Computer Science 2317, Springer, pp. 112–115. Available at http://dx.doi.org/10.1007/3-540-46037-3_15.

13. Zinovy Diskin (2005): Mathematics of Generic Specifications for Model Management. In Laura C. Rivero, Jorge Horacio Doorn & Viviana E. Ferraggine, editors: Encyclopedia of Database Technologies and Applications, Idea Group, pp. 351–366.

14. Zinovy Diskin (2008): Algebraic Models for Bidirectional Model Synchronization. In Czarnecki et al. [7], pp. 21–36. Available at http://dx.doi.org/10.1007/978-3-540-87875-9_2.

15. Zinovy Diskin (2009): Model Synchronization: Mappings, Tiles, and Categories. In Joao M. Fernandes, Ralf Lammel, Joost Visser & Jo˜ao Saraiva, editors: GTTSE, Lecture Notes in Computer Science 6491, Springer, pp. 92–165. Available at http://dx.doi.org/10.1007/978-3-642-18023-1_3.

16. Zinovy Diskin & Boris Cadish (1997): A Graphical Yet Formalized Framework for Specifying View Systems. In: ADBIS, Nevsky Dialect, pp. 123–132. Available at http://www.bcs.org/upload/pdf/ewic_ad97_paper17.pdf.

17. Zinovy Diskin, Steve M. Easterbrook & J¨urgen Dingel (2008): Engineering Associations: From Models to Code and Back through Semantics. In Richard F. Paige & Bertrand Meyer, editors: TOOLS (46), Lecture Notes in Business Information Processing 11, Springer, pp. 336–355. Available at http://dx.doi.org/10.1007/978-3-540-69824-1_19.

18. Zinovy Diskin, Boris Kadish, Frank Piessens & Michael Johnson (2000): Universal Arrow Foundations for Visual Modeling. In Michael Anderson, Peter Cheng & Volker Haarslev, editors: Diagrams, Lecture Notes in Computer Science 1889, Springer, pp. 345–360. Available at http://link.springer.de/link/service/series/0558/bibs/1889/18890345.htm.

19. Zinovy Diskin, Tom Maibaum & Krzysztof Czarnecki (2012): Intermodeling, Queries, and Kleisli Categories. In Juan de Lara & Andrea Zisman, editors: FASE, Lecture Notes in Computer Science 7212, Springer, pp. 163–177. Available at http://dx.doi.org/10.1007/978-3-642-28872-2_12.

20. Zinovy Diskin & Uwe Wolter (2008): A Diagrammatic Logic for Object-Oriented Visual Modeling. Electr. Notes Theor. Comput. Sci. 203(6), pp. 19–41. Available at http://dx.doi.org/10.1016/j.entcs.2008.10.041.

21. Zinovy Diskin, Yingfei Xiong & Krzysztof Czarnecki (2010): Specifying Overlaps of Heterogeneous Models for Global Consistency Checking. In: MoDELS Workshops, Lecture Notes in Computer Science 6627, Springer, pp. 165–179. Available at http://dx.doi.org/10.1007/978-3-642-21210-9_16.

22. Zinovy Diskin, Yingfei Xiong & Krzysztof Czarnecki (2011): From State- to Delta-Based Bidirectional Model Transformations: the Asymmetric Case. Journal of Object Technology 10, pp. 6: 1–25. Available at http://dx.doi.org/10.5381/jot.2011.10.1.a6.

23. H. Ehrig, K. Ehrig, U. Prange & G. Taenzer (2006): Fundamentals of Algebraic Graph Transformation.

24. J. L. Fiadeiro & T. S. E. Maibaum (1995): A Mathematical Toolbox for the Software Architect. In J. Kramer & A. Wolf, editors: 8th Int. Workshop on Software Specification and Design, IEEE CS Press, pp. 46–55.

25. Jose Luiz Fiadeiro (2004): Software Services: Scientific Challenge or Industrial Hype? In Zhiming Liu & Keijiro Araki, editors: ICTAC, Lecture Notes in Computer Science 3407, Springer, pp. 1–13. Available at http://dx.doi.org/10.1007/978-3-540-31862-0_1.

26. Jose Luiz Fiadeiro & T. S. E. Maibaum (1992): Temporal Theories as Modularisation Units for Concurrent System Specification. Formal Asp. Comput. 4(3), pp. 239–272. Available at http://dx.doi.org/10.1007/BF01212304.

27. Jose Luiz Fiadeiro & T. S. E. Maibaum (1995): Interconnecting Formalisms: Supporting Modularity, Reuse and Incrementality. In: SIGSOFT FSE, pp. 72–80. Available at http://doi.acm.org/10.1145/222124.222141.

28. J. N. Foster, M. Greenwald, J. Moore, B. Pierce & A. Schmitt (2007): Combinators for bidirectional tree transformations: A linguistic approach to the view-update problem. ACM Trans. Program. Lang. Syst. 29(3), doi:10.1145/1232420.1232424.

29. Joseph A. Goguen (1991): A Categorical Manifesto. Mathematical Structures in Computer Science 1(1), pp. 49–67. Available at http://dx.doi.org/10.1017/S0960129500000050.

30. Frank Hermann, Hartmut Ehrig, Fernando Orejas, Krzysztof Czarnecki, Zinovy Diskin & Yingfei Xiong (2011): Correctness of Model Synchronization Based on Triple Graph Grammars. In Whittle et al. [51], pp. 668–682. Available at http://dx.doi.org/10.1007/978-3-642-24485-8_49.

31. M. Hofmann, B. Pierce & D.Wagner (2011): Symmetric Lenses. In: POPL. Available at http://doi.acm.org/10.1145/1328438.1328487.

32. M. Johnson, R. Rosebrugh & R. Wood (2002): Entity-relationship-attribute designs and sketches. Theory and Applications of Categories 10(3), pp. 94–112.

33. Michael Johnson & Robert D. Rosebrugh (2007): Fibrations and universal view updatability. Theor. Comput. Sci. 388(1-3), pp. 109–129. Available at http://dx.doi.org/10.1016/j.tcs.2007.06.004.

34. Michael Johnson & Robert D. Rosebrugh (2012): Lens put-put laws: monotonic and mixed. To appear. http://www.easst.org/eceasst.

35. Michael Johnson, Robert D. Rosebrugh & Richard J. Wood (2010): Algebras and Update Strategies. J. UCS 16(5), pp. 729–748. Available at http://dx.doi.org/10.3217/jucs-016-05-0729.

36. Jose Fiadeiro (2004): Categories for Software Engineering. Springer.

37. Stefan Jurack & Gabriele Taentzer (2009): Towards Composite Model Transformations Using Distributed Graph Transformation Concepts. In Andy Sch¨urr & Bran Selic, editors: MoDELS, Lecture Notes in Computer Science 5795, Springer, pp. 226–240. Available at http://dx.doi.org/10.1007/978-3-642-04425-0_17.

38. Hongzhi Liang, Zinovy Diskin, J¨urgen Dingel & Ernesto Posse (2008): A General Approach for Scenario Integration. In Czarnecki et al. [7], pp. 204–218. Available at http://dx.doi.org/10.1007/978-3-540-87875-9_15.

39. M. Makkai (1997): Generalized Sketches as a Framework for Completeness Theorems. Journal of Pure and Applied Algebra 115, pp. 49–79, 179–212, 214–274.

40. Kazutaka Matsuda, Zhenjiang Hu, Keisuke Nakano, Makoto Hamana & Masato Takeichi (2007): Bidirectionalization transformation based on automatic derivation of view complement functions. In Ralf Hinze & Norman Ramsey, editors: ICFP, ACM, pp. 47–58. Available at http://dx.doi.org/10.1145/1291151.1291162.

41. Object Management Group (2008): MOF Query / Views / Transformations Specification 1.0. http://www.omg.org/docs/formal/08-04-03.pdf.

42. Rachel Pottinger & Philip A. Bernstein (2003): Merging Models Based on Given Correspondences. In: VLDB, pp. 826–873. Available at http://www.vldb.org/conf/2003/papers/S26P01.pdf.

43. Alessandro Rossini, , Juan de Lara, Esther Guerra, Adrian Rutle & Yngve Lamo (2012): A Graph Transformation-based Semantics for Deep Metamodelling. In: AGTIVE 2012. Available at http://dx.doi.org/10.1016/j.jlap.2009.10.003. To appear.

44. Alessandro Rossini, Adrian Rutle, Yngve Lamo & Uwe Wolter (2010): A formalisation of the copy-modifymerge approach to version control in MDE. J. Log. Algebr. Program. 79(7), pp. 636–658. Available at http://dx.doi.org/10.1016/j.jlap.2009.10.003.

45. Adrian Rutle, Alessandro Rossini, Yngve Lamo & Uwe Wolter (2010): A Formalisation of Constraint-Aware Model Transformations. In David S. Rosenblum & Gabriele Taentzer, editors: FASE, Lecture Notes in Computer Science 6013, Springer, pp. 13–28. Available at http://dx.doi.org/10.1007/978-3-642-12029-9_2.

46. Adrian Rutle, Alessandro Rossini, Yngve Lamo&UweWolter (2012): A formal approach to the specification and transformation of constraints in MDE. J. Log. Algebr. Program. 81(4), pp. 422–457. Available at http://dx.doi.org/10.1016/j.jlap.2012.03.006.

47. Bran Selic (2008): Personal reflections on automation, programming culture, and model-based software engineering. Autom. Softw. Eng. 15(3-4), pp. 379–391. Available at http://dx.doi.org/10.1007/s10515-008-0035-7.

48. M. Shaw (1996): Three patterns that help explain the development of software engineering (position paper). In: Dagstuhl Workshop on Software Architecture.

49. Stefano Spaccapietra & Christine Parent (1994): View Integration: A Step Forward in Solving Structural Conflicts. IEEE Trans. Knowl. Data Eng. 6(2), pp. 258–274. Available at http://doi.ieeecomputersociety.org/10.1109/69.277770.

50. Perdita Stevens (2010): Bidirectional model transformations in QVT: semantic issues and open questions. Software and System Modeling 9(1), pp. 7–20. Available at http://dx.doi.org/10.1007/s10270-008-0109-9.

51. Jon Whittle, Tony Clark & Thomas K¨uhne, editors (2011): Model Driven Engineering Languages and Systems, 14th International Conference, MODELS 2011, Wellington, New Zealand, October 16-21, 2011. Proceedings. Lecture Notes in Computer Science 6981, Springer. Available at http://dx.doi.org/10.1007/978-3-642-24485-8.

52. Uwe Wolter & Zinovy Diskin: From Indexed to Fibred Semantics The Generalized Sketch File. Technical Report 361, Department of Informatics, University of Bergen, Norway. http://www.ii.uib.no/publikasjoner/texrap/pdf/2007-361.pdf, year = 2007,.

53. Y. Xiong, D. Liu, Z. Hu, H. Zhao, M. Takeichi & H. Mei (2007): Towards automatic model synchronization from model transformations. In: ASE, pp. 164–173. Available at http://doi.acm.org/10.1145/1321631.1321657.

There is an appendix to this article that is not available in this version. To view this additional information, please use the citation on the first page of the chapter.

PART II

MDE IN PRACTICE

CHAPTER 6

INTEGRATING SOFTWARE ARCHITECTURE CONCEPTS INTO THE MDA PLATFORM WITH UML PROFILE

ADEL ALTI, TAHAR KHAMMACI, AND ADEL SMEDA

6.1 INTRODUCTION

Software architecture description provides an abstract representation of components and their interactions of a software system by means of Architecture Description Languages (ADLs)[7]. This technique is called Component-Based Software Architecture (CBSA). CBSA helps software architects to abstract the details of implementation and facilitates the manipulation and the reuse of components.

Recent developments in software techniques, i.e. Component-Based Software Development (CBSD), are based on the assembling prefabricated components. CBSD helps software developers to abstract the details of implementation and to facilitate the manipulation and reuse of components. Actually, there are several middleware platforms (CORBA, J2EE,

This chapter was originally published under the Creative Commons Attribution License or equivalent. Alti A, Khammaci T, and Smeda A. Integrating Software Architecture Concepts into the MDA Platform with UML Profile. Journal of Computer Science 3,10 (2007); pp 793–802.

NET, etc.) focus on developing component-based systems. Middleware as an abstraction layer is completely integrated in middleware platforms for resolving heterogeneity and guaranteeing the transparency communication of distributed components. The major problems consist of:

- The complexity to control interactions of distributed components
- The inter-connections among the components make the architecture complex
- The reuse of components in the implementation level is therefore limited

During the last decade, UML becomes a standard language for specifying, visualizing, constructing and documenting architectural description concepts[10]. However, UML lacks the support for some architectural concepts such as connectors, roles, etc., but it provides a suitable base to define profiles for software architecture and implementation platforms. The notion of transformation is an essential element for Model Driven Architecture (MDA)[8] aiming at automated model transformations. Furthermore, UML profiles can be integrated within an MDA context to define a chain of model transformations, from architectures to implementations[3,8].

Given the central importance of integrating Software Architecture (SA) concepts into MDA platform, concepts of the ADL are considered as PIM and explored in MDA platform as PSM. The different metamodels with different architecture concepts make the transformation rules complex. In this article, we try integrate SA concepts into MDA platform. We also discuss the usefulness and the importance of standard UML profiles in the definition of mapping rules between software architecture elements and its corresponding implementation elements for a given MDA platform. Our strategy focuses on separation of different abstraction levels, translates and integrates SA concepts into MDA platform more easily and more quickly.

The principal contribution of our work is, on the one hand to profit from the advantages of SA concepts including the explicit definition and support of connectors into MDA platform to treat the complex dependences among components and on the other hand to satisfy a higher level of abstraction for MDA platform by adopting high abstraction level from ADL.

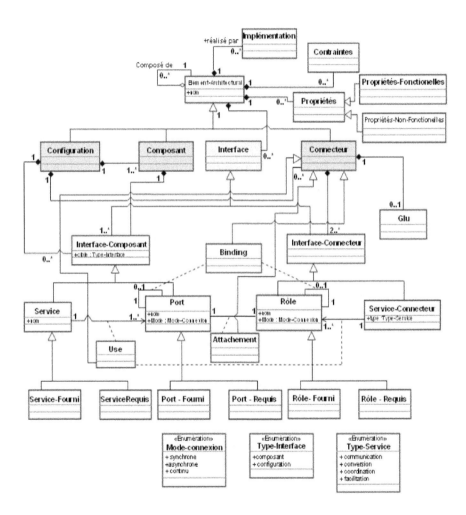

FIGURE 1: Meta model of the COSA approach

6.2 COSA SOFTWARE ARCHITECTURE

Component-Object based Software Architecture (COSA) describes systems as a collection of components that interact with each other using connectors.

Components and connectors have the same level of abstraction and are defined explicitly. COSA takes into account most of operational mechanisms used in the approach object-oriented such as instantiation, inheritance, composition, etc.

Figure 1 presents a meta-model of the COSA approach. COSA supports number of architectural elements including components, connectors and configurations[13]. These architectural elements are types that can be instantiated to construct several architectures. An architectural element can have its own properties and its own constraints.

The key role of configurations in COSA is to abstract the details of different components and connectors. A configuration has a name and defined by an interface (ports and services), which are the visible parts of the configuration and support the interactions among configurations and between a configuration and its components.

Components represent the computational elements and data stores of a system. Each component may have an interface with multiple ports and multiple services. The interface consists of a set of points of interactions between the component and the external world that allow the invocation of the services. A component can be primitive or composite[13].

Connectors represent interactions among components; they provide the link for architectural designs. A COSA connector is mainly represented by an interface and a glue specification[13]. In principle, the interface shows the necessary information about the connector, including the roles, service type that a connector provides (communication, conversion, coordination, facilitation). Connectors can be composite or primitive.

Interfaces in COSA are first-class entities. They provide connection points among architecture elements. Likewise, they define how the communication between these elements can take place. The interface of a component/configuration is called port and the interface of a connector is called role. In addition to ports and roles interfaces have services that express the semantics of the element with which they are associated.

Properties represent additional information (beyond structure) about the parts of an architectural description. Typically they are used to represent anticipated or required extra functional aspects of architectural design. There are two types of properties: functional properties and non-functional properties. Functions that relate to the semantics of a system and represent the requirements are called functional properties. Meanwhile non-functional properties represent additional requirements, such as safety, security, performance and portability.

Constraints are specific properties, they define certain rules and regulations that should be met in order to ensure adherence to intended component and connector uses.

6.3 COSA UML PROFILE

The goal of the COSA profile is to extend UML 2.0 in order to represent COSA architectural concepts. This profile aims to provide a practical way for integrating software architecture in the framework MDA (Model Driven Architecture), which unifies all modelling approaches[12].

A high level profile model provides the basic concepts to define COSA architecture. The meta-model of COSA is described as a UML stereotype package named «COSA». This package defines number of stereotypes: «COSAComponent», «COSAConnector», etc. These stereotypes correspond to the metaclasses of UML meta-model with all tagged values and its OCL 2.0 constraints[11]. Fig. 2 shows this meta-model. The second level permits to describe a particular architecture with the application of the profile. We can also define the value of each tagged value related to each stereotype. In this level the OCL constraints are checked and the final mapped system must conform to the UML profile. The third level presents a set of instances for component, connector and configuration types[12].

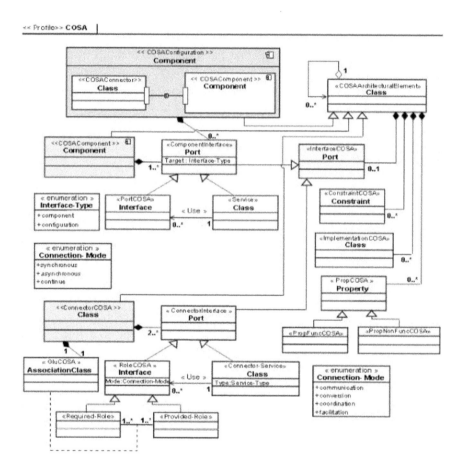

FIGURE 2: The COSA profile

6.4 INTEGRATION OF COSA SOFTWARE ARCHITECTURE CONCEPTS INTO MDA

MDA (Model Driven Architecture) provides means to separate preoccupations of architectural aspects from implementation aspects by supporting the automation of the transformation from modelling to implementation. The main point is the independent of the model definition from the implementation platforms (CORBA, J2EE, etc.).

MDA Platform provides simplicity of development by assembling prefabricated components but it does not support high levels of abstraction, especially composite components and connector concept. Most software architecture models such as COSA support composite components and define connectors explicitly as abstract concepts. Hence, it is very useful to define an automatic transformation from SA model (as an MDA PIM) to platform model (as an MDA PSM). The primary interest is a rapid mapping and smooth integration of software architecture concepts into MDA platforms to achieve a higher level of abstraction and to help solving the problems of interactions among heterogeneous components. Comparing to SA model, platform has concrete aspects and fully realizing designs. MDA takes into account the architecture description language as COSA; while integrating their description in two abstraction levels, at the PIM (Platform Independent Model) and in the PIM transformations toward PSM (Platform Specific Model).

6.4.1 SOFTWARE ARCHITECTURE AT THE PIM LEVEL

PIM metamodel includes all architectural concepts relative to the COSA model. Using the mechanisms provided by UML profiles, we realize PIM transformations toward PSM and integrates all software architecture concepts into MDA platforms

6.4.2 SOFTWARE ARCHITECTURE AT THE PSM LEVEL

The PIM transformations into PSM specify the way of which the MDA platforms (CORBA, J2EE, etc.) using models of COSA architectures contains all intended architectural concepts for exploitation.

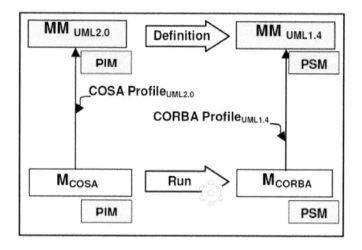

FIGURE 3: COSA (PIM) to CORBA (PSM) transformation

6.5 PROFILE TRANSFORMATION

Let us transform the COSA architecture model as PIM, which conforms
to the COSA-metamodel, into another model of specific MDA platform
which conforms to another metamodel (PSM). PIM and PSM have not the
same architecture concepts. That makes the transformation rules between
models more complex. Consequently, we propose means of direct profile
transformations to facilitate the elaboration of architectural concepts.

The mechanisms provided by UML profiles are very well suited to
describing any implementation platform and the transformation rules between models. The definition of transformation process starts with defining a UML model conforms to the COSA metamodel, next producing automatically an implementation UML platform model as a target platform.
After that, the model is evaluated by the platform profile.

We need to define the mapping rules from elements of the PIM to elements
of PSM that make up the platform profile. The idea of elaborating these

rules is to take each UML element of a PIM and find its corresponding PSM (the same semantically UML elements of PIM). Each element of transformation contains OCL expression [11], which permits transformation between the elements of COSA UML profile and platform UML profile and a filter to permit distinction between them. In addition, if the UML profile of the platform includes the specification of element relationships, then the transformation may be specified using operations deduced from theses relationships.

6.6 ILLUSTRATED TRANSFORMATION: FROM COSA (PIM) TO CORBA (PSM)

To illustrate how our strategy of mapping can be used, we apply it to COSA (PIM) to CORBA (PSM) transformation. Figure 3 presents the process of transformation from COSA software architecture to CORBA standard platform.

CORBA is a standard platform that provides simplicity of development by assembling prefabricated components but it does not support high levels of abstraction, especially composite components and connector concept. Meanwhile COSA supports composite components and defines connectors explicitly as abstract concepts.

Therefore, it is very useful to define an automatic transformation from COSA UML profiled (as an MDA PIM) to CORBA UML profiled (as an MDA PSM). The primary interest is a rapid mapping and smooth integration of COSA concepts into CORBA platform to achieve a higher level of abstraction and to help solving the problems of interactions among CORBA components. Compared to COSA, CORBA has concrete aspects and fully realizing designs.

COSA to CORBA transformation must follow incremental process that generates CORBA concepts from its corresponding COSA. This process starts with defining a UML model conforms to the COSA metamodel, next producing automatically a UML CORBA model as a target platform. After that, the model is evaluated by the CORBA UML profile. Figure 3 presents the process of transformation from COSA software architecture to CORBA platform.

TABLE 1: COSA-CORBA correspondence

COSA concepts	CORBA concepts
«COSAConfiguration» Component	«CORBAModule» Package
«COSAComponent» Component	«CORBAHome» Class
«COSAConnector» Class	
«Component-Interface» Port	«CORBAComponent» Class
«Connector-Interface» Port	
«COSAPort» Interface	«CORBAInterface» is synchronous
«COSARole» Interface	«CORBAEvent» is asynchronous
«Service» Class	«CORBAEvent» Class
«Connector-Service» Class	
«COSAGlu» Association Class	«IDL-Operation» Operation
«COSAUse» Delegate connector	«CORBAComponent» with two interfaces provided and required
«COSABinding» Delegate connector	
«COSAAttachment» Assembly	connector
«COSAProp» Property	«IDL-Attribute» Attribute

6.6.1 CORRESPONDENCE CONCEPTS

COSA UML profile[12] and CORBA UML profile[9] are based on two different UML meta-models; we need to map each COSA concept into CORBA concepts. The COSA-CORBA correspondence can be deduced easily from the same semantics between UML elements. COSA components are represented by UML 2.0 components. Since UML 2.0 component corresponds to a UML 1.4 class (the name of the class is the name of the component), a UML 2.0 component «COSAComponent» may be transformed to UML class «CORBAHome». COSA connectors, which are abstractions that include mechanisms of communication, are not defined explicitly in CORBA platform; we tried to find the closest CORBA concepts semantically. COSA connectors are represented by UML 2.0 classes. Since UML 2.0 class matches UML 1.4 class, so UML 2.0 Class «COSAConnector» is mapped to UML class «CORBAHome». Table 1 shows the concepts of COSA and their CORBA correspondence.

```
rule COSAComponent2CORBAHome {
from inComp : UML2!Component
(inComp. hasStereotype('COSAComponent'))
to outHome:UML14!Class (
name <- inComp.name,
feature<-inComp.getCOSAProps(),
constraint<-inComp.getCOSAConsts(),
clientDependency <-inComp.getCOSAImps(),
stereotype <- 'CORBAHome'
)
}
```

FIGURE 4: Mapping rule from COSA component to CORBA home using ATL

6.6.2 MAPPING RULES

Mapping rules must follow COSA to CORBA correspondence concepts. To elaborate each mapping rule we affect all elements relationships of source model (COSA) to its corresponding relationships on the target model (CORBA).

For example, COSA components, which are abstraction that includes mechanisms of computation, are represented by UML 2.0 components. Since UML 2.0 component corresponds to a UML 1.4 class (the name of the class is the name of the component), a UML 2.0 component «COSAComponent» may be transformed to UML class «CORBAHome». We include operations for acquiring attached elements   (getCOSAProps for acquired component properties, getCOSAImps for acquired component implementations and getCOSAContsraints for acquired component constraints) because COSA components contain only properties, implementations and constraints and then we impose this to the corresponding CORBA element (Fig. 4). This rule is expressed in ATL (Atlas Transformation Language)[2] .

COSA connectors, which are abstractions that include mechanisms of communication, are not defined explicitly in CORBA platform; we tried to find the closest CORBA concepts semantically. COSA connectors are represented by UML 2.0 classes (Fig. 5). Since UML 2.0 class matches UML 1.4 class, so UML 2.0 Class «COSAConnector» is mapped to UML class «CORBAHome».

```
rule COSAComponent2CORBAHome {
 from inComp : UML2!Component
 (inComp.hasStereotype('COSAComponent'))
 to outHome:UML14!Class (
 name <- inComp.name,
 feature<-inComp.getCOSAProps(),
 constraint<-inComp.getCOSAConsts(),
 clientDependency <-inComp.getCOSAImps(),
 stereotype <- 'CORBAHome'
 )
 }
```

FIGURE 5: Mapping rule from COSA connector to CORBA home using ATL

```
rule COSAPort2CORBAInterface{
 from InPort:UML2!Interface
 (InPort.hasStereotype('Required-Port')
  or(InPort.hasStereotype('Provided-Port')
 to utIntf:UML14!Interface(
 name <- InPort.name,
 namespace<-thisModule.CORBAModule,
 )
 do{
  let tp:String = InPort.getStereotype()
  if InPort.getPropObj(tp, 'Mode')=#synchnous
     outIntf.stereotype<-'CORBAInterface'
  else
  outIntf.stereotype<- 'CORBAEventPort'
  feature<-inComp.getCOSAProps(),
 }
```

FIGURE 6: Mapping rule from COSA port to CORBA interface using ATL

```
rule COSAConfiguration2CORBAModule {
 from inConfig :UML2!Component
   (Config.hasStereotype('COSAConfiguration'))
 to outHome:UML14!Package (
  name <- Config.name,
  feature<-inComp.getCOSAProps(),
  constraint<-inComp.getCOSAConsts(),
  clientDependency <-inComp.getCOSAImps(),
  namespace<- thisModule.CORBAModel,
  ownedElement<- Config.ownedMember,
  stereotype <-'CORBAModule'
 )
}
```

FIGURE 7: Mapping rule from COSA connector to CORBA home using ATL.

```
System client-server
{
   Class Component Server {
     Interface {
         Connection-Mode =synchronous
         Ports provide {provide :}
         }
         Constraints {max-clients=1;}
   }
   Class Component Client {
     Interface {
         Connection-Mode =synchronous
         Ports request {request :}
         }
   }
   Class Connector RPC {
      Interface {
         Connection-Mode =synchronous
         Roles provide {callee :}
         Roles request {caller :}
      }
      Glue {....}
   }
}
```

FIGURE 8: The Client-Server system in COSA

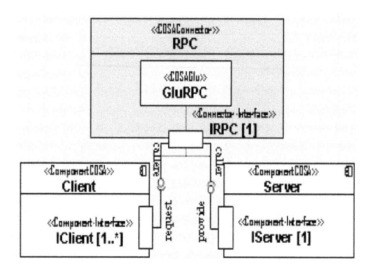

FIGURE 9: The Client-Server system using COSA UML 2.0 profile

COSA component/connector interfaces match UML 2.0 ports. Ports correspond to UML classes (name of the class is name of the port). So, a UML class (that represents a UML 2.0 component) must be attached to another class (that represents ports). Every class that represents a port (a UML class corresponds to «CORBAComponent») must be attached to a UML class that represents a component or a connector (components and connectors correspond to «CORBAHome»). COSA provided ports/roles (or required ports/roles) are transformed to facets (or receptacles) for synchronous communication or to event sinks (or event sources) for asynchronous communication (Fig. 6). This rule is expressed in ATL (Atlas Transformation Language)[2].

An important aspect of COSA architecture is to offer a graph of component and connector types called configurations. A UML 2.0 component can contain subcomponents and subclasses. COSA configurations are represented by UML 2.0 components. Since UML 2.0 component matches UML 1.4 Class (Fig. 7), UML 2.0 Component «COSAConfiguration» is mapped into UML class «CORBAModule».

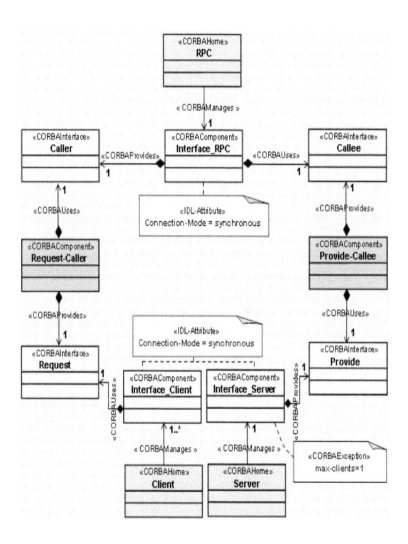

FIGURE 10: The Client-Server system using COSA UML 2.0 profile

Specific COSA connectors such as Use, Binding and Attachment are mapped into UML class (which is «CORBAComponent») and bound a provided interface (or event sink) into required interface (or event source). The principle of transformation using COSA and CORBA profiles is based on mapping each element in the COSA UML 2.0 profile into an element of the CORBA UML 1.4 profile.

6.6.3 IMPLEMENTING THE TRANSFORMATION

To illustrate how the COSA-CORBA transformation can be used, we apply it to the Client-Server system. Figure 8, shows the description of the system using COSA and Figure 9 presents the system after applying the profile. Figure 10 shows the architecture in CORBA after applying the transformation.

COSA to CORBA transformation is implemented in IBM Rational Software Modeler (RSM) for Eclipse 3.1. This visual modeling tool supports creating and managing UML models for software applications independent of their programming language. It has been used to define profiles for different applications, to convert meta-models and models into .ecore files and to elaborate the transformation from a source model to a target model. The Plug-In is developed in four steps:

- The meta-model of COSA (and CORBA) with all tagged values and OCL constraints is defined by the UML 2.0 (UML 1.4) profile
- The COSA-CORBA transformation is created. This transformation describes how COSA model elements are matched and navigated, to create and initialize the elements of CORBA models
- The meta-model of COSA (and CORBA) with all tagged values and OCL constraints is defined by the UML 2.0 (UML 1.4) profile
- COSA to CORBA transformation is configured and executed. The elaborated CORBA model is evaluated by its profile

COSA-CORBA transformation is defined using ATL transformation language[2] of RSM. Figure 11 shows the meta-models COSA and CORBA (in the left side) and the mapping rules (in the right side).

For the client-server example, we elaborated the client-server system by a components diagram and OCL constraints. The model is validated by COSA profile. The COSA-CORBA transformation is applied to the COSA

FIGURE 11: COSA-CORBA transformation

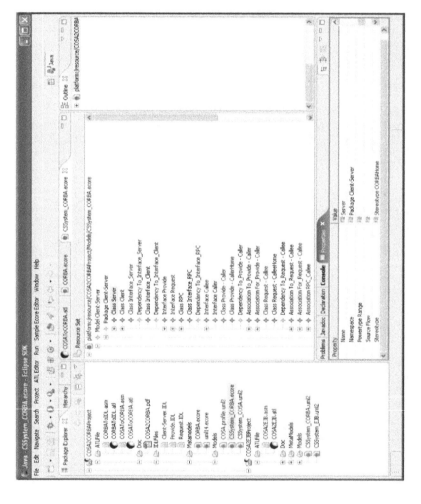

FIGURE 12: The CORBA model of Client-Server system

model for elaborating its correspondent CORBA model. Figure 12 shows the applied CORBA model of Client-Server system.

6.7 RELATED WORK

In[4], Garlan points out that the world of software development and the context in which software is being used are changing in significant ways and these changes promise to have a major impact on how architecture is practiced. Rodrigues at al.[14], defined a mapping rules to transform an ACME description into a CORBA IDL specification. They focused on composing systems by exploring the ACME extensions facilities to include input/output ports in an ACME specification. They transformed almost every thing as an IDL interface, therefore, they did not really profit from the concepts available in CORBA IDL. ACCORD RNTL Project[1] is an open and distributed environment that aims to ease assembling components. It defines a semi-automated matching of concepts and an automated transformation of ACCORD model into CCM. This work is based on UML profiles to represent ACCORD and CCM architectural concepts. It defines an intermediate filter model for adapting transformation process. Then assembling components are defined using XML files, this makes it difficult to promote components reuse. Manset at al.[5], defined a formal architecture-centric model-driven development (ACMDD) process on top of the powerful architecture description languages and platform, ArchWare. They used a formal semantics for building architectural models and refining to multilayered architecture specifications. Marcos at al.[6], integrated true architectural design aspects in MDA architecture and followed a transformation approach on the level of architecture models from Platform- Independent Architecture models (PIAs) free from all technological constraints to a Platform-Specific Architecture models (PSAs) depending on specific needs and technologies. They studied the integration software architecture as a new aspect at PIM and PSM levels into MDA for better manageability and administration. Its approach allows a well separation between differentes aspects, but disagrees in the more integration of architecture concepts and architectural styles available in ADLs. More recently, in[15] Sanchez proposed an automatic transformation between requirement and architecture models for achieving a comfortable MDA framework.

Our approach of profile transformations can be seen as a base for mapping architectural concepts into an implicational plat-form. It offers number of advantages compared to related works, including:

- Fast mapping and smooth integration of most of SA concepts especially the concepts that are not defined explicitly such as connector, configuration, roles, to achieve a complete MDA framework
- Satisfying the higher level of abstraction of MDA plate-form by adopting high abstraction level from the UML Profile
- Automatic elaboration rules at the transformation process by using the same UML meta-models

However, our approach does not include the description architectural styles available and the capacity of automatic elaboration of the correspondence specification concepts between MDA PIM and MDA PSM meta-models for the transformation process.

6.8 CONCLUSION

In this research, we propose the integration of software architecture concepts into MDA platform and also we define a strategy of direct transformation using UML profile by mapping software architecture model and platform models in UML meta-model then elaborate correspondences concepts between results UML meta-models in mapping rules. We illustrated our strategy using an automatic transformation from COSA concepts to CORBA concepts. This strategy allows the mapping of COSA software architecture concepts that are specified in the UML profile (PIM) into CORBA platform (PSM).Related benefits of profile transformations is a higher abstraction level of MDA platform and more easily and more quickly integrating architectural concepts within MDA.

For our future work, we are considering the mapping at the meta-meta level, i.e. from an architectural meta-meta model into MOF. We are also considering the transformation in the other MDA platform and in the other SA-based.

REFERENCES

1. ACOORD RNTL Project, www.infres.enst.fr.
2. ATLAS group LINA. and INRIA Nantes, 2007. ATL: Atlas Transformation Language. ATL User Manual version 7.0.
3. Fuentes-Fernández, L. and A. Vallecillo-Moreno, 2004. An Introduction to UML Profiles. European J. Inform. Prof., 7 (2): 6-13.
4. Garlan, D., 2000. Software Architecture: A Roadmap. Proc. of 22nd International Conference on Software Eng., pp: 91-101.
5. Manset, D., R.H.,Verjus and F. Oquendo, 2006. A formal architecture-centric, model-driven approach for the automatic generation of grid applications. Proc. of the 8th Int. Conf. on Enterprise Inform. Systems.
6. Marcos, E., C.J., Acua and C.E. Cuesta, 2006. Integrating Software Architecture into a MDA Framework. Proc. of the 3th European Workshop on SA (EWSA'2006), France, pp: 128-143.
7. Medvidovic, N. and R.N. Taylor, 2000. A classification and comparison framework for software architecture description languages. IEEE Trans. Software Eng., 26: 70-93.
8. Model Driven Architecture, www.omg.org/mda.
9. OMG, 2002. UML profile for CCM: Revised Submission. document mars/03-01-01
10. OMG, October 2004. UML 2.0 Superstructure Specification: Revised Final Adopted Specification.www.omg.org/docs/ptc/04-10-02.pdf.
11. OMG, June 2005. UML OCL 2.0 Specification: Revised Final Adopted Specification. www.omg.org/docs/ptc/05-06-06.pdf.
12. Alti, A., T. Khammaci and A. Smeda, 2007. Representing and Formally Modeling COSA software architecture with UML 2.0 profile. IRECOS Review., 2 (1): 30-37.
13. Oussalah, M., A. Smeda and T. Khammaci, 2004. An explicit definition of connectors for component based software architecture. Proc. of the 11th IEEE Conference Engineering of Computer Based Systems (ECBS'2004), Czech Republic, pp: 44-51.
14. Rodrigues, M.N., L. Lucena and T. Batista, 2004. From Acme to CORBA: Bridging the Gap. First European Workshop on Software Architecture (EWSA'04)., pp: 103-114.
15. Sánchez, P., J. Magno, L. Fuentes, A. Moreira and J. Araújo, 2006. Towards MDD Transformation from AORE into AOA, Proc. of the 3th European Workshop on Software Architecture, pp: 159-174.

CHAPTER 7

MODEL-DRIVEN ENGINEERING USING UML: A PRAGMATIC APPROACH

LIVIU GABRIEL CRETU

7.1 INTRODUCTION

More than a a decade ago, Object Management Group (OMG) proposed the Model Driven Architecture (MDA™) [1] to deal with the separation of platform dependent and independent aspects in information systems and the transformation rules between them. Since then, MDA has become a well established discipline both in practice and research in information systems and software engineering. However, since MDA is a proprietary trade mark specifying the process and artifacts to be used, people cannot easily modify and adapt to their needs while still using the brand name. A similar situation is, for example, the use of RESTful services and Web APIs where the first imposes strict rules on creating HTTP-based services while the later is just general enough to cover any kind of services acces-

This chapter was originally published as an open access article. Republished with permission by the author. Cretu LG. Model Driven Engineering Using UML: A Pragmatic Approach. International Journal of Computer Science and Information Technologies *4,2 (2013); pp. 309–314.*

sible via HTTP. As a consequence, today we have multiple acronyms in use for model-driven paradigm:

- MDA—Model Driven Architecture—a process with three translation steps: Computational Independent Model (CIM) to Platform Independent Model (PIM) to Platform Specific Model (PSM) and finally to the generated code;
- MDE—Model Driven Engineering [2]—the usual general term used instead of MDA. It proposes the same approach of modelling multiple abstraction layers and translation rules as MDA, only there is no recommendation regarding the number and content of these layers. MDE is being increasingly promoted as the discipline to manage separation and combination of various kinds of concerns in software or data engineering.
- MDD—Model Driven Development—focuses more on code generation instead of multiple modelling layers. It is usually seen as a two steps process: from model to code.

This paper will present an MDE method specifically designed to seamlessly adopt the principles of model-driven paradigm within the day-to-day software development process using the de-facto standard in software modelling: UML. However obvious it may sound that UML should be used with MDE, the literature mainly offers domainspecific model-driven examples or partial solutions to specific issues. Actually, one cannot easily find a step-bystep guide in MDA/MDE with UML. And this is the main rationale of this paper. We will start with a short literature review, then the MDE with UML method will be presented along with a list of useful MDE shortcuts, and finally an example will validate the proposed method.

7.2 MODEL-DRIVEN ENGINEERING PRACTICES

A quick literature review on the subject of MDA/MDE reveals two main areas of research:

1. Domain-Specific Languages (DSL)
2. Meta-models and UML profiles

Most of the domain engineering methodology emphasizes domain modelling as an important mechanism for the development of software systems made of software products (components) with similar architecture. Domain- Specific Languages are specifically tailored to directly represent the concepts of an application domain as programming primitives. Domain-specific languages lift the platform's level, reduce the underlying APIs' surface area, and let knowledgeable end users live in their data without complex software-centric models [8]. We can find DSLs combined with MDA principles used in the development of different types of software. For example, HyperDe is presented in [4] as an environment that supports the design and implementation of web-based applications combining model-based development with domain specific languages for flexible and rapid prototyping of applications. Moreover, in [5] one may find an interesting approach where MDE is applied to compose "programs" written in different DSLs, which will enable the use of the DSL approach to build applications spanning different domains.

The second widely recognized approach is to put metamodels at the very base of the MDA principles [6] and to incorporate them in the software engineering process using manual or automated model-to-model transformers. Metamodels are intended to define a set of related concepts and each meta-model defines a language for describing a specific domain of interest. The associated transformers use this language to generate new models from input models by interpreting the concepts in the meta-model.

Since UML is the standard in software engineerign, the first question is how can one define meta-models with this language, associate them with domain models and apply MDE transformations. In UML, a model element may specify a relationship to the meta-model elements by means of stereotypes and tagged-values. These are modelled using UML profiles. Profiles can play a particularly important role in describing the platform model and the transformation rules between models according to MDE principles. XMI [7] may then be used to transfer metamodels from one project to another, no matter the modelling tool, as long as it is UML based.

Regarding the usage of UML with model-driven paradigm , there are some works showing the natural relationship between UML profiles and the meta-modelling phase in MDA [9, 10] while a large number of papers are proposing domain specific profiles such as for critical infrastructures [11], distributed service models[12], embedded systems [13], web services [14], semantic web services [15] etc. An important number of papers are also dedicated to special languages needed to define and execute MDA Transformers such as in [15].

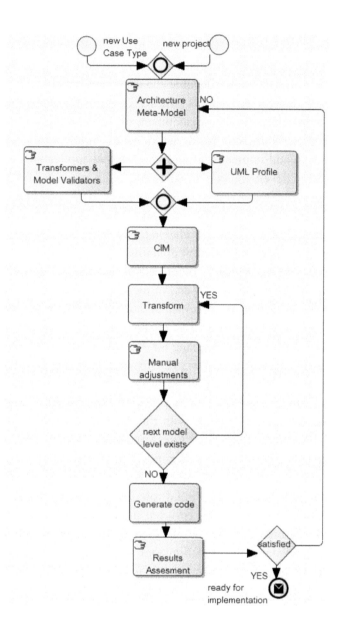

FIGURE 1: The MDE process using UML

7.3 A PRAGMATIC METHOD FOR MDE USING UML

MDE can leverage the software development process only if the latter does follow a set of well-defined principles:

- Reference architecture—the system has a clear architecture which both is well documented and a development framework has been built around it. This will provide the meta-model for the new systems. In other words, the development team will never have to raise any questions of the kind: "where should I put this piece of code?"
- Typed Use Cases—development tasks are usually organized around Use Cases and if the Use Case is associated with a meta-model (also known as pattern) then we call it a Typed Use Case (TUC). Typed Use Cases lead to typed development tasks for which the domain model abstractions as well as the software pattern to be implemented are known. In these cases the implementation can be estimated with very high level of accuracy, both in time and quality of the work.
- Just-enough automation—although MDE does not necessary mean any automation, this is one of the usual goals. In such case the development process automation will not have to generate 100% functional code. The trick is to automate the routine development work and to let the designers and developers concentrate on specific details or some behavioural exotic algorithms. The automation has to focus on two main areas: productivity and bug-free product. For example, generating the main interfaces as well as concrete class structures with inheritance to some abstract behaviour may lead to a productivity boost for junior developers as they will easily add the specific behaviour only in the right place. Not to mention they will also quickly learn the structure of the code for that type of Use Case.

Once we have a reference architecture and TUCs we can apply MDE principles with UML, and even automate the development process, taking into account the pragmatic goal of just-enough automation. UML offers two extension mechanisms very useful for MDE: stereotypes and tagged values. Stereotypes are used to associate UML artifacts with your own meta-model artifacts. Thus, using stereotypes one can further classify Classes, Use Cases, Relationships, and so on in order to bridge the gap between UML meta-model and the target system's meta-model. Tagged values are very useful to specifically define custom association types or other meta-data which have a meaning for an external processor. Both stereotypes and tagged values can be packaged into profiles to create the software development meta-model based on the reference architecture.

The UML-based MDE process is illustrated in figure 1. We still use the MDA artifacts (CIM, PIM, PSM) for convenience. However, since it is an iterative process, there is no restriction on the number of modelling layers.

In short, the UML-based MDE process starts with a meta-model for the system to be developed. This metamodel is derived from the reference architecture of the system. Then, a UML profile (stereotypes and tags) is created together with a set of rules to guide the creation of CIMs and the subsequent transformations. Finally, the stereotypes and tagged values are used to create the individual CIMs (or domain CIMs), models are validated and the transformations are applied (manually or automated).

7.3.1 THE UML-BASED MDE PROCESS

There are 4 phases of this process:

1. Phase 1: create the meta-model based on the reference architecture. The meta-model has three parts: a) an UML profile whose elements will be the labels of the software artifacts to be obtained from each UML element annotated with that stereotype; b) profile usage rules to guide the association of stereotypes and tagged-values to individual CIMs; c) transformation rules to guide the transformation of one model into another. For example, a Use Case may have a kind of relationship to the domain classes in order to specify the input/ output parameters. Then, the transformation rules specifically state how the Use Case will be transformed into a Service (PIM), then into a Web Service, RESTful Service or EJB Service (PSM). If MDE automation is the goal, then a collection of Transformers is also created in this phase.

2. Phase 2: the business analyst will create the domain analysis CIMs using standard UML elements annotated with the meta-model elements defined in Phase 1. The number and the types of diagrams to be used in this phase will be derived from the reference architecture of the system to be developed. The only two important things

to note are the followings: UML elements have to be annotated with meta-model stereotypes and the relationships needed by the MDE process have to be properly defined (based on the same meta-model elements) in order to generate the required modelling or code artifacts. In this phase the developers may also be involved to enrich the models for the MDE Transformers. A set of MDE shortcuts, as defined below, may be used.

3. Phase 3: transformation rules are applied (manually or automated) to generate PIMs and then PSMs and finally the code. Even if the process is automated, specific manual adjustments may be needed before each transformation. Also, model validators should be defined to check the metamodel semantics associated with the domain CIM.

4. Phase 4 consists in the analysis of the results, progress assessment, and refinements with the final goal to obtain a higher degree of control and predictability of the development process. Among many tools, CMMI [18] proposes one of the most trusted methods to measure this kind of progress.

7.3.2 B. MDE SHORTCUTS

Code generation implies working with highly formalized models, thus leaving no place for ambiguity. However our experience shows that strict MDA compliance may be quite undesirable in practice. Not only that the distinction between PIM and PSM is vague for most of the developers (mainly because they are using the same technologies and platforms for a long time) but also the time spent to put the Transformers stack in synchronization one with another may simply not be accepted by the management team.

To address these kinds of pragmatic issues, the MDE method proposed in this paper takes into consideration what we have called MDE Shortcuts. An MDE Shortcut may be defined as a systematic usage of links between elements appearing in different models for different viewpoints (e.g. a CIM element may have a link to some PIM element). There are three valid such shortcuts which may be taken into consideration:

1. A CIM element may have a link to PIM or PSM elements (even if the later may have been obtained by means of transformations and the link is added afterwards, just before generating the next model). This shortcut is obviously needed when one needs to re-use some existing components or services or add new modules to an existing system. The natural way to go is to reverse engineer the code to PSM. If one will have no time to define the required reverse-transformers till the CIM level, one will surely still need to use the existing classes in order to create the new extension of the system. Another scenario for this shortcut comes from the natural order of steps in software development: having the concept of a Service clarified, the first step will be to implement the Service then the Client (usually the user interface) that will connect to the Service using the provided interface. When one describes the Client's behaviour in CIM, there are two options: a) to link somehow the Client model elements (CIM) to the generated or re-engineered Service interface in PSM, or b) to add tagged-values specifying the concrete interfaces to be used later in the transformation process. In practice, we have found that the first approach seems more appropriate as it provides a unified way for models transformations (first iteration generates the Service models and code, then the second iteration comes back to Client CIM and adds the links to the new Services).

2. A PIM element may include PSM concepts – since CIM describes the business logic from the business viewpoint, to be able to generate some code one will have to enrich the model with enough technical information needed by transformers. This process is very much like writing code: no room for ambiguity. As a consequence, the CIM usually needs to incorporate enough information for direct code generation. Moving this information from one model to another may become quite a risky and error prone job. As such, the PSM operation implementation can be generated from the beginning (CIM-to-PIM Transformer) and attached to the corresponding class until the final code generation (usually as a tagged value or a scenario implementation UML element).

3. Developers may interfere with the MDE multiple transformation steps in order to add necessary features to PIM/PSM models, before code generation. This way, specific adjustments that have not yet been captured by Transformers will bring the opportunity to obtain 100% executable code.

By using MDE Shortcuts the number of Transformers (and consequently the eventual logical mappings errors) may decrease dramatically, while still keeping enough models to coherently describe the software from all the required perspectives. Following this pragmatic MDE approach proved to bring the promised productivity boost in practice.

7.4 MDE WITH UML APPLIED

In order to validate the proposed method we take the example of a business application which needs to implement various business processes. We will name it the Alpha system and we will take a simple example of a business process shown in fig 2. It is an over-simplified order management process where each morning a service gathers all the orders received by means of different channels (e-mail, web site, other systems), the orders

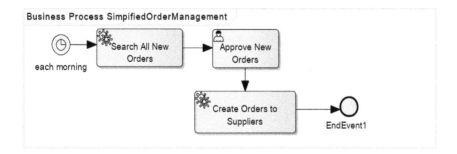

FIGURE 2: Simplified Order Process using BPMN.

then have to be approved by the manager using some web interface and finally the missing items have to be ordered further from the suppliers. To model the Alpha system we use both BPMN and UML since the modelling tool (Enterprise Architect from Sparx Systems) offers a flexible platform and a powerful transformation language to work with both notations. However, UML classical activity diagrams may be also an option with satisfactory results.

7.4.1 THE REFERENCE ARCHITECTURE

According to the process described earlier, we define the reference architecture for the Alpha system (fig 3) as a message based system involving business rules (BR) and business process management (BPM) engines, and an enterprise service bus (ESB).

Extended Domain Model: models the internal structure and behaviour of one service. It includes:

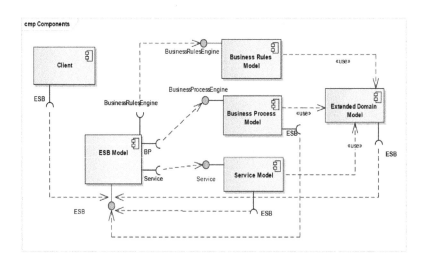

FIGURE 3: The reference architecture for the Alfa system

1. Domain Model: this is one of most used pattern from Martin Fowler's [17] collection of patterns for enterprise system architectures.
2. Message Model: defines the messages the service may respond to. Each Message corresponds to a business Use Case or Use Case Scenario encapsulating the input data (parameters), necessary for the service execution,.

Service Model: includes those classes that expose the functionality to the world. We call these Domain Services to distinguish them from other services (ESB, business rules, BPM). There is only one public method a Service interface exposes: handleMessage (message:Message). Thus, we call such a service a MessageHanlder. Routing one message to the corresponding processing Service will be the ESB's responsibility.

ESB Model: includes components, language and runtime to implement a messaging system, namely to create the configuration of channels, endpoints, routing and transformations to achieve ad-hoc services orchestrations.

Business Process Model: provide components, language and runtime to implement a business process management system.

Business Rules Model: provides components, language and runtime to declaratively define business rules, to associate them as pre-conditions or post-conditions for certain Messages and to execute them against that Message instances when they occur. By separating business rules in a different model, this architecture creates the opportunity for dynamically change the rule set to be applied to one Message instance, depending on the environmental variables accessible from execution context.

Client Model: represents the outside world of the Extended Domain Model. Usually the client refers to the graphical user interface of a system (the presentation layer) or another application/service. Clients execute system's behaviour by sending Messages to the ESB. Thus the client will become dependent only of the Domain Model not the Service Model.

7.4.2 THE MDE PROCESS

We apply the MDE process defined in the III.A section above for this reference architecture.

Phase 1: the business analyst will create a CIM version agreed by the customer. Three models will be created in this phase: the Business Process Model, the Domain Model and the Business Rules Model. The Message Model and the Service Model will be generated later on. According to the reference architecture we may create an UML profile as depicted in figure 4. For demonstration purposes, the profile has been simplified to the minimum number of elements needed here. To note: there are two specialized types of <<Service>>UseCases, namely <<Search>> and <<CRUD>> (Create, Read, Update, Delete) with the corresponding message handlers (according to the reference architecture). Dependencies of types Input and Output will be used to specify the input/output parameters for some Use-Cases (e.g. <<Search>> and <<CRUD>>.

Table 1 shows some of the most important transformation rules we have defined.

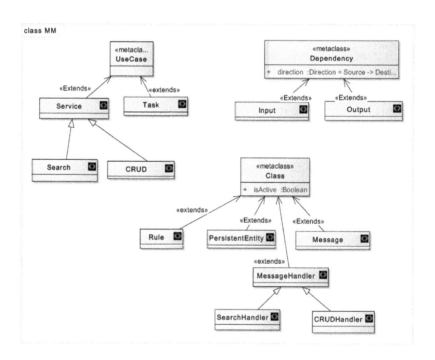

FIGURE 4: The UML profile for the reference architecture

TABLE 1: Transformation Rules for the Alpha System

		Transformations
	CIM	CIM
1	BPMN Service Activity	<<Service>> UseCase
2	BPMN Human Task	<<Task>> UseCase
	CIM	PIM
	<<Service>> UseCase	<<Message>> Class
		<<MessageHanlder>> Class implementing the Service interface
	<<Search>>UseCase	<<Message>> Class
		<<SearchHandler>>Class
	<<CRUD>>UseCase	<<Message>> Class
		<<CRUDHanlder>>Class
	<<PersistentEntity>>Class	<<PersistentEntity>>Class
	PIM	<<JavaEE> PSM
	<<Message>>Class	<<Message>Class
	<<MessageHandler>>Class	<<EJB>>Class implementing the Service interface from reference architecture
	<<PersistentEntity>>Class	<<PersistentEntity>>Class with the Java Persistence API annotations

Phase 2:the business analyst develops the CIM using the right stereotypes (figure 5). As seen in Table 1, we have one CIM-to-CIM transformation: from BPMN process to UseCase diagram. Once the UseCases are generated, the business analyst may change the <<Service>> stereotype to one of the specialized UseCase types: <<Search>> or <<CRUD>>. This is the case here with the UseCases derived from "Search All New Orders" and "Create Orders to Suppliers" BPMN activities (figure 2). Also in this phase the domain model is created and the links between some UseCases and Classes in order to specify the input and output for some of the UseCases according to the metamodel specification.

Phase 3 consists in executing the transformations and performing the manual adjustments if needed. Based on the rules defined in Table 1, a Transformer may be crated to automate the transformation activity. An example of the result may be found in figure 6. As for the manual adjust-

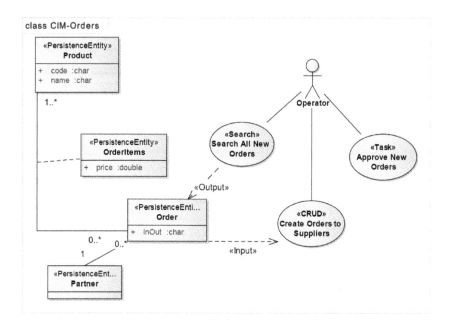

FIGURE 5: CIM for Order Process using stereotypes from Alpha meta-model.

ments, we apply the MDE shortcuts described earlier. In this example, one manual adjustment was needed: since the <<Input>> and <<Output>> stereotypes are based on Dependency UML meta-class, there is no option to specify the multiplicity of the relationship. Thus, a manual intervention is needed to correct the attribute type of the generated message type. In the specific case of Create Orders to Suppliers, the input may refer to multiple received orders and the output may be a collection of orders to different suppliers.

7.5 CONCLUSIONS

This paper introduced a well defined method for MDE using UML. The short literature review revealed there is strong orientation, both in research and practice, towards model-driven paradigm. The argument for this work has been the acknowledgement that there is still a lack of such complete

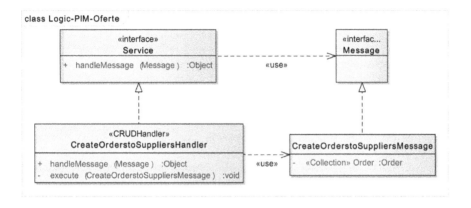

FIGURE 6: PIM for Order Process generated from CIM (partial).

guidelines to show how to adopt MDE principles in day-to-day software development business.

We have shown that mastering the relationship between software architecture and UML profiles leads to domainagnostic MDE process. This is the key aspect which positions this paper as a distinct approach in literature since we have seen a large number of works focusing on domainspecific MDE solutions. The so-called MDE shortcuts has been also presented as valid actions to reduce the number and complexity of MDE Transformers while pushing the level of productivity even further. An example has been provided to better illustrate the process and to validate the method.

REFERENCES

1.   OMG. MDA Guide version 1.0.1. OMG document omg/2003-06-01, 2003

2. J. Bézivin, "sNets: A First Generation Model Engineering Platform", in: Lecture Notes in Computer Science, Berlin, Germany: Springer, 2005 vol. 3844, pp. 169—181.

3. O. Pastor, S. España, J. I. Panach and Nathalie Aquino, "Model- Driven Development", Informatik-Spektrum, Volume 31, Issue 5, pp. 394-407, October 2008.

4. D. A. Nunes and D. Schwabe, "Rapid prototyping of web applications combining domain specific languages and model driven design," in Proceedings of the 6th international conference on Web engineering, 2006, ACM, New York, USA, pp. 153-160.

5. J. Estublier, G. Vega, A. D. Ionita, "Composing Domain-Specific Languages for Wide-Scope Software Engineering Applications", Model Driven Engineering Languages and Systems, ser. Lecture Notes in Computer Science, Berlin, Germany: Springer 2005, vol 3713, pp 69-83.

6. J. Bézivin, "In Search of a Basic Principle for Model Driven Engineering", European Journal for the Informatics Professional, Vol. V, No. 2, April 2004.

7. XML Model Interchange (XMI), Object Management Group standard, 1998, http://www.omg.org/docs/ad/98-10-05.pdf

8. T. Dave, "MDA: Revenge of the Modelers or UML Utopia?", Software, IEEE, Vol 21, no. 3 15-17, 2004

9. F.F. Lidia and A. Vallecillo-Moreno, "An introduction to UML profiles.", in UML and Model Engineering, Vol 2, 2004.

10. O. Rahma and B. Coulette, "Applying Security Patterns for Component Based Applications Using UML Profile." in IEEE 15th International Conference on Computational Science and Engineering (CSE), 2012, IEEE, pp. 186-193.

11. B. Ebrahim and A. A. Ghorbani, "Towards an MDA-oriented UML profile for critical infrastructure modeling." In Proceedings of the 2006 International Conference on Privacy, Security and Trust: Bridge the Gap Between PST Technologies and Business Services, 2006, ACM, p. 66..

12. S. Raul, F. Fondement, and A. Strohmeier, "Towards an MDAoriented UML profile for distribution." In Proceedings of EDOC 2004, Eighth IEEE International Conference on Enterprise Distributed Object Computing, 2004, pp. 227-239.

13. S., I. Wisniewski, L. T. Wiedermann Agner, P. C. Stadzisz, and J. M. Simão, "Modeling of embedded software on MDA platform models." Journal of Computer Science & Technology Vol 12, 2012.

14. S., Hassina, I. Bouacha, and M. S. Benselim, "Development of context–aware web services using the MDA approach." In International Journal of Web Science vol 1, no. 3, pp. 224-241, 2012

15. A. B. Djamel and M. Malki, "Development of semantic web services: model driven approach." In Proceedings of the 8th international conference on New technologies in distributed systems. ACM, 2008.

16. M. B. Kuznetsov, "UML model transformation and its application to MDA technology", Programming and Computer Software, Berlin, Germany: Springer 2007, Volume 33, Issue 1, pp 44-53.

17. M. Fowler, Patterns of Enterprise Application Architecture, Addison-Wesley Longman Publishing Co., Inc., Boston, MA, 2002.

18. S. Meena and R. G. Vishwakarma, "CMMI based software metrics to evaluate OOAD." Proceedings of the Second International Conference on Computational Science, Engineering and Information Technology. ACM, 2012.

CHAPTER 8

MODEL-BASED REUSE FOR CROSSCUTTING FRAMEWORKS: ASSESSING REUSE AND MAINTENANCE EFFORT

THIAGO GOTTARDI, RAFAEL SERAPILHA DURELLI, ÓSCAR PASTOR LÓPEZ, AND VALTER VIEIRA DE CAMARGO

8.1 CONTENT

This article is organized as follows: In Section 2 is presented the introduction of this article. Section 3 presents the necessary background to understand this article. More specifically, it is split into three sections, they are: Section 3.1 presents the concepts of Model-Driven Development, Section 3.2 showns the general notion of Aspect oriented programming and in Section 3.3 is presented the concepts of Crosscutting frameworks. In Section 4 is presented the proposed approach. In Section 5 is presented the evaluation of our approach. In Section 7 is presented some related works. Finally, in Section 8 we present the conclusion of this article.

Gottardi T, Durelli RS, López OP, and de Camargo VV. Model-Based Reuse for Crosscutting Frameworks: Assessing Reuse and Maintenance Effort. Journal of Software Engineering Research and Development 1,4 (2013); doi:10.1186/2195-1721-1-4. © 2013 Gottardi et al.; licensee Springer. This chapter was originally published under the Creative Commons Attribution Licenses, http://creativecommons.org/licenses/by/2.0

8.2 INTRODUCTION

Aspect-Oriented Programming (AOP) is a programming paradigm that overcomes the limitations of Object- Orientation (Programming) providing more suitable abstractions for modularizing crosscutting concerns (CC) such as persistence, security, and distribution. AspectJ is one of the programming languages that implements these abstractions (AspectJ Team 2003). Since the advent of AOP in 1997, a substantial effort has been invested in discovering how such abstractions can enhance reuse methodologies such as frameworks (Fayad and Schmidt 1997) and product lines (Clements and Northrop 2002). One example is the research that aims to design a CC in a generic way so that it can be reused in other applications (Bynens et al. 2010; Camargo and Masiero 2005; Cunha et al. 2006; Huang et al. 2004; Kulesza et al. 2006; Mortensen and Ghosh 2006; Sakenou et al. 2006; Shah and Hill 2004; Soares et al. 2006; Soudarajan and Khatchadourian 2009; Zanon et al. 2010). Because of the absence of a representative taxonomy for this kind of design, in our previous work we have proposed the term "Crosscutting Framework" (CF) to represent a generic and abstract design and implementation of a single crosscutting concern (Camargo and Masiero 2005).

Most of the CFs which are found in the literature adopt white-box reuse strategies in their reuse process, relying on writing source code to reuse the framework (Bynens et al. 2010; Camargo and Masiero 2005; Cunha et al. 2006; Huang et al. 2004; Kulesza et al. 2006; Mortensen and Ghosh 2006; Sakenou et al. 2006; Shah and Hill 2004; Soares et al. 2006; Soudarajan and Khatchadourian 2009; Zanon et al. 2010). This strategy is flexible in terms of framework evolution; however, application engineers need to cope with details not directly related to the requirements of the application under development. Therefore, the following problems exist when using such strategies: (i) the learning curve is steep because application engineers need to learn the programming paradigm employed in the framework design; (ii) a number of errors can be inserted because of the manual creation of the source code.; (iii) the development productivity is negatively affected as several lines of code must be written to define a small number of hooks, and (iv) the reuse processes can only be initiated during the implementation phase as there is no source code available in earlier phases.

To overcome these problems, we present a new approach for supporting the reuse of CFs using a Model-Driven Development (MDD) strategy. MDD consists of a combination of generative programming, domain-specific languages and model transformations. MDD aims at reducing the semantic gap between the program domain and its implementation, using high-level models that screen software developers from complexities of the underlying implementation platform (France and Rumpe 2007). Our approach is based on two models: the Reuse Requirements Model (RRM) and the Reuse Model (RM). Built by a framework engineer, RRM documents all the features and variabilities of a CF. Application engineers can then select just the desired features from the RRM and generate a more specific model, referred to as the RM. Later, the application engineer can conduct the reuse process by completing the RM fields with information from the application and automatically generate the reuse code.

Furthermore, we present the results of two comparative experiments which used the same Persistence CF (Camargo and Masiero 2005). The first experiment aimed to compare the productivity of conducting a reuse process when using our model-based approach versus the ad-hoc approach, i.e., writing the source code manually. The purpose of the second experiment was to compare the effort of maintaining applications developed with both our model-based approach versus the ad-hoc way. Our approach presented clear benefits for the instantiation time (productivity); however, no differences were identified regarding the maintenance effort. Therefore, the main contribution of this paper is twofold: (i) introduction of a model-based approach for supporting application engineers during the reuse process of CFs and (ii) presentation of the results of two experiments.

8.3 BACKGROUND

This section describes the background necessary to understand our proposed models. It is split into three subsections: the first one contains the concepts of Model-Driven Development, the second subsection has a basic description of aspect-oriented programming and the third one exposes the general notion of Crosscutting Frameworks.

8.3.1 MODEL-DRIVEN DEVELOPMENT

Software systems are becoming increasingly complex as customers demand richer functionality be delivered in shorter timescales (Clark et al. 2004). In this context, Model-Driven Development (MDD) can be used to speed up the software development and to manage its complexity in a better way by shifting the focus from the programming level to the solution-space.

MDD is an approach for software development that puts a particular emphasis upon making models the primary development artifacts and upon subjecting such models to a refinement process by using automatic transformations until a running system is obtained. Therefore, MDD aims to provide a higher abstraction level in the system development which further results in the improved understanding of complex systems (Pastor and Molina 2007).

Furthermore, MDD can be employed to handle software development problems that originate from the existence of heterogeneous platforms. This can be achieved by keeping different levels of model abstractions and by transforming models from Platform Independent Models (PIMs) to Platform Specific Models (PSMs) (Pastor and Molina 2007). Therefore, the automatic generation of application specific code offers many advantages such as: a rapid development of high quality code; a reduced number of accidental programming errors and the enhanced consistency between the design and the code (Schmidt 2006).

It is worth highlighting that models in MDD are usually represented by a domain-specific language (Fowler 2010), i.e., a language that adequately represents the information of a given domain. Instead of representing elements using a general purpose language (GPL), the knowledge is described in the language which domain experts understand. Besides, as the experts use a suitable language to describe the system at hand, the accidental complexity that one would insert into the system to describe a given domain is reduced, leaving just the essential complexity of the problem.

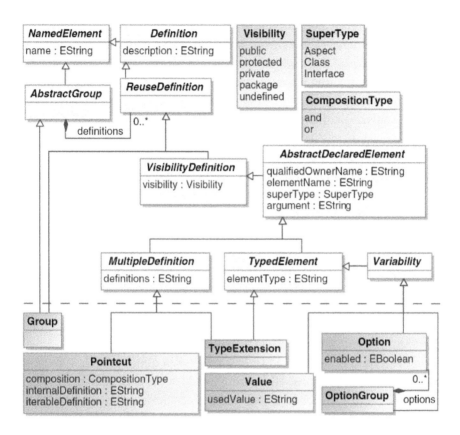

FIGURE 1: Metamodel of the proposed models. A metaclass diagram of 'CFReuse', which contains all metaclasses and enumerations.

8.3.2 ASPECT-ORIENTED PROGRAMMING

Aspect-Oriented Programming (AOP) aims at improving the modularization of a system by providing language abstractions that are dedicated to modularize crosscutting concerns (CCs). CCs are concerns which cannot be accurately modularized by using conventional paradigms (Kiczales et al. 1997). Without proper language abstractions, crosscutting concerns become scattered and tangled with other concerns of the software, affecting maintainability and reusability. In AOP, there is usually a distinction between base concerns and crosscutting concerns. The base concerns (or Core-concerns) are those which the system was originally designed to deal with. The crosscutting concerns are the concerns which affect on other concerns. Examples of crosscutting concerns include global restrictions, data persistence, authentication, access control, concurrency and cryptography (Kiczales et al. 1997).

Aspect-Oriented Programming languages allow programmers to design and implement crosscutting concern decoupled from the base concerns. The AOP compiler has the ability to weave the decoupled concerns together in order to attain a correct software system. Therefore, on the source-code level, there is a complete separation of concerns and the final release delivers the functionality expected by the users.

In this work we have employed the AspectJ language (Kiczales et al. 2001), which is an aspect-oriented extension for Java, allowing the Java code to be compiled seamlessly by the AspectJ compiler. The main constructs in this language are: aspect—a structure to represent a crosscutting concern; pointcut—a rule used to capture join points of other concerns; advices—types of behavior to be executed when a join point is captured; and intertype declarations—the ability to add static declarations from the outside of the affected code. In our work, intertype declarations are used to insert more interface realizations into classes of the base concern.

8.3.3 CROSSCUTTING FRAMEWORKS

Crosscutting Frameworks (CF) are aspect-oriented frameworks which encapsulate the generic behavior of a single crosscutting concern (Camargo and Masiero 2005; Cunha et al. 2006; Sakenou et al. 2006; Soudarajan and Khatchadourian 2009). It is possible to find CFs to support the implementation of persistence (Camargo and Masiero 2005; Soares et al. 2006), security (Shah and Hill 2004), cryptography (Huang et al. 2004), distribution (Soares et al. 2006) and other concerns (Mortensen and Ghosh 2006). The main objective of CFs is to make the reuse of crosscutting concerns a reality and a more productive task during the development of an application.

As well as other types of frameworks, CFs also need specific pieces of information regarding the base application to be reused correctly and to work properly. We name this kind of information "Reuse Requirements" (RR). For instance, the RR for an Access Control CF includes: 1) the application methods that need to have their access controlled; 2) the roles played by users; 3) the number of times a user is allowed get an incorrect password. This information is commonly documented in manuals known as "Cookbooks".

Unlike application frameworks, which are used to generate a whole new application, a CF needs to be coupled to a base application to become operational. The conventional process to reuse a CF is composed by two activities: instantiation and composition. During the instantiation, an application engineer chooses variabilities and implements hooks, while during the composition, he/she provides composition rules to couple the chosen variabilities to a base code.

CF-based applications, i.e, applications which were developed with the support of CFs, are composed by three types of modules: a base code module, a reuse code module and framework itself. The "base code" represents the source code of the base application and the "framework code" is the CF source code, which is untouched during the reuse process. The "reuse module" is the connection between the base application and the framework and it is developed/written by the application engineer. Applications can be composed by several CFs, each one coupled by one reuse module. The source code created specifically to reuse a CF, is referred here as "reuse code".

In our previous work we have developed a Persistence CF (Camargo et al. 2004) which is used here as a case study. This CF was designed like a product-line, so it has certain mandatory features, for instance, "Persistence" and "Connection". The first one aims to introduce a set of persistence operations (e.g., store, remove, update, etc) into application persistence classes. The second feature is related to the database connection and identifies points in the application code where a connection needs to be established or closed. This feature has variabilities as the Database Management System (e.g., MySQL, SyBase, Native and Interbase). This CF also has a set of optional features such as "Caching", which is used to improve the performance by keeping copies of data in the local memory, and "Pooling", which represents a number of active database connections.

8.4 MODEL-BASED REUSE APPROACH

In this section we present our approach and the models that support during the instantiation and composition of CFs: Reuse Requirements Model (RRM) and Reuse Model (RM). These models have been formulated on top of Eclipse Modeling Framework and Graphical Modeling Framework (Eclipse Consortium 2011). The formal definition of both models is speci-

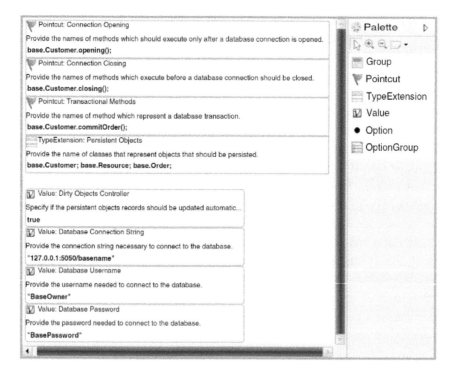

FIGURE 2: Reuse requirements models and a reuse models editor. A graphical user interface of the model editor. The editor is capable of editing Reuse Requirement Models and Reuse Models. The pallete on the right of the figure lists every concrete metaclass, which can be modelled on model level by dragging and dropping.

fied by the metamodel shown in Figure 1. It is comprised of a set of enumerations, abstract and concrete metaclasses.

The metamodel was built based on the vocabulary commonly used in the context of CFs, for example: pointcuts, classifier extensions, method overriding, and variability selection. These concepts were mapped into concrete metaclasses, which are visible under the dashed line of Figure 1.

Above the dashed line, there are also the following enumerations: "Visibility", "SuperType" and "CompositionType", which are sets of literals used as metaclass properties. The other elements above the line are abstract metaclasses, which were created after generalizing the properties of the concrete metaclasses. These abstract metaclasses can be applied in similar approaches and are also important to improve modularity and to avoid code replication of the reuse code generator.

Both of our proposed models are identical, however they are employed in different moments of the process. The first proposed model, the RRM, is a graphical documentation for Reuse Requirements, i.e., it graphically documents all the information needed to couple a CF to a base application. Conventionally, this is known as "cookbooks". This model involves information regarding all CF features and must be developed/provided by a framework engineer. The second model, the RM, is a subset of the RRM and contains only the selected features for conducting a reuse process. Since both models share the same metamodel, it is possible to employ a direct model transformation to instantiate a RM from a RRM by selecting a valid set of features. Both of our models are represented as forms containing boxes, as seen in Figure 2. Each box is an instance of a concrete metaclass element and represents a reuse requirement. Each box contains three lines. The first one contains both an icon representing the type of the element, (which is the same type visible in the "Palette") and the name of the reuse requirement. The second line shows a description and the last line must be filled by the application engineer to provide the necessary information regarding the base application. Notice that the last line is used only in RMs.

By analyzing a RRM, the application engineer can identify all the information required by the framework to conduct the reuse process. For example, this model represents the variabilities that must be chosen by the application engineer and also indicates join-points of the base code where crosscutting behavior must be applied to, as well as classes, interfaces, or aspect names that must be affected.

Framework variabilities that must be chosen during reuse process are also visible. For example, to instantiate a persistence CF, several activities must be done, among them: i) informing points of the base application in which the connection must be open and closed; ii) informing methods that represent data base transactions and iii) choosing variabilities, e.g., the driver that should be used to connect to the database.

The another model, the RM, is shown in Figure 2. It supports the reuse process of a crosscutting framework by filling in the third line of the boxes. Therefore, RM must be used by the application engineer to reuse a framework. For instance, the value "base.Customer.opening()" is a method of the base application that was inserted by the application engineer into the third line of the "Connection Opening" box to inform that the DB connection must be established before this method runs.

The code generator transforms the Reuse Model into the Reuse Code, which consists of pieces of AspectJ code used to couple the base application to the crosscutting framework. This transformation is not a one to one conversion, i.e., every element in the model not always generates the same number of code elements. This was a special underlying challenge we have experienced when implementing this approach. The code generator needs to read the RM completely and to aggregate all data to identify how many files need to be generated.

The reuse model elements contain attributes to define the super classes to be extended; several elements may identify the same superclass. Therefore, the code generator must identify every superclass in order to create a single subclass per superclass when generating "Pointcuts", "Options" and "Value Definitions".

The generation of "Type Extensions" is slightly different. Whenever there is a single type extension, the code generator creates a single aspect that aggregates every type extension using "declare parents"; a specific type of intertype declaration.

The architecture of the generator is represented in Figure 3. Initially, the XTend (Efftinge 2006) library is used as a front end of the compiler, loading the data of the model into a hierarchical structure in memory, similar to a Domain Object Model. After the structure is loaded, it is processed

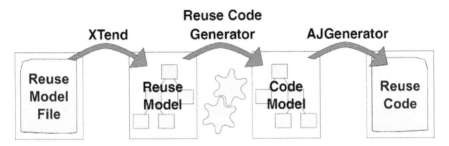

FIGURE 3: Reuse code generator architecture. The reuse code generator creates a reuse code by processing a reuse model. This process is divided into three sub processes, which are shown in this figure.

in order to identify the units that must be generated. This process creates another structure that represents the resulting code, which is similar to an abstract syntax tree. The "AJGenerator" is a back end of the generator that we have also created; it is capable of transforming this tree into actual files of valid AspectJ code.

8.4.1 REUSE PROCESS

This subsection explains the reuse process that is defined when using the new proposed models (RRM and RM). From this point it is important to clarify the distinction between the terms model and diagram. Model is a more generic term and it is physically represented by XML files, while a diagram is a visual representation of a model. So, in our case, the Reuse Requirements Diagram (RRD) is a diagram that represents the Reuse Requirements Model and the Reuse Diagram (RD) is a diagram that represents the Reuse Model. It is also worth mentioning that these diagrams are similar to forms, in which they must be filled in. In order to explain the new process, there is an activity diagram in Figure 4 illustrating the perspective of both developers: framework engineers and application engineers.

Since the CF must be completely defined before its reuse process is started, this explanation begins from the framework engineer's point of view. At the right side of the Figure 4, the framework engineer starts developing a new CF for a specific crosscutting concern. The first activity is to develop the framework itself (marked with 'A'). Then, the engineer should make the CF code available for reuse ('B') and should create the RRD ('C'), graphically indicating the information required to couple his CF to a base application. This diagram ('D') will be available for the application engineer. Upon finishing this process, the framework engineer has two artifacts that will be used by the application engineer: the Reuse Requirements Diagram ('D') and the Framework code ('B').

The reuse process starts on the left side of the figure, where the perspective of application engineers is considered. This engineer is responsible for developing the application, which is composed by both the "Base"

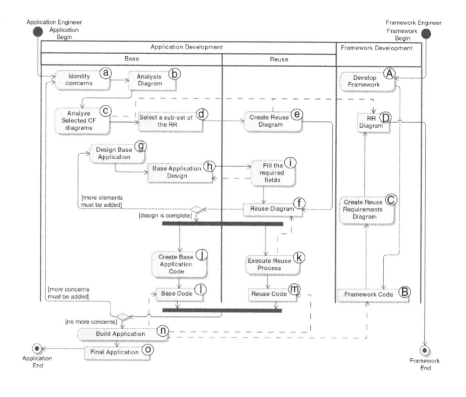

FIGURE 4: Reuse process activity diagram. A UML activity diagram that represents the reuse process to be employed when using the proposed models and the tools.

and "Reuse" modules. By analyzing the application being developed ('a'), the application engineer must identify the concerns that would affect the software, possibly by using an analysis diagram ('b'). By having these concerns identified, the application engineer is able to select the necessary frameworks and to start the reuse process since the earlier development phases. After selecting and analyzing the RRD of the selected frameworks ('c'), it is necessary to select a subset of the optional variabilities ('d') because some elements may not be necessary (since the framework may be supplied with default values), or to select mutually exclusive features. The selected elements will be carried to a new "Reuse" diagram ('e'). If there are more than one CF being reused, then there should be a "Reuse" diagram for each one of them. The application engineer should then design

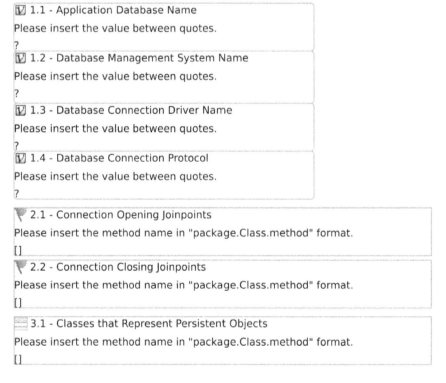

FIGURE 5: Reuse model template. A reuse model template that must be provided by the domain engineer in order to allow the application engineers to apply the process.

the base application ('g') documenting the name of the units, methods and attributes found on the base application ('h'). By designing the names of elements needed by the framework, they will become available, meaning that it is already possible to enter these names in the RD. This should be done before all required elements of the iteration are designed. After defining these names, which are the values needed by the reuse portion, they must be filled ('i') in the reuse diagram ('f') to enable the coupling among the modules.

The base application can be developed ('j') in parallel with the reuse process execution ('k'), which is a model transformation to generate the "Reuse Code" ('m') from the "Reuse Diagram" ('f'). After completing the "Base Code" ('l') and the "Reuse Code" ('m'), the application engineer may choose between adding a new concern (and extending the base application) or finishing the process. At that moment, the following pieces of code are available: the "Base Code" ('l'), the "Reuse Codes" ('m') and the selected "Framework Codes" ('B'). All of these codes are processed to build ('n') the "Final Application" ('o') and to conclude the process.

The transformation employed to create the RD avoids manual creation of this model. This is possible by identifying the selected framework and by processing its RRD. Besides accelerating the creation of this model, this also allows the RD to take all the needed elements from the earlier diagram to the code generation. However, the values regarding the base application are still needed and must be informed by the application engineer. The RRD contains information needed by the framework being reused. By identifying that information during earlier development phases it is easier to define it correctly. Consequently, the base application is not oblivious of the framework and its behaviors, however, the modules are completely isolated and have no code dependency among them. It is important to point out that the Reuse Code itself depends on the Base Code during the creation process, however, its definition can be made as soon as the base application design is complete.

8.4.2 APPROACH USAGE EXAMPLE

An usage example of our approach is described in this section. Firstly, we briefly describe the domain engineering which contains the creation of the

☑ 1.1 - Application Database Name

Please insert the value between quotes.

"airlinedb"

☑ 1.2 - Database Management System Name

Please insert the value between quotes.

"derby"

☑ 1.3 - Database Connection Driver Name

Please insert the value between quotes.

"org.apache.derby.jdbc.EmbeddedDriver"

☑ 1.4 - Database Connection Protocol

Please insert the value between quotes.

"jdbc:derby:"

2.1 - Connection Opening Joinpoints

Please insert the method name in "package.Class.method" format.

[baseapp.Airplane.landing,baseapp.Airport.opening,baseapp.Luggage.dispatch...

2.2 - Connection Closing Joinpoints

Please insert the method name in "package.Class.method" format.

[baseapp.Airplane.takeoff,baseapp.Airport.closing,baseapp.Luggage.retrieve...

3.1 - Classes that Represent Persistent Objects

Please insert the method name in "package.Class.method" format.

[baseapp.Airplane,baseapp.Airport,baseapp.Luggage,baseapp.Passenger...

FIGURE 6: Complete reuse model. A complete reuse model after the application engineer provides the information regarding the base application, which will allow framework reuse by code generation.

framework reuse model. Finally, the application engineering is described, which consists of reuse model completion and reuse code generation, thus completing the process.

8.4.3 DOMAIN ENGINEERING

The domain engineer must create a reuse model which contains the information necessary to reuse a crosscutting framework. In the example provided herein, every information needed to create a reuse model for a persistence framework. After the model creation, its completion is shown during application engineering to reuse the framework and couple it to an example application.

The reuse model template for the crosscutting framework in Figure 5, which was derived from a reuse requirements model by describing the framework hotspots. In Figure 6, the reuse model is shown after its completion.

The model elements are defined as follows: there are four value objects, two pointcut objects, and one type extension object. The value objects are used to define strings needed by the framework in order to connect it to the database. They are used to define the database name, the name of the database management system, the database connection driver, and the database connection protocol. Every property of these items are then represented on Tables 1, 2, 3 and 4.

TABLE 1: Application database name

Value object: application database name	
Name	Name
"1.1 - Application database name"	
Description	Description
"Please insert the value between quotes."	
Qualified name of the owner	QualifiedOwnerName
"persistence.instantiation.helper.ExtendedConnectionVariabilities"	
Method to be overridden	ElementName
"ExtendedConnectionVariabilities.setDatabaseName"	
Value data type	ElementType
"String"	
Select supertype (aspect, class or interface)	SuperType
"Class"	

A string needed by the database connection API in order to connect to a specific database managed by the database system.

TABLE 2: Database management system name

Value object: database management system name	
Name	Name
"1.2 - Database management system name"	
Description	Description
"Please insert the value between quotes."	
Qualified name of the owner	QualifiedOwnerName
"persistence.instantiation.helper.ExtendedConnectionVariabilities"	
Method to be overridden	ElementName
"ExtendedConnectionVariabilities.setSpecificDatabase"	
Value data type	ElementType
"String"	
Select supertype (aspect, class or interface)	SuperType
"Class"	

A string needed by the database connection API in order to select the database connection driver.

TABLE 3: Connection driver protocol

Value object: database connection driver name	
Name	Name
"1.3 - Database connection driver name"	
Description	Description
"Please insert the value between quotes."	
Qualified name of the owner	QualifiedOwnerName
"persistence.instantiation.helper.ExtendedConnectionVariabilities"	
Method to be overridden	ElementName
"ExtendedConnectionVariabilities.getDriver"	
Value data type	ElementType
"String"	
Select supertype (aspect, class or interface)	SuperType
"Class"	

A string needed by the database connection API in order to select the database connection driver.

TABLE 4: Connection driver protocol

Value object: database connection protocol	
Name	Name
"1.4 - Database connection protocol name"	
Description	Description
"Please insert the value between quotes."	
Qualified name of the owner	QualifiedOwnerName
"persistence.instantiation.helper.ExtendedConnectionVariabilities"	
Method to be overridden	ElementName
"ExtendedConnectionVariabilities.getJDBC"	
Value data type	ElementType
"String"	
Select supertype (aspect, class or interface)	SuperType
"Class"	

A string needed by the database connection API in order to connect to the database system.

TABLE 5: Connection opening joinpoint definition

Pointcut Object: connection opening joinpoints	
Name	Name
"2.1 - Connection opening joinpoints"	
Description	Description
"Please insert the method name in "package.Class.method" format."	
Qualified name of the owner	QualifiedOwnerName
"persistence.instantiation.helper.ExtendedConnectionCompositionRules"	
Pointcut to be overridden	ElementName
"openConnection"	
Composition operator	Composition
"or"	
Internal pointcut definition	InternalDefinition
""	
Iterable pointcut definition	IterableDefinition
"execution (* %s(..))"	
Select supertype (aspect, class or interface)	SuperType
"Class"	

The second pointcut object is used to define methods that run right after the database connection must be open.

The pointcut objects are used to define joinpoints of the base application. The first pointcut object is represented on Table 5 and it must be used to inform where DB connections must be established. To do that, the application engineer needs to inform which methods execute right after a DB connection is established, i.e., methods that operate properly only if there is a connection open. The second point cut object is represented on Table 6 and it is used to inform methods that execute right before the connection is closed, therefore, the last method that needs an open connection.

The last object is represented on Table 7, which is used to define the classes found in the base application. These base application define object types that must be persisted on the database.

This reuse model is provided along with the crosscutting framework to be used by the application engineer in order to instantiate the framework, which is described in Section 4.3.

TABLE 6: Connection closing joinpoint definition

Pointcut object: connection closing joinpoints	
Name	Name
"2.2 - Connection closing joinpoints"	
Description	Description
"Please insert the method name in "package.Class.method" format."	
Qualified name of the owner	QualifiedOwnerName
"persistence.instantiation.helper.ExtendedConnectionCompositionRules"	
Pointcut to be overridden	ElementName
"closeConnection"	
Composition operator	Composition
"or"	
Internal pointcut definition	InternalDefinition
""	
Iterable pointcut definition	IterableDefinition
"execution (* %s(..))"	
Select supertype (aspect, class or interface)	SuperType
"Class"	

The second pointcut object is used to define methods that run right before the database connection must be closed.

TABLE 7: Persistent objects definition

Type extension object: persistent objects	
Name	Name
"3.1 - Classes that represent persistent objects"	
Description	Description
"Please insert the class name in "package.Class" format."	
Qualified name of the owner	QualifiedOwnerName
"persistence.PersistentRoot"	
Select supertype (aspect, class or interface)	SuperType
"Interface"	

The last object from the example that is used to define the persistent objects of the application.

8.4.4 APPLICATION ENGINEERING

An example of an application development is given in this subsection. This application is referred to as Airline Ticket Management and must be coupled to the persistence CF previously mentioned. This application uses the Apache Derby Database Management System (Apache Software Foundation 2012). The design of this application is shown on Table 8.

Upon the reuse model completion, the resulting reuse model is similar to that shown in Figure 7. Despite not being shown in the application details, every base application class was created inside the package "base-app". After validating the model, the reuse code is generated; it is divided into three units.

The first generated unit is an aspect that extends a framework class. The overridden methods are used to return constant values that are necessary for the framework to successfully get connected to the database. It is important to emphasize that the four values have been defined in the same unit because they are owned by the same superclass. This would not happen if their superclasses were different.

TABLE 8: Base application details

Constant definition		
Application database name	"airlinedb"	
Database management system name	"derby"	
Database connection driver name	"org.apache.derby.jdbc.EmbeddedDriver"	
Database connection protocol	"jdbc:derby:"	
Joinpoint definition (method execution)		
Joinpoints	Method execution	
Connection opening joinpoints	Class	Method
	Airplane	Landing
	Airport	Opening
	Luggage	Dispatch
	Checkin	Confirm
	Passenger	Onboard
	Flight	Depart
Connection closing joinpoints	Class	Method
	Airplane	Takeoff
	Airport	Closing
	Luggage	Retrieve
	Checkin	Cancel
	Passenger	Unboard
	Flight	Arrive
Type extensions		
Classes that represent persistent objects	Class	
	Airport	
	Luggage	
	Checkin	
	Passenger	
	Flight	

Details of a base application that needs to be coupled to the crosscuting framework.

```
                           ConcreteExtendedConnectionVariabilities0.aj

package persistence.reuse;
import persistence.instantiation.helper.ExtendedConnectionVariabilities;
public aspect ConcreteExtendedConnectionVariabilities0 extends
 ExtendedConnectionVariabilities {
    public String ExtendedConnectionVariabilities.setDatabaseName (){
        return "airlinedb";
    }
    public String ExtendedConnectionVariabilities.setSpecificDatabase (){
        return "derby";
    }
    public String ExtendedConnectionVariabilities.getDriver (){
        return "org.apache.derby.jdbc.EmbeddedDriver";
    }
    public String ExtendedConnectionVariabilities.getJDBC (){
        return "jdbc:derby:";
    }
}
```

FIGURE 7: Reuse code - first unit. The first generated reuse code fragment contains an aspect that is used to define the "Connection Variabilities" of the framework: these "Connection Variabilities" are provided by overriding methods.

```
                                            ParentsDeclaration.aj

package  persistence.reuse;
public aspect  ParentsDeclaration  extends  Object {
    declare parents : baseapp.Airplane    implements
        persistence.PersistentRoot;
    declare parents : baseapp.Airport     implements
        persistence.PersistentRoot;
    declare parents : baseapp.Luggage     implements
        persistence.PersistentRoot;
    declare parents : baseapp.Checkin     implements
        persistence.PersistentRoot;
    declare parents : baseapp.Passenger   implements
        persistence.PersistentRoot;
    declare parents : baseapp.Flight      implements
        persistence.PersistentRoot;
}
```

FIGURE 8: Reuse code - second unit. The second generated reuse code fragment contains an aspect that is used to define the "Composition Rules" of the framework. The "CompositionRules" are provided by overriding pointcuts.

```
                                        ParentsDeclaration.aj

package   persistence.reuse;
public aspect   ParentsDeclaration   extends  Object {
      declare parents  : baseapp.Airplane     implements
            persistence.PersistentRoot;
      declare parents  : baseapp.Airport      implements
            persistence.PersistentRoot;
      declare parents  : baseapp.Luggage      implements
            persistence.PersistentRoot;
      declare parents  : baseapp.Checkin      implements
            persistence.PersistentRoot;
      declare parents  : baseapp.Passenger    implements
            persistence.PersistentRoot;
      declare parents  : baseapp.Flight       implements
            persistence.PersistentRoot;
}
```

FIGURE 9: Reuse code - third unit. The third generated reuse code fragment contains an aspect that is used to define static crosscutting features needed during the framework reuse. By default, all static crosscutting declarations are merged into a single aspect.

The second unit is shown in Figure 8, which is an aspect that overrides pointcuts openConnection and closeConnection. These pointcuts are used to capture base application joinpoints that trigger the database connections and disconnections. They are defined in a single aspect because they also share the same superclass.

Figure 9 shows another aspect, which uses static crosscutting features to define classes that extend the interface specified by domain engineer by using the "Declare Parents" syntax.

Our model generator is also capable of generating a validation code, which checks if the base element names inserted into the reuse model are valid.

8.5 METHODS

Two experiments have been conducted to compare our model-based reuse approach with the conventional way of reusing CFs, i.e., manually creating the reuse code. The first experiment is called Reuse Study and was planned to identify the gains in productivity when reusing a framework. The second experiment is denominated "Maintenance Study" and was designed to identify whether the our models help or not in the maintenance of a CF-based application. This second study is important because maintenance activities are usually performed more often than the reuse process. Each experiment has been performed twice. In this paper, the first execution is referred to as "First" and the second execution is referred to as "Replication". Since there have been only two executions for each experiment, we present four study executions in this section. The structure of the studies has been defined according to the recommendations of Wohlin et al. (2000).

8.5.1 REUSE STUDY DEFINITION

The objective was to compare the effort of reusing frameworks by using a conventional technique with the effort of using a model-based technique. The Persistence CF, briefly presented in Subsection 3.3, has played the role of "study subject" and it was used in both reuse techniques (conventional and model-based). The quantitative focus was determined considering the time spent in conducting the reuse process. The qualitative focus was to determine which technique takes less effort during the reuse process. This experiment was conducted from the perspective of application engineers reusing CFs: the study object was the 'effort' to perform a CF reuse.

8.5.2 REUSE STUDY PLANNING

The first experiment was planned considering the following question: "Which reuse technique takes less effort to reuse a CF?";

8.5.2.1 CONTEXT SELECTION

Both studies have been conducted by students of Computer Science. In this section, they are referred to as "participants". Sixteen participants took part in the experiments, eight of those were undergraduate students and the other eight were post-graduate students. Every participant had a prior AspectJ experience.

8.5.2.2 FORMULATION OF HYPOTHESES

Table 9 contains our formulated hypotheses for the reuse study, which are used to compare the productivity of our tool with the conventional process.

TABLE 9: Hypotheses for the reuse study

$H0_r$	There is no difference between using our tool and using an ad-hoc reuse process in terms of productivity (time) to successfully couple a CF with an application.
	Then, the techniques are equivalent.
	$Tc_r - Tm_r \approx 0$
Hp_r	There is a positive difference between using our tool and using an ad-hoc reuse process in terms of productivity (time) to successfully couple a CF with an application.
	Then, the conventional technique takes more time than the model-based tool.
	$Tc_r - Tm_r > 0$
Hn_r	There is a negative difference between using our tool and using an ad-hoc reuse process in terms of productivity (time) to successfully couple a CF with an application.
	Then, the conventional technique takes less time than the model-based tool.
	$Tc_r - Tm_r < 0$

Considering the Reuse Study, there are three hypotheses for the outcome. In the first one, both are equivalent, while in two of them, a technique is faster.

There are two variables shown on the table: " Tc_r " and " Tm_r ". " Tc_r " represents the overall time necessary to reuse the framework using the conventional technique while " Tm_r " represents the overall time necessary to reuse the framework using the model-based technique. There are three hypotheses shown on the table: " $H0_r$ ", " Hp_r " and " Hn_r ". " $H0_r$ " represents the null hypothesis, which is true when both techniques are equivalent; then, the time spent using the conventional technique minus the time spent using the model-based tool is approximately zero. " Hp_r " represents the first alternate hypothesis, which is true when the conventional technique takes longer than the model-based tool; then, the time spent to use the conventional technique minus the time of the model-based tool is positive. " Hn_r " represents the second alternate hypothesis, which is true when the conventional technique takes longer than the model-based tool; then, the time taken to use the conventional technique minus the time taken to use the model-based tool is negative. As these hypotheses consider different ranges of a single resulting real value, then, they are mutually exclusive and only one of them is true.

8.5.2.3 VARIABLE SELECTION

The dependent variable in this work is the "time spent to complete the process". The independent variables are Base Application, Technique and Execution Types, which, are controlled and manipulated.

8.5.2.4 PARTICIPANT SELECTION CRITERIA

The participants were selected through a non-probabilistic approach by convenience, i. e., the probability of all population elements belong to the same sample is unknown. We have invited every student from the computing department of Federal University of São Carlos that attended the AOP course, a total of 17 students. Every student had to be able to reuse the framework by editing code during the training. Because of that, one undergraduate student was rejected before the execution.

8.5.2.5 DESIGN OF THE STUDY

The participants were divided into two groups. Each group was composed by four graduate students and four undergraduate students. Each group was also balanced considering a characterization form and their results from the pilot study. Table 10 shows the planned phases.

TABLE 10: Study design

Phase	Group 1	Group 2
General training	Reuse and maintenance training	
	Repair shop	
1 st Reuse	Conventional	Models
Pilot phase	Hotel application	
2 nd Reuse	Models	Conventional
Pilot phase	Library application	
1 st First	Conventional	Models
Reuse phase	Deliveries application	
2 nd First	Models	Conventional
Reuse phase	Flights application	
1 st Replication	Conventional	Models
Reuse phase	Medical clinic application	
2 nd Replication	Models	Conventional
Reuse phase	Restaurant application	
1 st First	Conventional	Models

The Study Design contains every phase from both studies. It contains the sequence of operations, technique and the conidered applications.

8.5.2.6 INSTRUMENTATION FOR THE REUSE STUDY

Base applications were provided together with two documents. The first document was a manual regarding the current reuse technique, and the second document was a list of details, which described the classes, methods and values regarding the application to be coupled.

The provided applications had the same reuse complexity. The participants had to specify four values, twelve methods and six classes in order to reuse the framework and to couple it to each application. These applications were designed with exactly the same structure of six classes. Each class contained six methods plus a class with a main method which is used to run the test case.

Each phase row of the Table 10 is divided into sub-rows that contain the name of the application and the technique employed to reuse the framework. For instance, during the First Reuse Phase, the participants of the first group coupled the framework to the "Deliveries Application" by using the conventional technique. The participants of the second used the model-based tool to perform the same exercise.

8.5.3 OPERATION FOR REUSE STUDY

8.5.3.1 PREPARATION

During the maintenance study, the students had to fix a reuse artifact to complete the process. Every participant had to fix every application by using only one of the techniques in equal numbers.

8.5.3.2 EXECUTION

The participants had to work with two applications; each group started with a different technique. The secondary executions were replications of the primary executions with two other applications They were created to avoid the risk of getting unbalanced results during the primary execution, since some data that we gathered during the pilot study were rendered invalid.

8.5.3.3 DATA VALIDATION

The forms filled by the participants were confirmed with the preliminary data gathered during the pilot study. In order to provide a better controllability, the researchers also watched the notifications from the data collector to check if the participants had concluded the maintenance process and had gathered the necessary data.

8.5.3.4 DATA COLLECTION

The recorded timings during the reuse processes with both techniques are listed on the Table 11. Each table has five columns. Each column is defined by a letter or a word: "G" stands for the group of the participant during the activity; "A" stands for the application being reused; "T" stands for the reuse technique which is either "C" for conventional or "M" for model-based tool; "P" column lists an identifying code of the participants (students), whereas, the least, eight values are allocated to graduate students and the rest are undergraduate students; "Time" column lists the time the participant spent to complete each phase. The raw data we have gathered during the reuse study is also available as Additional file 1.

We have developed a data collector to gather the experiment data. This system has stored the timings with milliseconds precision considering both the server and clients' system clocks. However, the values presented in this paper only consider the server time. The delays of transmission by the computers are not taken into consideration; preliminary calculations considering the clients' clocks have indicated that these delays are insignificant, i.e., have not changed the hypothesis testing results. The server's clock was considered because we could verify that its clock had not been changed throughtout the execution.

That system was able to gather the timings and the supplied information transparently. The participants only had to execute the start time, which was supervised, and to work on the processes independently. After the test case had provided successful results, which meant that the framework was correctly coupled, the finish time was automatically submitted to the server before notifying the success to the participant.

8.5.4 DATA ANALYSIS AND INTERPRETATION FOR REUSE STUDY

The data of the first study is found on Table 11, which is arranged by the time taken to complete the process. The first noteworthy information found on this table is that the model-based reuse tool, which is identified by the letter 'M', is found in the first twelve results. The conventional process, which is identified by the letter 'C', got the last four results.

The timings data of Table 11 is also represented graphically in a bar graph, which is plotted on Figure 10. The same identifying code for each participant and the elapsed time in seconds are visible on the graph. The

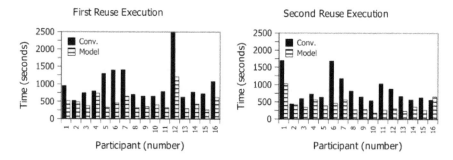

FIGURE 10: Reuse process timings bars graph. A graph in which the reuse experiment timings are plotted. Each bar represents the time taken by each participant in order to complete the reuse activities, which is identifiable by the participant number.

bars for the used conventional technique and the used model tool are paired for each participant, allowing easier visualization of the amount of time taken by each of them. In other words, the taller the bar, the more time it took to complete the process with the specified technique.

The second significant information found during the first study was that not a single participant could reuse the framework faster by using the conventional process than by using the reuse tool in the same activity.

Table 12 shows the average timings and their proportions. If we analyze the average time that the participants from both groups have taken to complete the processes, we could conclude that the conventional technique took approximately 97.64% longer than the model-based tool.

TABLE 12: Reuse study average timings

A.	Tech.	Avg.	Sum of Avg.	Percents
First	Conv.	16:13.44008	30:03.79341	66.7766%
Replication	13:50.35333			
First	Model	08:04.980525	14:57.441176	33.2234%
Replication	06:52.460651			
Total		45:01.234586		100.0000%

The Study Average Timings table contains averages for the Reuse Study. It is possible to compare the general time effort needed to complete the activities of both techniques.

8.5.5 MAINTENANCE STUDY DEFINITION

It is necessary to remind here that our objective was to compare the effort in modifying a CF-based application by editing the reuse code (conventional technique) with the effort in modifying the same application by editing the RM. The Persistence CF, shown in the Section 3.3 was again used in the two maintenance exercises. The quantitative focus was measured by means of the time spent in the maintenance tasks and the qualitative focus was to determine which artifact (source code or RM) takes less effort during maintenance. This experiment was conducted from the perspective of application engineers who intended to maintain CF-based applications. Therefore, the study object is the 'effort' of maintaining a CF-based application.

8.5.6 MAINTENANCE STUDY PLANNING

The core question we wanted to answer here was: "Which artifact takes less editing effort during maintenance: the reuse model or the reuse code?" During this experiment we have gathered and analyzed the timings taken to complete the process for each activity.

8.5.6.1 CONTEXT SELECTION

Both studies were conducted by students of the Computer Science Department. In this section, they are referred to as "participants". Sixteen participants took part in the experiments: eight of them were undergraduate students and the other eight were graduate students. Every participant had a prior AspectJ experience.

8.5.6.2 FORMULATION OF HYPOTHESES

Table 13 contains three variables. " Tc_m " represents the overall time to edit the reuse code during maintenance. " Tm_m " represents the overall time to edit the reuse model during maintenance. " $H0_m$ " represents the null hypothesis, which is true when the edition of both artifacts is equivalent. " Hp_m " represents the first alternate hypothesis, which is true when the edition of the reuse code takes longer than editing the RM. " Hn_m " represents the second alternate hypothesis, which is true when the edition of the reuse code takes less time than editing the RM. These hypotheses are also mutually exclusive: only one of them is true.

TABLE 13: Hypotheses for the maintenance study

$H0_m$	There is no difference between using editing a reuse model and editing the reuse code in terms of productivity (time) when maintaining an application that reuses a CF.
	Then, it is equivalent to edit any of the artifacts. $Tc_m - Tm_m \approx 0$
Hp_m	There is a positive difference between using editing a reuse model and editing the reuse code in terms of productivity (time) when maintaining an application that reuses a CF.
	Then, editing the reuse code takes more time than editing a reuse model during maintenance. $Tc_m - Tm_m > 0$
Hn_m	There is a negative difference between using editing a reuse model and editing the reuse code in terms of productivity (time) when maintaining an application that reuses a CF.
	Then, editing the reuse code takes less time than editing a reuse model during maintenance. $Tc_m - Tm_m < 0$

Considering the Reuse Study, there are three hypotheses for the outcome. In the first one, both are equivalent, while in two of them, a technique is faster.

8.5.6.3 VARIABLE SELECTION

The dependent variable analyzed here was the "time spent to complete the process". The independent variables, which were controlled and manipulated, are: "Base Application", "Technique" and "Execution Types".

8.5.6.4 PARTICIPANT SELECTION CRITERIA

The participants were selected through a non probabilistic approach by convenience, i. e., the probability of all population elements belong to the same sample is unknown. Both studies share the same participants.

8.5.6.5 DESIGN OF THE MAINTENANCE STUDY

The participants were divided into two groups. Each group was composed of four graduate students and four undergraduate students. Each group was also balanced considering the characterization form of each participant and their results from the first study. The phases for this study are shown in Table 14.

TABLE 14: Maintenance study design

Phase	Group 1	Group 2
General training	Maintenance training	
	Deliveries application	
2 nd First	Models	Conventional
Maintenance phase	Flights application	
1 st Replication	Conventional	Models
Maintenance phase	Medical clinic application	
2 nd Replication	Models	Conventional
Maintenance phase	Restaurant application	

The Study Design contains every phase from both studies. It contains the sequence of operations, technique and the conidered applications.

8.5.6.6 INSTRUMENTATION FOR THE MAINTENANCE STUDY

The base applications provided for the second study were modified versions of the same applications that had been supplied during the first study. These applicationswere provided with incorrect reuse codes (conventional) and incorrect reuse models (model-based): these incorrect artifacts had to be fixed by the participants. The participants received a document describing possible generic errors that could happen when a reuse code or a model are defined incorrectly. It is important to point out that that document did not have details regarding the base applications; the participants had to find the errors by browsing the source code.

The provided applications had the same reuse complexity: the reuse codes and models had the same amount of errors. In order to fix each CF coupling, the participants had to fix three outdated class names, three outdated method names, and three mistyped characters. It is also important to emphasize that errors specific for the manual edition of reuse codes were not inserted in this study. Each phase row of the Table 14 is divided into sub-rows that contain the name of the application and the technique employed during the maintenance. For instance, the participants of the first group had to fix the reuse code of the "Deliveries Application" during the First Maintenance Phase, while the participants of the second group had to fix the reuse model to perform the same exercise.

8.5.7 OPERATION FOR MAINTENANCE STUDY

8.5.7.1 PREPARATION

During the maintenance study, the students had to fix a reuse artifact to complete the process. Every participant had to fix every application. They have fixed each application only once, by using only one of the techniques in equal numbers.

8.5.7.2 OPERATION EXECUTION

The participants had to work with two applications; each group started with a different technique. The secondary executions were replications of the primary executions with two other applications They were created to avoid the risk of getting unbalanced results during the primary execution, since some data that we gathered during the pilot study were rendered invalid.

8.5.7.3 DATA VALIDATION

The forms filled by the participants were confirmed with the preliminary data gathered during the pilot study. In order to provide a better controllability, the researchers also watched the notifications from the data collector to check if the participants had concluded the maintenance process and had gathered the necessary data.

8.5.7.4 DATA COLLECTION

The timings for the maintenance study are presented in Table 15. The column "G" stands for the group of the participant; "A" stands for the application being reused; "T" stands for the reuse technique which is either "C" for conventional or "M" for model-based tool; "Time" column lists the time the participant spent to complete each phase, and finally; and "P" column lists an identifying code of the participants. At least eight values are allocated to graduate students and the rest are undergraduate students; The raw data we have gathered during the maintenance study is also available as Additional file 2.

The data collector that was employed to gather the experiment data stored the timings with milliseconds precision: both the server and clients' system clocks were taken into consideration. However, the values presented in this paper consider only the server time. The delay of data transmission over the network was not taken into consideration. We believe that they are insignificant in this case because preliminary calculations considering the clients' clocks did not change the order of results.

That system was able to gather the timings and the supplied information transparently. The unique task of the participants was to click in a button to initialize the starting time. Once the provided test case had succeed (meaning that the framework was correctly coupled) the finishing time was automatically submitted to the server before notifying the success to the participant.

8.5.8 DATA ANALYSIS AND INTERPRETATION FOR MAINTENANCE STUDY

The data of the second study is found on Table 15. This study has provided results similar to the first study. The first eleven values are related to the model-based tool, while the last four are related to the conventional technique. Only the Participant 16 was able to reuse the framework faster by applying the conventional process, which contradicts the results of the same participant in the previous study. This participant said he got confused when he had to correct the reuse model. That was the reason why he had to restart the process from the very beginning, causing this longer time.

The plots for the maintenance study are found on Figure 11. These plots follow the same guidelines that were used when plotting the graphs for the previous study. Considering the timings of the maintenance study, the reuse model edition does not provide any advantage in terms of productivity, since most of participants took longer to edit the model than the reuse code.

Table 16 illustrates the average timings and their proportions. Considering only the average time, the participants who applied the conventional technique took less time than their counterparts who used our model-based approach.

8.6 RESULTS AND DISCUSSION

8.6.1 HYPOTHESES TESTING FOR REUSE STUDY

In this section, we present statistical calculations to evaluate the data of the reuse study. We applied Paired T-Tests for each execution and another

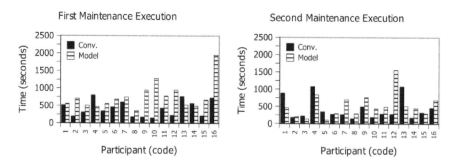

FIGURE 11: Maintenance process timings bars graph. A graph in which the maintenance experiment timings are plotted. Each bar represents the time taken by each participant in order to complete the maintenance activities, which is identifiable by the participant number.

T-Test after removing eight outliers. The time consumed in each execution was processed using the statistic computation environment "R" (Free Software Foundation, Inc 2012). The results of the T-Tests are shown on Table 17, which is actually a pair of tables. The time unit is "seconds".

TABLE 16: Maintenance study average timings

A.	Tech.	Avg.	Sum of Avg.	Percents
First	Conv.	06:57.498758	13:55.762733	39.5521%
Replication		06:58.263975		
First	Model	12:43.152626	21:17.305521	60.4479%
Replication		08:34.152895		
Total		35:13.068254		100.0000%

The Study Average Timings table contains averages for the Maintenance Study. It is possible to compare the general time effort needed to complete the activities of both techniques.

TABLE 17: Reuse study t-test results

T-Test	Data	Means	d.f.	t	p
Paired	First	488.4596	15	5.841634	$3.243855 \cdot 10^{-05}$
Paired	Replication	417.8927	15	5.285366	$9.156136 \cdot 10^{-05}$
Two-sided	Both	771.4236	43.70626	6.977408	$1.276575 \cdot 10^{-08}$
		409.4295			

T-Test is a statistical test used to determine the correct hypothesis for both studies. This table lists the results for the reuse study.

The first columns of these tables contain the type of T-Test and the second ones indicate the source of the data. The "Means" columns indicate the resultant mean for each T-Test. For a paired T-Test, there is one mean, which is the average of subtracting each set member by its counterpart in the other set. For the non-paired T-Tests, there are two means, which are the averages for each set. In this case, the first set represents the conventional technique; the second set represents the use of the model-based tool. The "d.t." columns stand for the degrees of freedom, which is related to how many different values are found in the sets; "t"and "p" are variables considered in the hypothesis testing.

The Paired T-Test is used to compare the differences between two samples related to each participant. In this case, the time difference of every participant is considered individually; then, the means of the differences are calculated. In the "Two-Sided" T-Tests, which are unpaired, the means are calculated for the entire group, because a participant may be an outlier in a specific technique, which breaks the pairs. It is referred to as two-sided because the two sets have the same number of elements, since the same number of outliers was removed from each group.

TABLE 18: Chi-squared test for outlier detection applied on reuse study

Study	T.	G.	X2	p	Position	Outlier
First	C	1	5.104305	0.02386654	highest	2489.414342
		2	2.930583	0.08691612	highest	1390.72776
	M	1	4.091151	0.04310829	highest	1203.920754
		2	2.228028	0.1355267	highest	482.570996
Replication	C	1	4.552248	0.03287556	highest	1698.301114
		2	5.013908	0.02514448	highest	1682.391335
	M	1	3.917559	0.04778423	highest	1029.073104
		2	2.943313	0.08623369	lowest	179.467569

Chi-squared test is a statistical test used to detect outliers. It was employed to detect eight outliers in the reuse study. These outliers are removed in the last t-test.

The "Chi-squared test" was applied to both studies in order to detect the outliers, which were then removed when calculating the unpaired T-Test. On the table, the unpaired T-Tests are refered as "Two-sided". The results of the "Chi-squared test" for the reuse study are found on Table 18. The 'M' in the techniques column indicates the use of our tool, while 'C' indicates the conventional technique. The group column indicates the number of the group. The X^2 indicates the result of subtracting each value

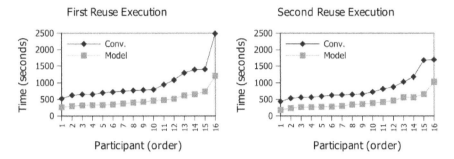

FIGURE 12: Reuse process timings line graph. A graph in which the reuse experiment timings are plotted. The timings are plotted as points in ascendant order, which are then linked with lines. This graph is useful to visualize the data dispersion.

by the variance of the complete set. The position column indicates their position on the set, i.e., highest or lowest. The outlier column shows the timings in seconds that were considered abnormal.

In order to achieve a better visualization of the outliers, we also provide two plots of the data sets. In Figure 12 there are line graphs which may be used to visualize the dispersion of the timing records. In these plots, the timings for each technique are ordered by their performance; therefore, the participant numbers in these plots are not related to their identification codes.

Considering the reuse study and according to the analysis from Table 17 we can state the following. Since all p-values are less than the margin of error (0.01%), which corresponds to the established significance level of 99.99%, then, statistically, we can reject the " $H0_r$" hypothesis that states the techniques are equivalent. Since every t-value is positive, we can accept the " Hp_r" hypothesis, which implies that the conventional technique takes more time than ours.

8.6.2 HYPOTHESES TESTING FOR MAINTENANCE STUDY

In this section, we present statistical calculations to evaluate the data of the maintenance study. Similarly to the reuse study, we applied Paired T-Tests for each execution and another T-Test after removing eight outliers. The seconds that were spent during the process were processed using the statistic computation environment "R" (Free Software Foundation, Inc 2012). The results of the T-Tests are shown on Table 19.

TABLE 19: Maintenance study t-test results

T-test	Data	Means	d.f.	t	p
Paired	First	-345.6539	15	-3.971923	0.001227479
Paired	Replication	-95.88892	15	-1.191781	0.2518624
Two-sided	Both	431.3323	24.22097	-2.662684	0.0135614
		641.0024			

T-Test is a statistical test used to determine the correct hypothesis for both studies. This table lists the results for the maintenance study.

The first column of this table contain the type of T-Test. The second columns indicate the source of the data, which refers to the datasets created for each technique. The "Means" columns indicate the resultant means. The "d.t." columns stand for the degree of freedom; "t" and "p" are variables considered in the hypothesis testing.

The "Chi-squared test" was applied in order to detect the outlier. The results of the "Chi-squared test" for the maintenance study are found on Table 20. These outliers were removed when calculating the unpaired T-Test. On the table, the unpaired T-Test is refered as "Two-sided". The 'M' in the techniques column indicates the use of our tool, while 'C' indicates the conventional technique. The group column indicates the number of the group. The X^2 indicates the results of an comparison to the variance of the complete set. The position column indicates their position on the set, i.e., highest or lowest. And finally, the outlier column shows the timings in seconds that were considered abnormal.

In order to achieve better visualization of the outliers, we also provide two plots of the data sets. In Figure 13, there are line graphs which may be used to visualize the dispersion of the timing records. In these plots, the timings for each technique are ordered independently. Therefore, the participant numbers in these plots are not related to their identification codes.

TABLE 20: Chi-squared test for outlier detection applied on maintenance study

Study	T.	G.	X^2	p	Position	Outlier
First	C	1	2.350449	0.1252469	lowest	182.751342
		2	2.152789	0.1423112	highest	458.576312
	M	1	5.788559	0.0161308	highest	1952.875079
		2	3.598538	0.05783041	highest	1283.533192
Replication	C	1	1.771974	0.183138	highest	1082.486509
		2	4.338041	0.03726978	highest	493.115942
	M	1	2.422232	0.1196244	highest	837.879299
		2	4.87366	0.02726961	lowest	1554.176697

Chi-squared test is a statistical test used to detect outliers. It was employed to detect eight outliers in the maintenance study. These outliers are removed in the last t-test.

If we take into consideration the maintenance study and its analysis illustrated on Table 19, we cannot reject the " H0m" hypothesis that states the techniques are equivalent because all p-values are bigger than the margin of error (0.01%), which corresponds to the established significance level of 99.99%. Therefore, statistically, we can assume that the effort needed to edit a reuse code and a reuse model is approximately equal.

8.6.3 THREATS TO VALIDITY

8.6.3.1 INTERNAL VALIDITY

- Experience Level of Participants. The different levels of knowledge of the participants could have compromised the data. To mitigate this threat, we divided the participants in two balanced groups considering their experience level and later we rebalanced the groups considering the preliminary results. Although all participants already had a prior experience in how to reuse the CF in the conventional way, during the training phase, they were

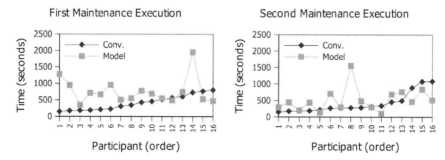

FIGURE 13: Maintenance process timings line graph. A graph in which the maintenance experiment timings are plotted. The timings are plotted as points in ascendant order, which are then linked with lines. This graph is useful to visualize the data dispersion.

taught how to make the reuse with the model-based tool and also how to reuse it in the normal way. So, this could have provided the participants even more experience with the conventional technique.

- Productivity under evaluation. The students could have thought that their results in the experiment will influence their grades in the course. In order to mitigate this, we explained to the students that no one was being evaluated and their participation was considered anonymous.
- Facilities used during the study. Different computers and configurations could have affected the recorded timings. However, participants used the same configuration, make, model, and operating system in equal numbers. The participants were not allowed to change their computers during the same activity. This means that every participant had to execute every exercise using the same computer.

8.6.3.2 VALIDITY BY CONSTRUCTION

- Hypothesis expectations: the participants already knew the researchers and knew that the model-based tool was supposed to ease the reuse process, which reflects one of our hypothesis. Both of these issues could affect the collected data and cause the experiment to be less impartial. In order to avoid impartiality, we enforced that the participants had to keep a steady pace during the whole study.

8.6.3.3 EXTERNAL VALIDITY

• Interaction between configuration and treatment. It is possible that the re-use exercises were not accurate for every reuse of a crosscutting framework for real world applications. Only a single crosscutting framework was considered in our study and the base applications were of the same complexity. To mitigate this threat, we designed the exercises with applications that were based on the ones existing in reality.

8.6.3.4 CONCLUSION VALIDITY

• Measure reliability. It refers to metrics used to measuring the reuse effort. To mitigate this threat, we have used only the time, necessary to complete the process, which was captured by a data collector in order to allow better precision;
• Low statistic power. The ability of a statistic test to reveal the reliable data. We applied three T-Tests to analyze the experiment data statistically to avoid the low statistic power.

8.7 RELATED WORK

The approach proposed by Cechticky et al. (2003) allows the reuse of object-oriented application framework by applying the tool called OBS Instantiation Environment. That tool supports graphical models to define the settings to generate the expected application. The model-to-code transformation generates a new application that reuses the framework.

In another related work, Braga and Masiero (2003) proposed a process to create framework instantiation tools. The process is specific for application frameworks defined by a pattern language. The process application assures that the tool is capable of generating every possible framework variability.

The approach defined by Czarnecki et al. (2006) defines a round-trip process to create domain specific languages for framework documentation. These languages can be employed to represent the information that the framework programming interfaces need during the instantiation and the description of these interfaces. This is a bilateral process, i.e., two transformers are fashioned: a transformer from model to code and a transformer from code to model. Generated codes are transformed back to models. This allow the comparison of the source model with the generated model, which should be perfectly equal. If differences are found, the language or the transformers should be improved in the activity called "conciliation".

Santos et al. proposed a process and a tool to suport framework reuse (Santos et al. 2008). In this approach, the domain engineer must supply a reuse example which must be tagged. These tags mark points of the reuse example that is to be replaced in order to create different applications.

The tags are mapped into a domain specific language that lists information that the application engineer should supply in order to reuse the framework. This domain specific language instances are, then, interpreted by a tool that is capable of listing the points to complete framework instantiation. This is the only related work that uses AspectJ and the aspect-oriented programming.

Our proposal differs from their approach on the following topics: 1) their approach is restricted to frameworks known during the development of the tool; 2) the reuse process is applied to application frameworks, which are used to create new applications.

Another approach was proposed by Oliveira et al. (2011). Their approach can be applied to a greater number of object oriented frameworks. After the framework development, its developer may use the approach to ease the reuse by writing the cookbook in a formal language known as Reuse Definition Language (RDL) which can also be used to generate the source code. This process allows us to select variabilities and resources during the reuse procedure, as long as the framework engineer specifies the RDL code correctly. These approaches were created to support the reuse procedure during the final development stages. Therefore, the approach that is proposed in this paper differs from others by supporting earlier development phases. This allows the application engineer to initiate the reuse process since the analysis phase while developing an application compatible to the reused frameworks.

Although the approach proposed by Cechticky et al. (2003) is specific for only one framework, it can be employed since the design phase. The other related approach can be employed in a greater number of frameworks:

however, it is used on a lower abstraction level, and does not support the design phase. Another difference is the generation of aspect-oriented code, which improves code modularization. Finally, the last difference that must be pointed out is the use of experiments to evaluate the approach, while the presented related works only show case studies employing their tools.

8.8 CONCLUSIONS

In this article we presented a model-based approach that raises the abstraction level of reusing Crosscutting Frameworks (CFs)—a type of aspect-oriented framework. The approach is supported by two models, called Reuse Requirements Model (RRM) and Reuse Model (RM). The RRM serves as a graphical view for enhancing cookbooks and the RM supports application engineers in performing the reuse process by filling in this model and generating the source-code. Considering our approach, a new reuse process is delineated allowing engineers to start the reuse in early development phases. Using our approach, application developers do not need to worry about either architectural or source-code details, shortening the time necessary to conduct the process.

We have evaluated our approach by means of two experiments. The first one was focused on comparing the productivity of our model-based approach to the ad-hoc approach. The results showed the improvement of approximately 97% in favor of our approach. We claim that this improvement can be influenced by the framework characteristics but not by the application characteristics. If a CF requires a lot of heterogeneous joinpoints we think this percentage will go down because the application engineer will need to write the joinpoints (method names, for instance) either using both our approach or the ad-hoc one. However, if the CF is heavily based on inter-type declarations and the returning of values, then we claim that the productivity can be even higher, as it is very straightforward to do so while using our approach.

The second experiment was focused on observing the effort in maintaining applications that were developed with our approach (CF-based applications) and with the ad-hoc one. It was not possible to conclude which process takes less effort in this case; however, we believe that they are approximately equivalent. The participants argued that the tool could be improved to avoid opening new forms while entering the model attributes, which, as they claim, had disrupted their work and prevented them from reaching a better performance in this case. It is important that in this experiment we did not provide errors that developers could create while using the conventional approach, since our model approach shields the developers from doing that. We have also provided the raw data gathered during the studies as Additional files 1 and 2.

As the possible limitations of our work, we can mention the following. Once the models have been created on top of the Eclipse Modeling Project, they cannot be used in another development environment. Besides, the code generator only produce codes for AspectJ, therefore, only crosscutting frameworks developed in this language can be currently supported. A simple extension is possible to allow this approach to support the reuse of non-crosscutting frameworks written in Java and AspectJ. Also, we have not yet evaluated how to deal with coupling of multiple CFs to a single base application. Although this functionality is already supported in our approach, some frameworks may select the same joinpoints, which may cause conflicts and lead to unpredictable results.

Long term future works are: (i) providing a support for framework engineers so that they do not have to build the RRM manually. The idea is to develop a tool which can assist them in creating this model in a more automatic way; (ii) performing an experiment to verify whether the abstractions of the model elements are on a suitable level (iii) analyzing the reusability of the metamodel abstract classes.

REFERENCES

1.   Antkiewicz M, Czarnecki K (2006) Framework-specific modeling languages with round-trip engineering. In: ACM/IEEE 9th international conference on model driven engineering languages and systems (MoDELS). Springer-Verlag, Genova. pp 692-706 http://www.springerlink.com/content/y081522127011160/fulltext.pdf
2.   Apache Software Foundation (2012) Apache Derby. http://db.apache.org/derby/
3.   AspectJ Team (2003) The AspectJ(TM) Programming Guide. http://www.eclipse.org/aspectj/doc/released/progguide/
4.   Braga R, Masiero P (2003) Building a wizard for framework instantiation based on a pattern language. In: Konstantas D, Léonard M, Pigneur Y, Patel S (eds) Object-

oriented information systems, Volume 2817 of Lecture notes in computer science. Springer, Berlin / Heidelberg. pp 95-106 http://dx.doi.org/10.1007/978-3-540-45242-3_10

5. Bynens M, Landuyt D, Truyen E, Joosen W (2010) Towards reusable aspects: the mismatch problem. In: Workshop on Aspect, Components and Patterns for Infrastructure Software (ACP4IS'10). Rennes and Saint Malo, France. ACM, New York, NY, USA. pp 17-20

6. Camargo VV, Masiero PC (2005) Frameworks Orientados A Aspectos. In: Anais Do 19° Simpósio Brasileiro De Engenharia De Software (SBES'2005). Uberlândia-MG, Brasil, Outubro.

7. Masiero PC, Camargo VV (2004) An approach to design crosscutting framework families. In: Proc. of the 2008 AOSD workshop on Aspects, components, and patterns for infrastructure software, ACP4IS '08. Brussels, Belgium. ACM, New York, NY, USA. http://dl.acm.org/citation.cfm?id=1404891.1404894

8. Cechticky V, Chevalley P, Pasetti A, Schaufelberger W (2003) A generative approach to framework instantiation. In: Proceedings of the 2nd international conference on Generative programming and component engineering, GPCE '03. Springer-Verlag, New York, Inc., New York. pp 267-286 http://portal.acm.org/citation.cfm?id=954186.954203

9. Clark T, Evans A, Sammut P, Willans J (2004) Transformation Language Design: A Metamodelling Foundation, ICGT, Volume 3256 of Graph Transformations, Lecture Notes in Computer Science. Springer-Verlag, Berlin, Heidelberg. pp 13–21

10. Clements P, Northrop L (2002) Software product lines: practices and patterns, 3rd edn. The SEI series in software engineering, 563 pages, first edition. Addison-Wesley Professional, Boston, United States of America. http://www.pearsonhighered.com/educator/product/Software-Product-Lines-Practices-and-Patterns/9780201703320.page

11. Cunha C, Sobral J, Monteiro M (2006) Reusable aspect-oriented implementations of concurrency patterns and mechanisms. In: Aspect-Oriented Software Development Conference (AOSD'06). Bonn, Germany. ACM, New York, NY, USA.

12. Eclipse Consortium (2011) Graphical Modeling Framework, version 1.5.0. Graphical Modeling Project. http://www.eclipse.org/modeling/gmp/

13. Efftinge S (2006) openArchitectureWare 4.1 Xtend language reference. http://www.openarchitectureware.org/pub/documentation/4.3.1/html/contents/core_ reference.html

14. Fayad M, Schmidt DC (1997) Object-oriented application frameworks. Commun ACM 40:32-38

15. Fowler M (2010) Domain specific languages, 1st edition. 640 pages, first edition. Addison-Wesley Professional, Boston, United States of America. http://www.pearsonhighered.com/educator/product/DomainSpecific-Languages/9780321712943.page

16. France R, Rumpe B (2007) Model-driven development of complex software: a research roadmap. In: 2007 Future of Software Engineering, FOSE 07. IEEE Computer Society, Washington. pp 37-54

17. Free Software Foundation, Inc (2012) R. http://www.r-project.org/

18. Huang M, Wang C, Zhang L (2004) Towards a reusable and generic aspect library. In: Workshop of the Aspect Oriented Software Development Conference at AOSD-SEC'04, AOSD'04. Lancaster, United Kingdom. ACM, New York, NY, USA.

19. Kiczales G, Lamping J, Mendhekar A, Maeda C, Lopes C, marc Loingtier J, Irwin J (1997) Aspect-oriented programming. In: ECOOP. Springer-Verlag, Heidelberger, Berlin, Germany.

20. Kiczales G, Hilsdale E, Hugunin J, Kersten M, Palm J, Griswold WG (2001) An overview of aspectJ. Springer-Verlag, Heidelberger, Berlin, Germany. pp 327–353

21. Kulesza U, Alves E, Garcia R, Lucena CJPD, Borba P (2006) Improving Extensibility of object-oriented frameworks with aspect-oriented programming. In: Proc. of the 9th Intl Conf. on software reuse (ICSR'06). Torino, Italy, June 12-15, 2006, Lecture Notes in Computer Science, Programming and Software Engineering, vol 4039. Springer-Verlag, Heidelberger, Berlin, Germany. pp 231-245

22. Mortensen M, Ghosh S (2006) Creating pluggable and reusable non-functional aspects in AspectC++. In: Proceedings of the fifth AOSD workshop on aspects, components, and patterns for infrastructure Software. Bonn, Germany. ACM, New York, NY, USA.

23. Oliveira TC, Alencar P, Cowan D (2011) ReuseTool-An extensible tool support for object-oriented framework reuse. J Syst Softw 84(12):2234-2252 http://dx.doi.org/10.1016/j.jss.2011.06.030

24. Pastor O, Molina JC (2007) Model-driven architecture in practice: a software production environment based on conceptual modeling. Springer-Verlag, New York, Secaucus.

25. Sakenou D, Mehner K, Herrmann S, Sudhof H (2006) Patterns for re-usable aspects in object teams. In: Net Object Days. Erfurt, Germany. Object Teams, Technische Universität Berlin, Berlin, Germany.

26. Santos AL, Koskimies K, Lopes A (2008) Automated domain-specific modeling languages for generating framework-based applications. Softw Product Line Conf Int 0:149-158

27. Schmidt DC (2006) Model-driven engineering. IEEE Computer 39(2): http://www.truststc.org/pubs/30.html

28. Shah V, Hill V (2004) An aspect-oriented security framework: lessons learned. In: Workshop of the Aspect Oriented Software Development Conference at AOSD-SEC'04, AOSD'04. Lancaster, United Kingdom. ACM, New York, NY, USA.

29. Soares S, Laureano E, Borba P (2006) Distribution and persistence as aspects. Software: Practice and Experience. 36(7):711-759 John Wiley & Sons, Ltd. Hoboken, NJ, USA. http://onlinelibrary.wiley.com/doi/10.1002/spe.715/abstract

30. Soudarajan N, Khatchadourian R (2009) Specifying reusable aspects. In: Asian Workshop on Aspect-Oriented and Modular Software Development (AOAsia'09). Auckland, New Zealand. AOAsia, Chinese University of Hong Kong, Hong Kong, People's Republic of China.

31. Wohlin C, Runeson P, Höst M, Ohlsson MC, Regnell B, Wesslén A (2000) Experimentation in software engineering: an introduction. First edition. 204 pages. Kluwer Academic Publishers, Norwell, MA, USA.

32. Zanon I, Camargo VV, Penteado RAD (2010) Reestructuring an application framework with a persistence crosscutting framework. INFOCOMP 1:9-16

Tables 11 and 15 are not available in this version of the article. To views these, along with several online supplemental files, please use the citation on the first page of this chapter.

CHAPTER 9

USING BUILT-IN DOMAIN-SPECIFIC MODELING SUPPORT TO GUIDE MODEL-BASED TEST GENERATION

TEEMU KANSTRÉN AND OLLI-PEKKA PUOLITAIVAL

9.1 INTRODUCTION

Model-based testing (MBT) as an advanced test automation concept has been gaining increasing interest in the industry in recent years. MBT can be defined in various ways, and in this paper we follow the definition by Utting and Legeard [14] as "Generation of test cases with oracles from a behavioral model". MBT can be a powerful approach in generating test cases to cover various aspects of the system under test from the test models. However, typically several different types of expertise are required to build useful test models and to effectively generate test cases from these models.

Firstly, creating models for MBT is essentially a programming activity, describing the system under test (SUT) at a high level and from the testing viewpoint. Although graphical modeling notations exist, such as using UML state charts, at some level the user always needs to describe the behavioral aspects in terms of some form of programming language constructs [14]. This aspect is highlighted by the use of the term model program to describe the test models [3].

Thus we can say that programming skills are required to produce the test models. Additionally, each MBT tool has its own notation for describing the test aspects (e.g., defining what constitutes a test step) on top of this test model [15], requiring the user to also have expertise in the specific modeling notations of the used tools. However, having programming skills and knowing the tool notations is typically not enough but one also requires domain expertise in order to be able to build useful test models. Typically all the required expertise can only be found in combination of several experts.

In this paper we view MBT from the viewpoint of domain-specific modeling (DSM) and how we can integrate support for more effective modeling and test generation for MBT tools with the help of DSM concepts. In DSM terminology, the person with the programming and tool expertise is termed here as the language expert and the person with domain knowledge as the domain expert.

We discuss the use of a MBT tool that transforms the test model into a DSM language, and how this can be used to more effectively guide test generation. We show how the language developer can use our OSMO-Tester MBT tool framework to develop test models using a full (Java) programming language and all the benefits it provides (reuse of skills, test libraries, IDE integration with debugging, refactoring and more). It is our experience that this type of a modeling language provides a powerful modeling basis and is as easier if not easier to learn than custom semi-graphical notations of many MBT tools. The OSMOTester toolset provides a framework for creating these test models, and from these test models automatically creates a DSM language that the domain expert can use to guide test generation.

The rest of this paper is structured as follows. Section 2 presents the background concepts of modelbased testing and domain-specific modeling in more detail, and also discusses related work. Section 3 presents the OSMOTester toolset and the approach it supports in detail. Section 4 provides discussion on the topic. Finally, section 5 concludes the paper.

9.2 BACKGROUND

This section briefly presents the relevant background concepts for this paper and discusses related work.

9.2.1 MODEL-BASED TESTING

As described before, model-based testing as discussed here is about using behavioral models as a basis to generate tests for a system. This requires various tools and expertise to provide a useful result. Several different MBT tools exist, each with their own set of features and test generation algorithms [15]. These also use various notations that are suited for generic representation of system behavior, such as statebased, transition-based, and function-based notations, and various combinations of such notations [15]. As noted, practically all of them require representing the system under test in terms of some programming language constructs to enable test generation with input data and oracles from the model.

In this regard, we borrow the term model program from [3] to describe the test models. Grieskamp et al. [3] define the model program as using guarded-update rules to modify the global data state. When a rule is invoked, a transition between the data states takes place and at the same time a method on the SUT test adapter is invoked. As a result, test steps (sometimes called actions) take place in an order defined by the model, the model traversal algorithms, and as executed by the test adapter.

With regards to the required expertise, it can be said that several different forms of expertise are required to produce useful models. Domain knowledge is required to produce test cases that link with the SUT, produce meaningful input data and evaluate the results in a useful way. Modeling expertise is required to understand how different aspects of the SUT behavior can be effectively described in the test models. Tool knowledge is required to understand the notation of the MBT tools used and to build models that effectively make use of the provided features of the tools modeling language and allow the tool to effectively generate test cases from these models. Test expertise in general is required to understand not only the vertical target domain but also the horizontal domain of test automation and how they should map together to produce a useful overall test environment.

In a practical context, with complexity of modern systems, it is unrealistic to expect one or few persons to have all this knowledge of different domains. The target domain expert is usually an expert on the application domain and should not be expected to know all the details of MBT to produce useful test cases. A test expert in the target domain may be an expert in applying test automation concepts in the specific domain with the help of the domain expert. Another expert may be an expert in using specific MBT tools and in expressing system behavior in terms of behavioral models. Different combinations of experts typically exist for different target domains and systems, some cross-domain experts in several areas, and several experts may be available in any domain. However, effectively working together is required by the different experts to produce useful test models that in the end allow for effective test generation for the target system. With sufficient resources, the overall MBT process can be carried out using only MBT tools and models, for example, using purely model programs as test models, with collaboration of the different (language and domain) experts at all points of the process. However, it is also useful to provide support for the domain experts to perform independent exploration of the test target with the help of the test models. To support this, we look at the concepts of domain-specific modeling.

9.2.2 DOMAIN-SPECIFIC MODELING

Domain-specific modeling can be defined as using models to raise the level of abstraction, using domain concepts to describe the solution [8]. From these models, it is possible to automatically generate the required product (code) as both the modeling language and the generators are created specifically for the company and the domain (application). The DSM approach consists of two main parts:

- Language and generator development, and
- Solution modeling.

In the first part, the modeling notation and the transformation from that notation to the actual end product are defined. The first part involves the domain expert and the language developer. The second part involves the developers who work on developing the actual end products. In case of DSM, this also includes domain experts as they can use the higher abstraction level of the domain specific language to develop products as well.

DSM works best and is most cost-effective when developing several end products which share characteristics but also vary in different ways. In this case the same modeling language can be used to create several products, justifying the cost of language development. In traditional domains the target systems have typically been product families, in which different products can be modeled using the same domain specific language. In the test automation domain, we observe that even a single system typically has numerous varying test cases, based on the same base language.

In our previous work we have used DSM to express test cases directly [11] and also to express test models in MBT with a transformation to a specific chosen MBT tool [6]. This means the domain expert is able to build test cases and test models using familiar domain concepts. However, these approaches require a language expert to define the language in a DSM tool which has no built-in support for the MBT tool notation, making the language development challenging without advanced editing support, requiring specific DSM tool skills, making development harder and complicating maintenance.

In this paper we describe a modeling approach for MBT where the DSM language creation is integrated into the model built using the MBT tool with only little or no extra effort required from the language developer. As the model is built on an existing popular programming language, it allows for re-use of skills, development environments, and other assets.

9.2.3 RELATED WORKS

Model-based testing has been reported as having been successfully applied in several domains. This includes aerospace [1], automotive [2, 10], medical [16], communication protocols [3], and information systems [12].

These studies typically show improvements and benefits in applying the MBT approach in the different domains. However, they also highlight the typical situation where the model is built by an expert in the MBT tools and their notation, with the help of information provided by the domain experts. Providing means for a domain expert without the need of deep MBT tool expertise is a topic where domain-specific modeling can be applied.

In MBT, the test model is typically created to describe a large set of potential SUT behavior. The number of potential test combinations that can be generated from such models is huge or even unbounded. To address this issue, Grieskamp et al. [3] have applied model slicing, where the expert defines constraints in the notation of the model program on how the test generator will generate test cases from the model. They use the term scenario-based test generation viewing the slices to define certain test generation scenarios. Our approach is similar while also providing a higher-abstraction level DSM language for the domain expert. Additionally, we also provide means to use this to manually create specific test scripts from the test models.

Specialized approaches for using MBT in specific domains have also been proposed. Takala et al. [13] have built a tool for model-based testing of Android smart-phone applications. This tool is intended to build test models for Android applications in terms of their common user-interface elements. This provides a specific DSM for MBT in for the Android application domain. We provide a generic approach that can be used as a basis for more specific approaches such as these.

Another example of applying DSM with MBT is presented by Kloos and Eschbach for the domain of railway control systems [9]. A specific language is presented for this domain and this can be used to create test models. This language requires detailed knowledge on domain aspects and formalisms such as Mealy machines and process calculi, which can be challenging for domain experts. We use a common programming language (Java) as the underlying notation to ease the language development, and provide a domain-specific abstraction on top of it to enable the domain expert to work with the model as well.

A related approach is presented by Katara and Kervinen [7] who use low-level keywords (e.g., press key X) and on top of those, higher-level domain-specific action words (e.g., take picture), and transitions between them, to describe the test model for MBT. Our approach is similar in using textual domainspecific language in the context of MBT. However, we automatically produce these domain languages from the test model and allow their use to guide test generation and effectively generate specialized versions of the model.

Finally, our previous work on creating graphical modelling DSM languages for MBT is also relevant [6]. In the previous work specific modeling languages are built for specific domains and complete model programs are generated, which are challenging to create, maintain and evolve in a graphical code generator not built for the MBT tools notation. In this paper, we present an approach where the DSM is automatically built as part of the provided test model. An interesting extension would be to add a graphical DSM layer on top of our automatically generated textual DSM language.

9.3 THE OSMOTESTER APPROACH

Our approach is implemented and available in a tool called OSMOTester [4]. Here we refer to our approach as the OSMOTester approach according to this implementation. This approach is based on two layers in line with

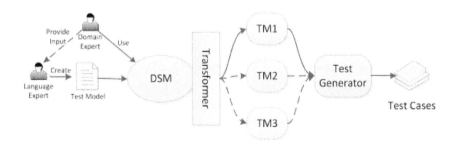

FIGURE 1: DSM elements in our approach

the definition of domain specific modeling we presented in section 2: one for language and generator (model program) development, and another for the solution development (DSM guided test generation). In this section we first present a high-level overview of the approach, followed by the support for developing the language and the test generator, and finally the support for the solution development. This approach works both for online (direct test execution in generation) and offline (generate scripts and execute later) MBT approaches.

9.3.1 HIGH-LEVEL OVERVIEW

From the test automation perspective, our approach in terms of DSM is illustrated in Figure 1. Together with the domain expert, the language expert defines the generic overall test model. From this model, OSMOTester automatically forms a higher-level DSM language that the domain expert can use to guide the test generation from this model. In DSM terminology, a transformation is applied by OSMOTester based on the constraints defined by the domain expert to produce constrained variants of the test model (TM1, TM2, TM3 in the figure). The OSMOTester test generator then generates test cases from these test model variants (or scenarios/slices as in [3]).

10.3.2 LANGUAGE AND GENERATOR DEVELOPMENT

The modeling notation supported by OSMOTester is the standard Java programming language with specific annotations and modeling objects to support test generation from the models. With the term model object we refer to Java classes containing transition methods and data-flow variable usage. The basics of the modeling notation and the composition of test models from this notation have been described in our previous work [5]. It is based on our experiences in test modeling and use of other tools (e.g., ModelJUnit [14] is a close relative). We recall here the basics of this modeling notation including the latest evolutions.

We view the models for model-based testing as composed of two main elements: control-flow and data-flow. We start here by presenting the control-flow aspects followed by the data-flow aspects.

9.3.2.1 CONTROL-FLOW MODELING

With control-flow we refer to the order in which the different test steps are executed. The test step refers to executing a transition method on the model program. As is common for this type of approach, the possible transitions that can be taken at any time are defined by their associated guard

LISTING 1: Model object example.

```
1   /** The global model state, shared across test models. */
2   private final ModelState state;
3   /** The scripter for creating/executing the test cases. */
4   private final CalendarScripter scripter;
5
6   @Transition("AddEvent")
7   public void addEvent() {
8     String uid = state.randomUID();
9     Date start = state.randomStartTime();
10    Date end = calculateEndTime(start);
11    ModelEvent event = state.createEvent(uid, start, end);
12    scripter.addEvent(event);
13  }
14
15  @Guard("RemoveOrganizerEvent")
16  public boolean guardRemoveOrganizerEvent() {
17    return state.hasEvents();
18  }
19
20  @Transition("RemoveOrganizerEvent")
21  public void removeOrganizerEvent() {
22    ModelEvent event = state.getAndRemoveOrganizerEvent();
23    scripter.removeEvent(event.getUid(), event);
24  }
```

statements. A transition can only be taken when the associated guard statements allow it to be taken.

To support for control-flow modeling OSMOTester defines two basic annotations, @Guard and @Transition. When a method in a model program is associated with a @Guard annotation, these methods must return a Boolean value of true to allow any associated transitions to be taken by the test generator. A guard method is associated to transitions by their naming, which is given as @Guard("name") and @Transition("name"). A guard can be associated to several transitions by using an array of names, or by leaving the name out completely which associates it to all transitions in the test model(s).

A transition is the central concept of the control-flow modeling as all other elements related to control-flow are executed together with associ-

LISTING 2: Data-flow example

```
1   @Variable
2   /** Used to generate start times between January 2000 and December 2010. */
3   private ValueRange<Long> startTime;
4
5   public ModelState() {
6     Calendar start = Calendar.getInstance();
7     start.setTime(new Date(0));
8     start.set(2000, 0, 1, 0, 0, 0);
9     Calendar end = Calendar.getInstance();
10    end.setTime(new Date(0));
11    end.set(2010, 11, 31, 23, 59, 59);
12    long startMillis = start.getTimeInMillis();
13    long endMillis = end.getTimeInMillis();
14    startTime = new ValueRange<Long>(startMillis, endMillis);
15  }
16
17  public Date randomStartTime() {
18    return new Date(startTime.next());
19  }
```

ated transitions. As it is out experience that transitions in test generation represent a form of test step in a test model, we also support using the annotation @TestStep instead of @Transition. Other control-flow related elements include the @Pre and @Post annotations, which cause any tagged methods to be executed before (@Pre) or after (@Post) the associated transitions. Association is similar as for @Guard annotations. For example, we have used @Post annotations to provide generic test oracles that should be executed after each test step (to evaluate model state vs SUT), and both @Pre and @Post annotations to provide logging information on the model state before and after test steps.

As described in [5], these elements can be embedded in different Java classes and then composed in a modular fashion by the OSMOTester tool. This allows one to specify different concepts, partial models, and their compositions in separate modules and configurations. Listing 1 shows an example of a model object using these elements.

9.3.3 DATA-FLOW MODELING

As an extension to our previous work, we also provide a set of objects to support data-flow modeling. The main modeling objects for data-flow currently are:

- Value range: defining a numerical range of values for a variable
- Value set: defining a set of values for a variable
- Readable words: defining character combinations that consist of commonly displayed humanreadable characters.

In order to use these data-flow objects, one initializes them at model-creation time and uses them to provide matching values where needed as input in the test steps. As each of the provided objects keeps a history of the values it has provided, it is possible to configure them with different algorithms for input generation. This includes random values, least covered values, or boundary values (for a value range). Each data-flow object can be configured separately with their own configuration of values and algorithms.

Listing 2 gives an example of defining a range of possible values for a start date of a calendar event using a value range object. New values for this variable are generated using the next() method, which is part of an interface shared by all data-flow objects.

Beyond these specific object types, also primitive values (e.g., integers, Strings, Booleans) and custom objects of any type can be recorded by OSMOTester. While their generation and updates may not be handled by OSMOTester itself, it will still record values of all @Variable tagged variables in the model objects regardless of their type. All values are recorded by their object instance, and can be compared to their String representation if used as definitions in coverage algorithms or similar components.

9.3.4 COMPOSING THE MODELS AND GENERATING TESTS

Once the different elements of the control-flow and data-flow models have been specified, they still need to be composed together and we need to be able to invoke a test generator to generate tests based on these models. OSMOTester provides the test generator component that basically traverses the given model program steps according to their guards and chosen generation algorithms. As the generator traverses the transitions, it also explores the data-flow space by generating data from any encountered data-flow object.

The binding of the model objects together in practice consists of creating the test generator (Java) object and using its methods to add the (Java) model objects to it. For space reasons, we do not show this as an example here but one is available in [5]. The OSMOTester generator starts by parsing all the given model objects and associating all model elements to each other. It also stores references to all @Variable tagged variables to capture any values they produce. This allows for creation of more advanced algorithms and feature to support test generation without requiring specific action by the user.

It is possible to define a set of specific algorithms and constraints to guide the test generation also at this level. Test and suite end conditions provided with OSMOTester include:

- Length: end after generating a given number of steps or tests
- Probability: end after any step or test with a given probability
- Requirements coverage: end when the given requirements have been covered (identified by specific object calls in the test models)
- Step coverage: end when the defined set of transitions has been covered
- Data coverage: end when the defined set of values for given data variables has been covered
- And/Or compositions: allow composing several end conditions together with logical operators

Similarly, different algorithms for traversing the given models can be defined based on the different elements of the model objects. OSMOTester includes the following algorithms:

- Random: picks a random transition from the ones available
- Balancing: randomly picks an available transition but favors less covered ones
- Weighted: randomly picks an available transition but gives a higher probability to ones with higher weight.

Weight can be defined by the modeler as in @Transition("name", 5), where 5 is the weight.

9.3.5 DOMAIN SPECIFIC SCRIPTING LANGUAGES

In the previous subsection we described the first part of our DSM support, the language development framework. In this subsection we describe the second part of DSM in our MBT context: support for solution domain modeling. In our previous work we have created graphical domain-specific languages for manual test creation [11] and for test modeling for model-based test generation [6]. There approaches were based on using a specific domain-specific modeling tool to build the models separately from the test models.

Here the test models themselves are used as a basis for the domain language and the MBT tool as the test generator. The support for using such models has been integrated into the OSMOTester tool itself, requiring no external tools or practically no added effort on top of building the test models themselves as described in the previous subsection.

LISTING 3: DSM script example.

```
1   setting, value
2   model factory, osmo.tester.examples.gui.TestModelFactory
3   algorithm, random
4
5   step, times
6   add event, >=2
7   add overlapping event, >= 3
8   add task, == 1
9   add overlapping task, <=2
10
11  variable, coverage
12  event count, 5
```

The basis for this domain language is formed by the transitions defined in the test model as described in section 3.2.1. More specifically, the names given to the transitions in the annotations as in @Transition("name") form the vocabulary of the domain specific language. In our experience, as people work to build such models and give names to their model elements, they naturally tend to use names of familiar domain and test concepts. For example, OSMOTester comes with a calendar application example that has the following transitions:

- Add event: Adds a new event to the calendar for an existing user.
- Link event to user: Links an existing event to another user, making the new user a participant in the event organized by the first user.
- Remove organizer event: Removes an event completely by deleting it from the organizer and as a result from all linked participants.
- Remove participant event: Removes a participant from an event.
- Add task: Adds a task for an existing user. A task is like an event with no duration or participants.
- Remove task: Removes a chosen task from associated user.
- Add task overlapping event: Adds a task that overlaps a chosen event in time for the same user.
- Add overlapping event: Adds an event overlapping another event in time for the same user.

These are transitions (test steps) of the calendar example that describe its nominal (expected) behavior. Additionally, the calendar test model also defines a set of transitions for testing the error handling behavior of the calendar. These are the following transitions:

- Remove a task that does not exist: Tries to remove a task which does not exist (invalid data).
- Remove an event that does not exist: Tries to remove an event which does not exist (invalid data).

OSMOTester supports two different types of applications of these elements as a domain-specific testing language. In this subsection we will further demonstrate their use in terms of the calendar example.

9.3.5.1 ABSTRACT DOMAIN-SPECIFIC SCRIPTING

We can define constraints over the model programs to guide the OSMO-Tester test generator. The model defines the overall possible flows of test generation, while the scripting language allows for guiding it towards specific goals. This support is based on the observed needs in industrial application, where the domain experts wish to guide test generation to explore specific areas of interest at different times.

For example, considering the calendar example, we may wish to generate a set of test cases for having several overlapping events and some tasks, with several events active at a time (i.e., not removed before new ones are added). In this case, we can use the generic model program specified previously, and just define the specific requirements for the test cases in the scripting language. A script supporting this definition is shown in Listing 3.

This shows three different tables illustrating different aspects than can be defined for configuring the test generator. First, we provide a settings table specifying that the model objects for test generation are provided by a class called osmo.tester.example.gui.TestModelFactory. We also define that we wish to use the random algorithm for test generation.

Second, we define a step coverage requirement table specifying that we want the AddEvent step (transition) to occur in each generated test case a minimum of 2 times. We also define that we want the step AddOverlap-pingEvent to occur a minimum of 3 times. The AddTask step needs to be present exactly once in each generated test case, and the AddOverlapping-Task at most 2 times.

The third and final table in this example specifies that the variable EventCount should have the value of 5 at some point in each generated test case. As the model program uses the EventCount variable to express the total number of both organizer events and participant events, this ensures that their total sum as active events during a test case reaches 5 at some point. At the same time, the previously defined requirements for different types of transitions ensure that different types of events are also generated in each test case (organizer and participant).

A table missing in this example is one that allows the user also to over-ride what data values are generated for specific input values. This table is similar to the variable coverage table, defining variable names and their possible values to be generated. If there is no definition for a variable, the generic model program definitions are used instead.

These examples also illustrate the expertise required to build suitable models than can be used in a diverse way as a basis for test generation. For example, in the calendar example, the current model program does not let us specify how many users we wish to have included in the generated tests. In fact, the example provided with the OSMOTester distribution generates a number of users randomly between 3 and 5. If this becomes important to control, a specific transition for adding transitions could be defined and we could then define exact number of these transitions required. Alterna-tively, a data variable could be defined that is used by the model program to generate a matching number of users and thus allows the user to control the number through the scripting language.

In addition to manual script writing, OSMOTester also provides a graphical user interface (GUI) to create these scripts. This is illustrated in Figure 2. The useful part of this GUI is that given the set of model objects that compose the model-program it can automatically identify all possible transitions and data variables. Thus it can show the user the options avail-able for building the DSM scripts and also the operators available. An example of these is shown in Figure 2 for the calendar example.

Considering the end result, generating a number of tests using test generation algorithms to execute a model program produces a lot of variation but this may not always be the type of variation the domain expert wants at that time. Many MBT tools use static analysis techniques such as symbolic execution and constraint solving to generate specific test cases traversing the model in desired paths. As we take a more dynamic approach of executing the model as a normal program, we also provide support for optimizing the test set in this way. We support optimizing for transition, transition pair, requirements (specific definitions in model objects), variable (number of values) and variable value (specific values) coverage via a greedy optimizer. The optimizer takes a weight value for each of these coverage criteria and provides an optimized subset of specified size from the given overall set.

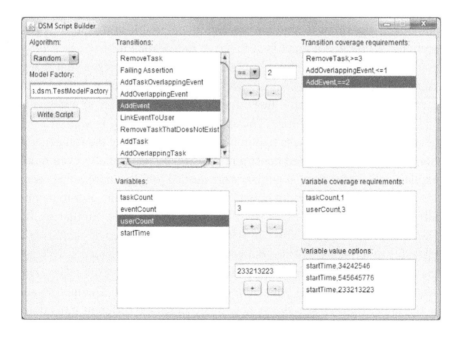

FIGURE 2: OSMO DSM GUI

In our experience test generation from the models is generally fast, and this provides a practical method for providing an optimized test suite. For example, generating 50000 test cases from the calendar example takes about 11 seconds, and optimizing this to find an optimized set of 50 tests with the algorithm takes about 17 seconds on an Intel CoreI5 2,67Mhz system utilizing a single core, with the Java virtual machine maximum heap size of 880MB (formed by Java default settings, not modified or monitored as memory use did not become an issue). As the test object OSMOTester creates for each generated test case gives the model program a possibility to store the test script with it, the user can then pick the optimized set of scripts for use.

9.3.5.2 MANUAL DOMAIN-SPECIFIC SCRIPTING

Model-based testing is commonly considered as a means for automated test generation from test models. The tests are generated by using some automated algorithm to traverse the test model as illustrated in previous sections. While it is a great goal to strive for creating all test cases automatically from such models, in practice it is our experience that many people still wish to see a set of specific manually crafted test cases that they can control and verify they cover a given set of paths, requirements and other elements of interest. The approach we presented in section 3.5.1 helps address many of these requirements through guiding the test generation through user-provided constraints. However, additionally even more explicit options for manual guidance are needed to fully address this need.

In this section we present how OSMOTester enables the user to manually generate exact test cases from the same test models. Similar to the DSM scripting language, this can also be manually scripted or guided via a GUI shown in Figure 3. This GUI consists of four main elements. The test log in the upper left corner shows the test steps that have been taken. The sequence number is reset when a new test case is started. The metrics set in the upper right corner shows how many times the different transitions have been taken in the current test suite.

The next transition choice in the lower left corner shows which transitions can be taken at a given time. By clicking on a transition in this

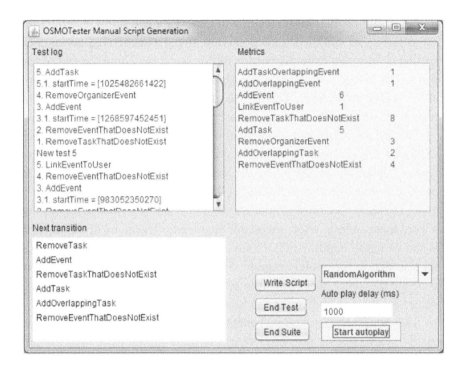

FIGURE 3: Manual GUI

list, the user can guide the OSMOTester generator to take that transition. Choosing one actually executes that step of the model program and updates the set of available transitions. As the GUI only displays the valid transitions for the current state, the user can only create valid test cases with it. The lower right corner contains the set of controls used to further guide the test generation. The write script button writes the generated test script to a file. It should be noted that this is not a test script for the SUT but a script for OSMOTester itself, defining which transitions to take and which values to provide for data variables. The end test button starts a new test case for the suite and end suite finishes the test generation. The algorithm, delay and start autoplay controls are all related to the autoplay feature. It enables the user to start and stop automated model traversal using a chosen algorithm, and to continue manual generation when preferred, always updating the GUI.

As an end result, OSMOTester will generate a test script matching the set of test cases and their transitions (test steps) as generated in this tool. Listing 4 shows an example portion of this script matching the end of test 4 and start of test 5. Notice that this also includes the values of model variables used in those steps. That is, the user can script both the sequence of transitions and variable values in those steps.

Beyond the transitions, the GUI also allows the user to specify the data values of relevant model variables. Figure4 shows an example of three types of dataflow variables. The (a) option shows a request for the user to provide a value for a numeric range (shown in red if an invalid number is give), (b) shows a choice from a set of values, and (c) shows a request for a word that can be any set of readable characters. The name of the variable is shown in the window title. Option OK inputs the given manual choice for this step in the model program, Skip uses the model program logic to generate the value once, and Auto sets the model program to generate all values for this variable in the future automatically.

This approach has several benefits. First of all, it enables the user to easily create specific test cases from the same model as is used for test generation. Thus test scripting can be done from a single source with less duplicated effort. It also eases test maintenance as updates to the model will also be directly updated to the test cases themselves. Thus changes required to test cases to adapt to changes in the test target can be handled in one place and are automatically updated to all test cases, both manually created and automatically generated.

FIGURE 4: Dataflow GUI (a) Value Range (b) Value Set (c) Readable words

LISTING 4: Manual test script example

```
1   action, name, value
2   ...
3   step, link event to user,
4   new test,,
5   step, add event,
6   variable, start time, 1268597452451
7   step, remove event that does not exist,
8   step, remove task that does not exist
```

9.4 DISCUSSION

As we have presented, our approach is based on using existing programming languages and tool as a basis for modeling. As the approach is only based on the basic programming language constructs, it does not require specific tool support for modeling such as a customized visualization and editing component. Instead, the user can choose any integrated development environment (IDE) they are familiar with and use that as they find best (within the Java programming language constraints). This also makes it much easier for us to build a modeling language and framework as we do not need to worry about features such as refactoring, syntax highlighting, debugging and code navigation. These are practically provided for free by the available tools (IDE).

In our experience, people working with test automation are often also experienced programmers. For them, working with this type of a modeling approach is easy as they can work using tools and notation familiar to them. This also keeps them informed exactly about how their tests are built, instead of hiding if behind the custom notations of tools. In practice our experience is also that the approach gives a lot of power that is not available in customized notations as popular general purpose programming languages typically have more resources put into their development and as well as available libraries.

However, as not all people are experts in programming or wish to write their test case using a programming language notation, higher levels of abstraction are also important. For example, a domain expert may be interested in testing their system using specific configurations of the test models with specific properties. Even if in theory it may be possible to show that a MBT tool will generate a set of impressive test cases, it is equally or even more important to provide confidence for different stakeholders that the important features and their important properties are covered in the provided test cases. By providing means to generate overall test cases from the model, constrain the test generation by using a DSM language, or to manually define specific test cases we enable these different goals to be achieved.

Many existing tools make extensive use of static analysis techniques such as symbolic execution and constraint solving [14]. These enable features such as generating test data to cover specific paths of the test model. In our case, we have opted not to use such techniques, beyond those provided by the IDE's, but to focus on supporting and effectively exploiting the runtime execution aspects. In this case, any programming language features can be used in the model programs without worrying about the scalability of the analysis techniques. At the same time, as the model program is executed it can also be easily used to provide features such as the manual test generation GUI we have presented here. As the model program is actually executed, the user can at all times be given exact information about the current state of the model and what actions are possible in that state.

While the approach in many ways gives the user power, it also puts a lot of responsibility to them. As the models are not extensively checked by the tool, they may require some more analysis effort by the user (which is not necessarily a bad thing as it increases the understanding of the system). For example, one has to realize that requiring 10 event removals will never terminate if only 5 event creations are allowed. The domain expert needs to have such understanding, but it is also possible to configure end conditions and create models that report such failures, or provide thresholds for breaking and report failure to achieve required constraints, if needed.

For optimization we apply test selection by allowing one to generate a large set and provide optimization algorithms to select a subset with specific properties. This works when generating offline test scripts to be executed after generation. However, if done in online mode where the tests are executed as generated this is not effective but rather manual tuning of the model becomes more important. In these scenarios it could be beneficial also to have more advanced analysis features from the static analysis domain as well, such as the model checking capabilities in Spec Explorer that also uses a form of model programs [3].

OSMOTester is currently being used by several companies in the embedded and software industry to support test automation. It has been our experience in case studies with industrial partners that the user naturally names the elements in the built model using familiar terms in the target domain. It has also been our experience that while a language expert (a role we commonly take) may help them build a model, they can make the most of it if given a simple way to guide the test generation for different aspects in their model. Yet in many cases they are not interested in learning all the details of the model internal elements as domain experts. Examples of real requirements include setting up a model to produce a certain number of users, varying the generated tests with a chosen subset of possible parameters, and using a specific set of values in specific set of generated tests. The approach we have presented here has helped address those needs.

9.5 CONCLUSIONS

Model-based testing is a powerful test generation technique and tools for this have come a long way and are increasingly adopted in the industry. However, their generic nature, required skills and exposed formalisms can hinder their potential in industrial context with domain experts. In this paper, we presented an approach to guide model-based test generation using domain-specific concepts through support integrated into a MBT tool. This approach starts from using a framework over a common programming language (Java) to build the test model program. The naming conventions used in this framework automatically turn this test model into a domain-specific language that can be used to guide the test generation from this model. The user can then either generate test from the generic test model, constrain it to generate varied test cases for specific scenario(s) or manually create specific test cases from the model.

This allows not only automated generation of a large set of test cases from the test model but also addressing more specific needs by domain experts without needing a language (test model) expert to help with model customization. It also allows one to build more confidence in covering specific elements of the system under test as required by test requirements. As the user can create test cases from the model using manual guidance they can have confidence the requirements are covered and how they are covered. This also helps in the general test maintenance issues as updating the model will also automatically update the manually created test scripts that are based on this model. In the future we plan to explore further means to ease the adoption and use of MBT with concepts such as specification mining input.

REFERENCES

1. M. Blackburn, R. Busser, A. Nauman, R. Knickerbocker & R. Kasuda (2002): Mars Polar Lander Fault Identification Using Model-Based Testing. In: 8th IEEE Int'l. Conf. on Engineering of Complex Computer Systems (ICECCS02), pp. 163–169, doi:10.1109/ICECCS.2002.1181509.
2. E. Bringmann & A. Kramer (2008): Model-Based Testing of Automotive Systems. In: IEEE Int'l. Conf. on Software Testing, Verification and Validation (ICST2008), pp. 485–493 doi:10.1109/ICST.2008.45.
3. W. Grieskamp, N. Kicillof, K. Stobie & V. Braberman (2011): Model-Based Quality Assurance of Protocol Documentation: Tools and Methodology. Journal of Software Testing, Verification and Reliability 21(1), pp. 55–71, doi:10.1002/stvr.427.
4. T. Kanstren (2011): OSMOTester. Available at http://code.google.com/p/osmo.
5. T. Kanstren, O-P. Puolitaival & J. Perala (2011): An Approach to Modularization in Model-Based Testing. In: 3rd Int'l. Conf. on Advances in System Testing and Validation Lifecycle (VALID2011).
6. T. Kanstren, O-P. Puolitaival, V-M. Rytky, A. Saarela & J. S. Ker¨anen (2012): Experiences in Setting up Domain-Specific Model-Based Testing. In: 13th IEEE Int'l. Conf. on Industrial Technology (ICIT2012).
7. M. Katara & A. Kervinen (2006): Making Model-Based Testing more Agile: A Use Case Driven Approach. In: Haifa Verification Conference (HVC2006), pp. 219–234, doi:10.1007/978-3-540-70889-6 17.
8. S. Kelly & J-P. Tolvanen (2008): Domain Specific Modeling: Enabling Full Code Generation. Wiley.
9. J. Kloos & R. Eschbach (2010): A Systematic Approach to Construct Compositional Behaviour Models for Network-structured Safety-critical Systems. Electronic Notes in Theoretical Computer Science 263, pp. 145– 160, doi:10.1016/j.entcs.2010.05.009.

10. A. Pretschner, W. Prenninger, S. Wagner, C. K¨uhnel, M. Baumgartner, B. Sostawa, R. Zolch & T. Stauner (2005): One Evaluation of Model-Based testing and its Automation. In: 27th Int'l. Conf. on Software Engineering (ICSE2005), pp. 392–401, doi:10.1145/1062455.1062529.

11. O-P. Puolitaival, T. Kanstren, V-M. Rytky & A. Saarela (2011): Utilizing Domain-Specific Modelling for Software Testing. In: 3rd Int'l. Conf. on Advances in System Testing and Validation Lifecycle (VALID2011).

12. P. Santos-Neto, R. Resende & C. Padua (2008): An Evaluation of a Model-Based Testing Method for Information Systems. In: ACM Symposium on Applied Computing, pp. 770–776, doi:10.1145/1363686.1363865.

13. T. Takala, M. Katara & J. Harty (2012): Experiences of System-Level Model-Based GUI Testing of Android Applications. In: 4th IEEE Int'l. Conf. on Software Testing, Verification and Validation (ICST2011), doi:10.1109/ICST.2011.11.

14. M. Utting & B. Legeard (2007): Practical Model-Based Testing: A Tools Approach. Morgan Kaufmann.

15. M. Utting, A. Pretschner & B. Legeard (2011): A Taxonomy of Model-Based Testing Approaches. Journal of Software Testing, Verification and Reliability, doi:10.1002/stvr.456.

16. M. Vieira, X. Song, G. Matos, S. Storck, R. Tanikella & B. Hasling (2008): Applying Model-Based Testing to Healthcare Products: Preliminary Experiences. In: 30th Int'l. Conf. on Software Engineering (ICSE2008), pp. 669–671, doi:10.1145/1368088.1368183.

CHAPTER 10

RECOVERY AND MIGRATION OF APPLICATION LOGIC FROM LEGACY SYSTEMS

WIKTOR NOWAKOWSKI, MICHAŁ SMIAŁEK,
ALBERT AMBROZIEWICZ, NORBERT JARZEBOWSKI,
AND TOMASZ STRASZAK

10.1 INTRODUCTION

It is more than obvious that the functioning of most companies and organizations is heavily dependent on software assets which automate or support most of their business processes. Many of such software applications have been in production for years being constantly evolved in order to adapt them to business changes resulting both from changing market needs as well as emerging new technologies providing new business opportunities. Service Oriented Architecture (SOA) and cloud computing are seen as the most dominant software engineering paradigms nowadays. They have dramatically changed the way software systems are designed, delivered and used, what also implies changes in the way business services are provided [1]. For many organizations the transition of their legacy applications to

This chapter was originally published under the Creative Commons Attribution License. Nowakowski W, Smiałek M, Ambroziewicz A, Jarzebowski N, and Straszak T. Recovery and Migration of Application Logic from Legacy Systems. Computer Science **13**,4 (2012); http://dx.doi.org/10.7494/csci.2012.13.4.53.

the new architectural patterns becomes problematic. This is mainly due to obsolescence of technologies, platforms and architectures on which legacy systems are based. Software systems introduced many years ago are often characterized by a complex monolithic structure (eg. without clear distinction between user interface, application logic and business model), technologies with non-common gateways, poor interoperability and lack of support, what makes the refactoring to the new structure (eg. component- or service-based architecture) or integration with other enterprise applications virtually impossible. The evolution is also hampered by the loss of knowledge, both technical and business, caused by insufficient documentation of changes introduced over years, changes in personnel, etc.

Most often, the only reasonable solution to the problems mentioned above is to build a new system that would accomplish the functionality of the old one yet enabling business and technology agility possible to achieve with new software paradigms. However, the cost of replacing the old system with a system built from scratch is often too high. Therefore, there is a call for methods and tools for automated recovery of the knowledge buried inside legacy systems facilitating migration to the new architectures or reuse of essential portions of existing systems.

An important initiative to provide standards for understanding and evolving existing software is the OMG's Architecture-Driven Modernization (ADM). It proposes the Knowledge Discovery Metamodel (KDM) [21] for representing the knowledge obtained from existing software in

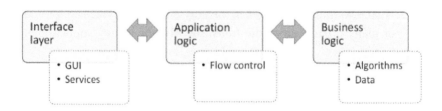

FIGURE 1: The role of application logic in IT systems.

the form of models. KDM provides constructs for representing knowledge about software systems mainly at the level of code. The constructs for representing domain and application logic abstractions are roughly defined.

In this paper we propose an approach for recovery and migration of application logic information from legacy systems. The understanding of application logic extraction from the system design is fundamental to the effective recovery of business value contained in the legacy system. The application logic of an IT system defines sequences of user-system interactions in relation to the domain logic within which the system operates. In our approach, such information can be extracted from any existing system by determining its observable behaviour and stored in the form of requirements-level models conformant to the RSL-AL language. This language is an extension of the Requirements Specification Language (described in Section 3.1 in this paper) and it serves as an intermediate language between the recovery and migration steps. The migration step uses the ReDSeeDS approach [25, 26] to generate the target system structure. Specifications in RSL-AL can be transformed to component architectures (eg. UML or SoaML), platform specific design (eg. specific cloud platform) and even to implementation (code). The proposed approach is supported by a tooling framework and is an important supplement to the methods for reuse and migration of legacy systems, that are being developed within the REMICS project [17].

The paper is structured as follows. Section 2 discusses the notion of application logic that is to be recovered. Section 3 describes capabilities of the RSL-AL language for capturing application logic related information. Section 4 presents the process and tools for recovery and migration of application logic from legacy applications. Finally, Section 5 concludes by presenting the results of evaluation performed so far and summarising future work.

10.2 THE NOTION OF APPLICATION LOGIC

Software systems architecture can be structured conforming to a number of design principles established within the IT industry. The popular architectural patterns are multilayered architecture [6, 7], Model-View-Controller [23] and Model-View- Presenter [22]. The common part of these and many other architectural approaches are components responsible for controlling the flows gathered by system interfaces from the outside of the system (as inputs from users or other systems), using them to trigger business processing inside the system and then passing responses to output interfaces (see Figure 1). This common part controlling internal flows in a software system is called application logic or workflow logic [9].

The notion of application logic varies in the implementation in regard to architectural patterns mentioned above. Application logic in a typical layered system is realized in one of the layers and it bridges the gap between the business logic (data handling and processing layers) and the user interface tier as depicted in Figure 1. These two latter layers conform to the limitation of calling modules of adjacent layers only (see [7] for discussion on this constraint) and communicate only through the application logic layer. In the MVP pattern the Presenter simply passes flows between the View and the Model. In an MVC-style architecture, most of the application logic processing resides in the Controller part, that handles the inputs captured by the View, makes calls to the Model and then sends signals to the View, so they can be passed on to the users.

The application logic carries information about the user-system dialogue in relation to domain-specific processing and platform-specific user interface appearance. Such information reflects the observable behavior of any IT system and defines the way in which it is operating internally. It can be argued that the re-discovery of knowledge residing in the legacy system through the aspect of application logic has advantages over other approaches. The application logic's dynamic aspect is a supplement to the information contained in static architectural models. Application logic analysis gives a more in-depth look into the system than observation the of the "exteriors" of a system (GUI design and user manual analysis). Also, most of the time, the flow of control contained in the application logic is easier to capture and understand than information contained in the source code.

10.3 CAPTURING APPLICATION LOGIC WITH RSL-AL

The Requirements Specification Language allows for conceptual modeling based on object-oriented ideas and user-interface specifications in the area of requirements engineering. Software requirements modeled in RSL have their behavioral and structural aspects distinguished: the descriptions of modeled domain elements are separated from the specification of their dynamics. In RSL, links between behavioral and static elements can be assigned roles and responsibilities and can have temporal ordering and variety of conditions specified. This allows for precise flow control in the resulting models.

The RSL notation is human-readable (based on popular notation, understandable to different audiences and using expressions as close as possible to the natural language), but on the other hand is precise enough to allow automated processing (like, for example, MDA-style transformations [16]). In Sections below we describe principles of RSL and its application to logic extension. For the extended overview of the RSL language please refer to [24] and to [13] for the formal language definition.

10.3.1 RSL CONCEPTS AND STRUCTURE

In RSL, a taxonomy of requirements is formulated. The most general requirement type, called simply "Requirement", is an expression of some feature defined for a software system. The Requirement's subtypes include functional and constraint requirements, as well as use cases specialized from the UML use cases [20].

Relationships from a fixed set defined in RSL may be used to interrelate requirements. This set includes several types for Requirement Relationships as well as use-case-specific relationship "Invoke" used to denote that another Use case (more precisely: one of its scenarios) can be invoked from within the currently performed Use case. The advantage of this relationship over UML «include» and «extend» mechanisms lies in its precision and unambiguity: the invoked scenario steps are executed in the exact position in the interaction sequence as defined by the relationship usage (see [4] for a discussion on vague semantics of the include/extend relationships).

RSL differentiates between requirement entities ("requirements as such") and their representations (their content). Requirements as such are names with identifiers, attributes and relations to other requirements.

Content representations carry the information contained within the requirements (e.g. for Use cases, an interaction information in the form of scenarios). This is illustrated in Figure 2 which can be used as an example for the following description of RSL.

Requirements can have multiple representations that carry equivalent information. Given that information included in different representations is the same, the representations can serve different purposes as they present the same requirements content in a disparate manner. While some of the representations are oriented towards human RSL users, the others are intended for automated machine processing. Some of the human-readable representations are easily read and understood by a business audience (for example software users or project sponsors' representatives), the others are more appealing to technical people (e.g. programmers, designers, or architects).

The current RSL version defines two main types of requirements representations: constrained language representations and schematic (or: diagrammatic) representations. Constrained language representations express requirement information as textual scenarios. The diagrammatic representations are based on UML activity diagrams and sequence (interaction) diagrams. All types of representations are defined in a formal way through a grammar. The grammar for diagrammatic representations is expressed as a MOF [19] metamodel.

The representations defined in RSL contain user-system interaction information and flow of events for a given requirement. This interaction is described by a set of scenarios (leading to one goal or showing a number of ways that fail in reaching that goal). Each scenario has a set of ordered sentences describing signals exchanged between actors and system components participating in the scenario. Special types of sentences, called control sentences, are used to express conditions in the flow of interaction. For more information on requirement representations refer to [27].

In RSL, the container for requirements as well as their representations is called the Requirements Specification. It consists of a hierarchy of requirement packages and a specialized package named the Domain Specification. This last package contains elements pertaining to the vocabulary of the problem domain separated from (or rather: pointed at by) a description of requirement dynamics carried by the requirements representations.

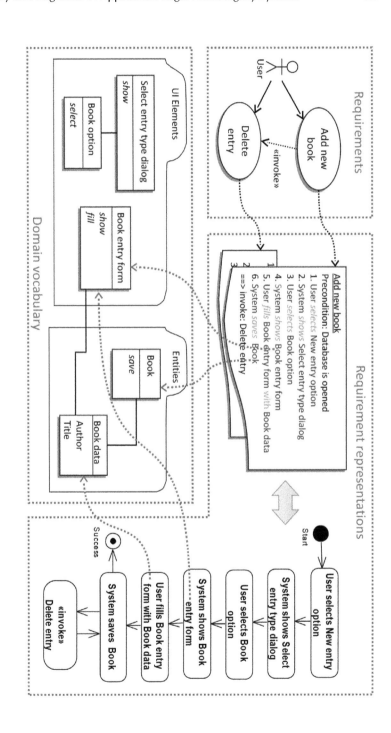

FIGURE 2: Summary of the RSL notation.

The domain specific vocabulary in RSL is centered around nouns. In RSL, a noun ("user", "ticket") is called a notion. An RSL noun may consist of multiple words (like "data form" or "user account"). Each such noun-based notion is a basic vocabulary element and it has a textual definition.

Notion can be part of many different phrases. Each of such phrases contains the notion with a supplement of other parts of speech (e.g. verbs or adjectives). For example "user account" may have phrases "delete user account" (with definition: "to delete from the system an account related to a user") and "expired user account" ("an account that was not renewed in a given period"). Definitions used to describe notions and phrases may contain other notions or phrases. Such use of domain element names in the definitions is a basis for creating associations among domain elements and resulting in a domain vocabulary having the characteristics of a static class-like model.

As it was pointed above, the domain vocabulary elements are used within the descriptions of behavioral aspects of the requirements and are referred to by requirement representations. Such references are called hyperlinks (this is also true for the situation when a textual definition of some domain element uses the name of other notion or other notion's phrase). Hyperlinks are the building blocks of textual representations and

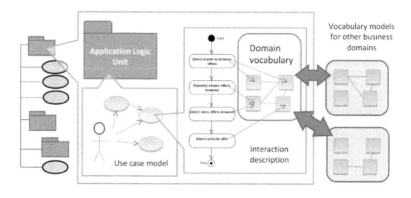

FIGURE 3: The levels of application logic management.

the domain element definitions. For the constrained representations, the sequence of hyperlinks used in a given expression conforms to a specified grammar.

RSL uses the SVO(O) grammar [10] [11]. The basic sentence structure for this grammar is Subject – Verb – Object – Indirect Object. In RSL, a sentence in the SVO(O) grammar contains one hyperlink to its subject (a noun phrase, in most cases just a notion) and a hyperlink to a verb phrase. This verb phrase may be a simple one (containing only a single object) or complex (with two objects and an optional preposition). Such sentences are used to precisely describe the dynamic aspect of a requirement: a sentence conforming to the SVO grammar defines an active interaction entity (the sentence subject) performing an action (the verb in the verb phrase) with the use of passive elements (the objects).

10.3.2 RSL EXTENSION FOR APPLICATION LOGIC

The core of RSL has been extended with capabilities for creating solution-independent application logic descriptions. The RSL-AL extension is based on RSL concepts like separation of elements' description and their dynamics specification, precise domain vocabulary and rigorous interaction definition, and at the same time it allows for the efficient management of application logic building blocks and application logic patterns.

While RSL is a language with capabilities for application logic specifications, the new elements in the extension are introduced to allow for the efficient management of application logic related information. This management can be done on different levels: on the functionality overview level and on the level of detailed interaction information (see Figure 3).

The upper level of abstracting the application logic information pertains to elements grouped in units collecting areas of functionality. These groupings, called Application Logic Units, are containers for elements of functionality (use cases) and can be interrelated by the use of precisely defined relationships. The granularity of application logic management on this level may be compared to package-level concepts of UML.

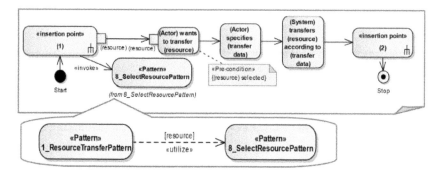

FIGURE 4: Insertion of application logic "snippet" into flow of interaction describing other functionality.

Relationships existing at the lower detail level (connecting units of functionality) are already covered extensively in RSL (see the «invoke» relationship above), but RSL-AL introduces the idea of linkages between snippets of functionality. Such partial functionalities do not describe interactions which allow reaching some kind of a goal or a significant value (as opposed to user-system dialogue found in use cases), but are important and/or repeatable elements of control flow descriptions within the software system. They can contain just the partial flow of interaction leading to an intermediate goal and are intended as basic functionality blocks. The RSL extension for application logic allows operating on such partial functionalities: they can be defined and then interrelated (put together, chained) to create more complete functional units. These relationships are represented at two levels of abstraction: at the level of a functional unit (use case level, sub-package level) and at the level of a requirement representation (as a textual scenario or an activity diagram).

In the RSL-AL approach, full utilization of the RSL concept of separating the vocabulary and behavior enables control of consistency of the vocabulary used in the chained snippets of functionality. Each of such elementary application logic building blocks has precisely defined notions it refers to and these notions are used as this functionality parameters. When one partial functionality is inserted into other one, all the uses of parametrized

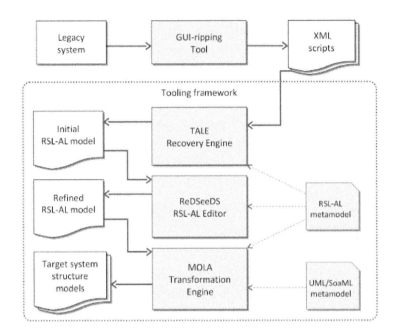

FIGURE 5: Overview of the recovery and migration process and tools.

notions in the inserted one are substituted with corresponding notions of the target unit of functionality. This ensures that the resulting interaction description uses consistent wording.

Figure 4 presents an example of inserting an application logic snippet (regarding a resource selection) into the interaction flow for transferring a resource. In the main interaction, a marker (insertion point) indicates the position at which other flows can be inserted (by the «invoke» relationship). UML pin-like notation indicates the vocabulary parameter of the interaction description. The higher-level view of this information (the diagram in the lower part of Figure 4) shows just two interactions and a relationship between them along with the vocabulary parameter used).

The above notion substitution mechanism is also used at other levels of application logic elements management and enables the use of patterns in the domain of application logic modeling. Elements of functionality (packages, units of functionality or atomic building blocks) can be abstracted from the business domain they describe (note interactions in Figure 4 that deal with very general notions like resource). Then, reusing them in different contexts (with different business vocabulary) needs minimal effort. Such a reuse process requires only mapping of abstracted domain vocabulary elements to a target (concrete) domain model. The descriptions of interaction flow are not changed in this process (see right-hand side of Figure 3). For a more detailed explanation of this mechanism refer to [3].

10.4 PROCESS AND TOOLS FOR APPLICATION LOGIC RECOVERY AND MIGRATION

Figure 5 shows an overview of the process and tools allowing for recovery and migration of application logic information from the existing systems. The recovery phase encompasses the idea of semi-automatic reverse engineering while the migration phase is based on model-driven forward engineering techniques. Throughout this process we use the "essential" specifications according to the presented RSL-AL language. We first analyse the legacy system's UI by using a GUI-ripping tool. Based on this semi-automatic analysis we generate the initial RSL-AL model which can then be modified by hand to refine it or to cater for new or changed functionality. By the fact, that the model is based on a metamodel, we can use a model transformation engine to generate the target system structure models (both platform independent and platform specific) and code. Subsequent steps of the process are described in detail in the sections below.

10.4.1 RECOVERY

The first step of the recovery process is performed using a GUI-ripping tool (see a discussion on this in [15]). This step is performed semi-automatically. It involves manual traversal through a system's user interface during which the system observable behaviour is systematically scanned. A user (preferably a person who normally works with the legacy system and is aware of its behaviour), simply interacts with the legacy system sequentially performing individual functionalities (use cases). An example of such interaction for searching a client (in Polish: Wyszukiwanie klienta) is illustrated in Figure 6a. During this, the GUI-ripping tool records the flows of interaction representing the system's application logic. This includes user inputs (buttons clicked, data entered, widget focus gained, etc.) and the respective system responses (windows displayed, messages shown to the user or even textual console behaviour). In order to capture the most extensive application logic knowledge, it is important to traverse through all possible functional paths, including exceptional system's behaviour resulting, for example, from entering invalid data, operation cancellation etc. The GUI-ripping tool stores all this information in XML-based scripts. In our tool chain we use IBM Rational Functional Tester as the GUI-ripping tool because it supports a wide range of UI technologies including those based on textual consoles. However, any tool allowing interaction recording to some form of structured text files may be integrated with our tooling framework.

The next step of the recovery process is to transform scripts obtained from the GUI-ripping tool into an RSL-AL model. This is done with the TALE tool (Tool for Application Logic Extraction) developed as part of this work. This novel tool automatically extracts sequences of user-system interactions producing scenarios with SVO sentences. Figure 6b shows an automatically extracted scenario representing the interaction illustrated in Figure 6a. All the extracted scenarios are attached to use cases as their representations and are grouped within the "Functional Requirements" package being a part of the recovered model (see the project tree in Figure 6b).

Furthermore, the TALE tool also re-creates the domain vocabulary containing domain notions (created mainly based on data passed to and from the user) and UI elements (windows, buttons, input fields, etc.) used in the recovered scenarios. What is important, the tool is able to extract information about the composition of specific notions. For example, when there is a form displayed to enter personal data (such as first name, last name, PESEL numer, etc.—see the "Osoba fizyczna" tab in Figure 6a), a composite notion for "Osoba fizyczna data" is created. Such a notion contains descriptions for every field filled on the form, instead of a number of unrelated notions reflecting these fields.

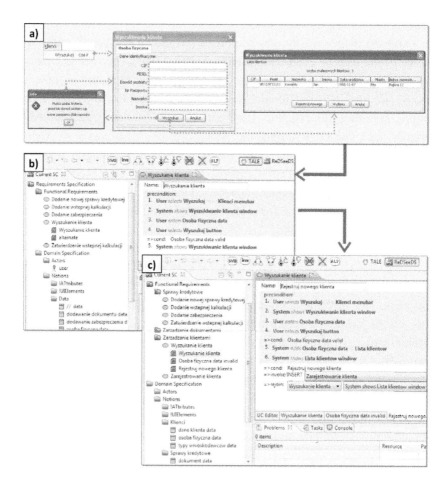

FIGURE 6: An example of GUI interaction (a), the automatically recovered RSL-AL model (b) and the manually refined final model (c).

This reduces the amount of simple notions created from the GUI record-ings, therefore reduces the unnecessary complexity of the recovered mod-el. All these elements are stored in the "Domain Specification" package.

The extracted use case scenarios linked to a domain vocabulary form the initial RSL-AL model. Thanks to the characteristics of the RSL-AL language, this model is easily understandable to people (even those barely knowledgeable of the original system) thus giving the possibility of its easy extension and modification. First of all, some modifications are need-ed because of the fact that not all of the application logic information can be automatically retrieved from the recording scripts. This includes sen-tences that control flow of scenario execution (conditions and «invoke» sentences) and sentences expressing internal system operations (eg. calls to business logic operations), such as "System verifies data", "System stores information", "System deletes item from item list" etc. Also domain vocabulary usually needs manual refactoring—mostly renaming some no-tions. Moreover, changes can be done to cater to the migrated system for new or changed functionality or just to optimize some scenario flows, eg. by applying standard application logic patterns [3].

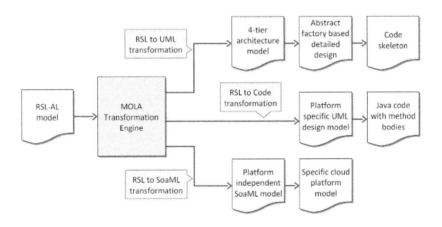

FIGURE 7: Transforming RSL-AL model into different target models.

All these modifications can be made in the ReDSeeDS tool, which offers a comprehensive RSL-AL editor. It allows for writing use case scenarios in accordance with the rules of the language grammar. Managing of domain specification elements from the level of the use case editor or using tree-like structures is possible as well. Also a basic application logic pattern library is supplied with the tool. Switching between TALE and ReDSeeDS is seamless since both tools are integrated within a single framework and they share a common data model which is an implementation of the RSL-AL metamodel. Figure 6c shows the recovered model after refinements.

10.4.2 MIGRATION

The refined RSL-AL model, containing both the still relevant "legacy" requirements and the "new" ones, is a starting point for the migration phase in which a new system structure is generated. The generation is realised through a model transformation within the ReDSeeDS tool that has a built-in transformation engine for the MOLA language [14]. In order to do this, we need to reorganize the requirements model according to the needs of the transformation rules that are to be applied (as shown in Figure 6c) and choose one of predefined transformation profiles. The structure and notation of the target model depends on the chosen transformation profile as shown in Figure 7.

Currently "RSL to UML" and "RSL to Code" transformations profiles are ready to use. "RSL to UML" transformation chain implements the MDA concepts with the requirements specification in RSL as the CIM (Computation Independent Model), multi-tier architecture model as the PIM (Platform Independent Model) and detailed design model based on abstract factory design pattern as the PSM (Platform Specific Model) [5]. The "RSL to Code" transformation is able to generate classes forming a full structure of the system following the MVP architectural pattern, including the complete code for the method bodies in the application logic (Presenter) and presentation (View) layers. It also provides a code skeleton with method stubs for the domain logic layer (Model).

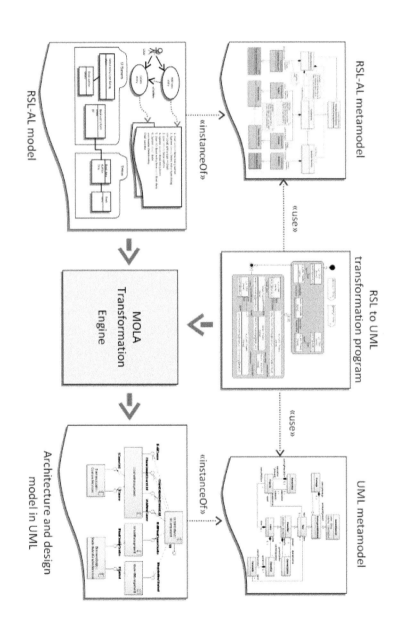

FIGURE 8: Transformation details.

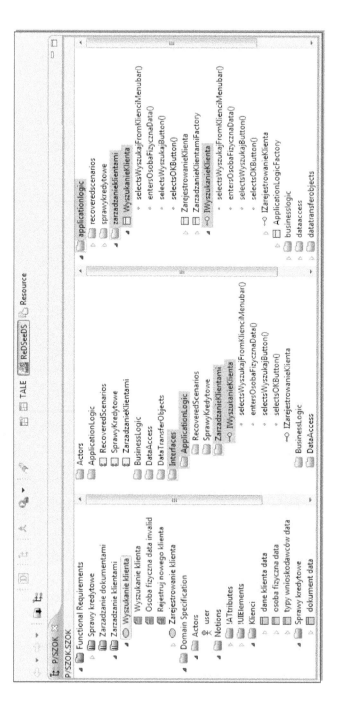

FIGURE 9: Target system structure generated with the RSL to UML transformation.

According to current trends in internet technologies, an expected target of the migration process is a cloud-enabled system. Thus, the new system structure should follow service-oriented architecture principles and should be expressed in SoaML [8]. This requires a specific transformation profile, which is under construction now.

The migration process, implemented within the ReDSeeDS tool, uses the MOLA engine. An example transformation scheme is shown in Figure 8. The MOLA transforamtion engine uses transformation programs written in MOLA transformation language, which offers very readable graphical notation. Any transformation expressed in MOLA consists of meta-models for the source and target models, along with one or more transition procedures. Source and target meta-models are defined in the MOLA meta-modelling language, which is close in specification to that of EMOF (Essential MOF — see [19]). MOLA procedures form the executable part of the MOLA transformation. Traceability associations, which link elements of the source meta-model and corresponding elements of the target meta-model, facilitate building of natural transformation procedures and document the performed transformations. This is illustrated in Figure 9. There is a trace from the "Wyszukanie klienta" use case leading to the "IWyszukanieKlienta" interface in the application logic tier in the solution architecture and its realisation within the "ZarzadzanieKlientami" component in the detailed design. This structure is the result of the "RSL to UML" transformation, where the target model is an instance of the UML meta-model.

By the fact that SoaML (see [2]) and UML have a common meta-model, transformations to SoaML are expected to be similar to the transformations which generate UML. The output model of both groups of transformations is an UML-based logical system design at different levels of abstraction, relevant to the structure of the source requirements specification (use cases, notions and packages). The "RSL to SoaML" transformations are expected to generate the structured model of services constructed with stereotyped packages, components, interfaces, classes. The target models is also expected to contain sequence diagrams describing the services behaviour based on the use case scenarios. All messages exchanged via services in sequence diagrams will have adequate operations in the corresponding interfaces thus keeping the target model coherent. An example of a sequence diagram generated with "RSL to UML" transformation is shown in Figure 10.

10.5 EVALUATION AND FUTURE WORK

Since the presented solution combines some existing approaches, it has been already partially validated. The results presented in [18] prove very good acceptance of the RSL as a specification language. Also usability of RSL-AL constructs when writing application logic specifications have been validated in a controlled experiment (see [3]). Moreover, evaluation results of the ReDSeeDS approach (see [12]) have shown the feasibility of transformation-supported path from semiformal requirements to code in a model-driven way. A nontrivial part of a software system can be generated by transformations from appropriately defined RSL models.

A comprehensive evaluation of the presented approach (including the recovery phase) in the industrial context is currently ongoing. A larger case study based on a legacy corporate banking system delivered by Infovide-Matrix S.A. (one of the major Polish software providers) is performed. In fact, the examples in this paper are taken from this case study (a bank credit management system). The main objective of this case study is to modernize the legacy system by migrating it into a cloud in the SaaS model in order to provide uniform access to the system functionality by the customers' external systems.

Early experiments on the case study system show promising levels of application logic that can be recovered. For a certain part of the system's functionality a set of test scripts were recorded in the GUI-ripping tool. With this input, the TALE tool was able to produce sensible RSL-AL model. It needed some manual modification of the interaction sequence in most of the scenarios (ca. 80 percent) as well as some modification of the domain vocabulary (ca. 50 percent of notions needed to be renamed). Although the recovery phase is not fully automatic, experience shows that it is still much faster than it would be if one had to manually write scenarios from scratch. Moreover, the recovery can be associated with the normal operation of the recovered system. The operators can work normally with the legacy system, at the same time recording its functionality.

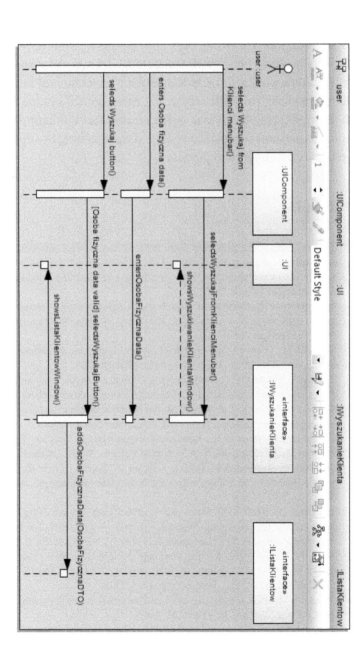

FIGURE 10: Dynamic architectural model generated with the RSL to UML transformation.

The ongoing work on the solution currently focuses on the development of transformations from the RSL-AL models into platform independent architectural SoaML models and, possibly, a full application logic code for a selected novel web technology. To make our approach more holistic, future work will include automatic generation of test cases from RSL-AL models. This will assure that the migrated system will comply with the observable behaviour of the legacy one. Furthermore, it will be possible to perform acceptance testing of the functionality updated during the recovery and migration process.

REFERENCES

1. Economic and social impact of software & software-based services, d2 – the european software industry. Pierre Audoin Consultants Report, July 30 2009.
2. Service oriented architecture Modeling Language (SoaML) Specification, version 1.0, formal/2012-03-01, 2012.
3. Ambroziewicz A., Smiałek M.: Application Logic Patterns — reusable elements of user-system interaction. In Proc. of MODELS'10, Oslo, Norway, LNCS 6394, pp. 241–255. Springer, 2010.
4. Astudillo H., G´enova G., Smiałek M., et al..: Use cases in model-driven software engineering. LNCS, 3844:262–271, 2006. MODELS'06.
5. Bojarski J., Straszak T., Ambroziewicz A., Nowakowski W.: Transition from precisely defined requirements into draft architecture as an mda realisation. In M. Smiałek, K. Mukasa, M. Nick, J. Falb, ed., Model Reuse Strategies, Can requriements drive reuse of software models?, pp. 35–42. Fraunhofer Verlag, 2008.
6. Buschmann F., Meunier R., Rohnert H., Sommerlad P., Stal M.: Pattern-Oriented Software Architecture, vol. 1: A System of Patterns. Wiley, Chichester, UK, 1996.
7. Clements P., Bachmann F., Bass L., Garlan D., Ivers J., Little R., Nord R., Stafford J.: Documenting Software Architectures: Views and Beyond. Addison-Wesley, 2003.
8. Elvesaeter B., Berre A.-J., Sadovykh A.: Specifying services using the service oriented architecture modeling language (soaml) — a baseline for specification of cloud-based services. In F. Leymann, I. Ivanov, M. van Sinderen, B. Shishkov, eds., Proc. of CLOSER 2011, Aachen, Germany, pp. 276–285. SciTePress, 2011.
9. Fowler M.: Patterns of Enterprise Application Architecture. Addison-Wesley Longman Publishing Co., Inc., Boston, MA, USA, 2002.
10. Graham I. M.: Task scripts, use cases and scenarios in object-oriented analysis. Object-Oriented Systems, 3(3):123–142, 1996.
11. Graham I. M.: Object-Oriented Methods Principles & Practice. Pearson Education, 2001.
12. Jedlitschka A., Mukasa K. S., Weber S.: Case creation verification and validation. Project Deliverable D6.1, ReDSeeDS Project, 2009. www.redseeds.eu.

13. Kaindl H., Smiałek M., Wagner P., Svetinovic D., Ambroziewicz A., Bojarski J., Nowakowski W., Straszak T., Schwarz H., Bildhauer D., Brogan J.P., Mukasa K. S., Wolter K., Krebs T.: Requirements specification language definition. Project Deliverable D2.4.2, ReDSeeDS Project, 2009. www.redseeds.eu.
14. Kalnins A., Barzdins J., Celms E.: Model transformation language MOLA. Lecture Notes in Computer Science, 3599:14–28, 2004. Proc. of MDAFA'04, Link"oping, Sweden.
15. Memon A. M., Banerjee I., Nagarajan A.: GUI ripping: Reverse engineering of graphical user interfaces for testing. In Proc. of the 10th Working Conference on Reverse Engineering, Victoria, Canada, pp. 260–269, November 2003.
16. Miller J., Mukerji J., editors. MDA Guide Version 1.0.1, omg/03-06-01. Object Management Group, 2003.
17. Mohagheghi P., Barbier F., Berre A., Morin B., Sadovykh A., Saether T., Henry A., Abherve A., Ritter T., Hein C., Smiałek M.: European Research Activities in Cloud Computing, chapter Migrating Legacy Applications to the Service Cloud Paradigm: The REMICS Project. Cambridge Scholars Publishing, 2012.
18. Mukasa K. S., et al.: Requirements specification language validation report. Project Deliverable D2.5.1, ReDSeeDS Project, 2007.
19. Object Management Group. Meta Object Facility Core Specification, version 2.0, formal/2006-01-01, 2006.
20. Object Management Group. Unified Modeling Language: Superstructure, version 2.2, formal/09-02-02, 2009.
21. Object Management Group. Architecture-Driven Modernization: Knowledge Discovery Meta-Model (KDM), version 1.3, formal/2011-08-04, 2011.
22. Potel M.: MVP: Model-View-Presenter the Taligent programming model for C++ and Java. Technical Report, Taligent Inc., 1996.
23. Reenskaug T.: Models-views-controllers. Technical Note, Xerox PARC, 1979.
24. Smiałek M., Ambroziewicz A., Bojarski J., Nowakowski W., Straszak T.: Introducing a unified requirements specification language. In Proc. CEE-SET'2007, Software Engineering in Progress, Poznan, Poland, pp. 172–183. Nakom, 2007.
25. Smiałek M., Ambroziewicz A., Bojarski J., Nowakowski W., Straszak T.: Od modelu do wdrozenia — kierunki badan i zastosowan inzynierii oprogramowania, chapter Narzedzie i metodyka dla systematycznego wytwarzania oprogramowania, pp. 23–34. Wydawnictwa Komunikacji i Łacznosci, 2009.
26. Smiałek M., Ambroziewicz A., Bojarski J., Nowakowski W., Straszak T., Wolter K., Hotz L., Mukasa K. S., Jedlitschka A., Bildhauer D., Falkowski K., Haas J., Horn T., Riediger V., Schwarz H., Kalnins A., Kalnina E., Sostaks A., Celms E., Rein M., Drejewicz S., Knab S., Falb J., C, etin S., T"ufek¸ci O., C, okke¸ceci I.: Case-driven software development comprehensive approach to produce and reuse model-based software cases. Project Deliverable D8.2.2, ReDSeeDS Project, 2009. www.redseeds.eu.
27. Smiałek M., Bojarski J., Nowakowski W., Ambroziewicz A., Straszak T.: Complementary use case scenario representations based on domain vocabularies. Lecture Notes in Computer Science, 4735:544–558, 2007. Proc. of MODELS'07, Nashville, TN, USA.

AUTHOR NOTES

CHAPTER 2

Acknowledgments

The authors wish to thank Clementine Nebut, Tewfik Ziadi, Paul Istoan, and Mathieu Acher for so many fruitful discussions on the topic of Model-Driven Engineering for Software Product Lines. This paper, largely based on common work with them, could not have been written without all their contributions to the field.

CHAPTER 3

Acknowledgments

This work has been developed with the support of MEC under the project SESAMO TIN2007-62894 and GVA ORCA PROMETEO/2009/015.

CHAPTER 5

Acknowledgments:

Ideas presented in the paper have been discussed at NECSIS seminars at McMaster and the University of Waterloo; we are grateful to all their participants, and especially to Michał Antkiewicz and Krzysztof Czarnecki, for useful feedback and stimulating criticism. We have also benefited greatly from discussions with Don Batory, Steve Easterbrook, Jos´e Fiadeiro, Michael Healy, Michael Johnson, Ralf Lammel, Bran Selic and Uwe Wolter. Thanks also go to anonymous referees for comments. Financial support was provided with the NECSIS project funded by the Automotive Partnership Canada.

CHAPTER 8

Acknowledgments

The authors would like to thank CNPq for funding (Processes 132996/2010-3 and 560241/2010-0) and for the Universal Project (Process Number 483106/2009-7) in which this article was created. Thiago Gottardi would also like to thank FAPESP (Process 2011/04064-8).

CHAPTER 10

Acknowledgments

This research has been carried out in the REMICS project and partially funded by the EU (contract number IST-257793 under the 7th framework programme), see http://www.remics.eu/.

INDEX